WRITING CULTURE AND
THE LIFE OF ANTHROPOLOGY

Writing Culture and the Life of Anthropology

Orin Starn, editor

DUKE UNIVERSITY PRESS *Durham and London* 2015

Designed by Amy Ruth Buchanan
Typeset in Galliard
by Westchester Publishing Services

Chapters 1, 2, 5, 6, 7, 8, 12, and 13
originally appeared in *Cultural Anthropology* 27(3), 2012. © 2012 American
Anthropological Association. Reprinted
with permission of the American Anthropological Association.

Cover art: (*left to right*) Nick Cave,
Soundsuit, 2009, mixed media, 72 × 22
1/8 inches. Nick Cave, *Soundsuit*,
2006, mixed media including buttons,
upholstery, metal, and mannequin;
78 × 26 × 14 inches. Nick Cave,
Soundsuit, 2009, mixed media,
74 × 24 × 21 inches. All © Nick Cave.
Photos by James Prinz Photography.
Courtesy of the artist and Jack Shainman
Gallery, New York.

Library of Congress Cataloging-
in-Publication Data
Writing culture and the life of anthropology /
Orin Starn, editor.
pages cm
Includes bibliographical references and index.
ISBN 978-0-8223-5862-6 (hardcover : alk. paper)
ISBN 978-0-8223-5873-2 (pbk. : alk. paper)
ISBN 978-0-8223-7565-4 (e-book)
1. Communication in ethnology.
2. Ethnology—Authorship.
3. Anthropology—Authorship. I. Starn, Orin.
GN307.7.W75 2015
306.01—dc23
2014036268

For Ken

CONTENTS

———————————

"It's a trap," Eminem warns us against dwelling too much in the past. "Fuck my last CD that shits in the trash."[1]

It's hard to disagree altogether with the aging hip-hop megastar. Our modern pieties enshrine remembering as our moral duty and a therapeutic necessity for individuals and nations alike. But sometimes, as others before Eminem have also suggested, forgetting may not be such a bad thing. Nietzsche claimed cows are happier than people because they can't remember anything that happened more than a few minutes before.

Then again, it may not be wise to take cows entirely for our model. We anthropologists, when we do bother to look back, sometimes lean on canned histories about complicity with colonialism and other real and imagined disciplinary failings. Our tendency is to adopt an almost childish enchantment with the latest trendy theories, theorists, and topics. It's a mark of vitality, and yet it can also leave one puzzling over just what waters the patched-up schooner of anthropology has crossed and where it may be headed next.

This collection is about anthropology's past, present, and possible future ports of call. A spirit of retrospection, *pace* Marshall Mathers, gave rise to the project in the first place. In 1986, the year of Halley's comet and the first IBM laptop, perhaps the single most influential anthropology book in recent decades appeared: *Writing Culture: The Poetics and Politics of Ethnography.* As the twenty-fifth anniversary of the book's publication neared (and, as these things do, soon passed), it provided an occasion for inviting the editors, George Marcus and James Clifford, and a group of leading anthropologists to offer their thoughts about the book and its legacies.[2] Their by turns wistful, optimistic, elusive, fragmentary, programmatic, and provocative essays about the field then and now come together in this book.

It's striking just how much anthropology has changed in just a few short decades. Our former fixation on those proverbial exotic tribal societies has given way to a brave new disciplinary world where just about anything anywhere has become fair ethnographic game. We may still work in archetypal anthropological stomping grounds like New Guinea and the Amazon (though with angles of inquiry very different from our disciplinary ancestors), but just as likely now in San Francisco BDSM dungeons, French magic clubs, or Brazil's plastic surgery wards.[3] And too we are no longer the stereotypical white male preserve of an older scientific day. If anthropology early on had its pioneering female luminaries, many more women and people of color and from the Third World have now entered the ranks, albeit too often still facing unpleasant obstacles of various kinds.[4] There has also been the ever-changing medley of sometimes overlapping, sometimes conflicting theoretical trends: Marxism and feminism in varied versions; the many stripes of poststructuralist and postcolonial theory; the interest in sovereignty and governmentality; Foucault, Agamben, Butler, Latour, Deleuze . . . and who knows what next.

Any attempt to reckon with these disciplinary changes should surely include *Writing Culture*. As a graduate student in the 1980s, I can testify to the book's big splash in our modest pond of a discipline. *Writing Culture* was the flagship text for the debates about reflexivity and representation that defined that whole decade in anthropology, or the "writing culture" moment, as some still call it. You simply had to read—and have an opinion about—the book unless you wanted to appear pathetically behind the times, which is never a good plan for a graduate student. (The middle-aged tenured professor, alas, can and sometimes does get away with it since we can't be fired—yet.)

Those opinions were quite radically polarized. Neither George Marcus nor James Clifford ever identified as a "postmodernist." That did not keep some critics from branding the two *Writing Culture* editors as the ringleaders of a sinister "postmodern movement." Along with Marcus and Michael M. J. Fischer's *Anthropology as Cultural Critique* (1986), Clifford's *The Predicament of Culture* (1988), and other influential new texts, the essays in *Writing Culture* seemed to threaten the traditional bedrock principles of truth, science, and objectivity with the relativizing epistemic murk of newfangled literary theory and other suspect influences.[5] Then, as now, job interviews at AAA meetings were conducted in those horrible little curtained booths at the convention hotel. You had to be ready to discuss your position on postmodernism as if it were self-evident what that notoriously slippery and by now antique-sounding term meant, let alone that one had to be "for" or "against" it. It sometimes felt, if you gave the wrong answer, as though someone might push the button to the trap door under your chair.

Why did *Writing Culture* generate such controversy? After all, others had already called for radically rethinking anthropology amid the turmoil of decolonization and social protest across the late 1960s and 1970s. A pair of earlier landmark anthologies, *Reinventing Anthropology* and *Anthropology and the Colonial Encounter*, had been especially influential in opening the discipline to serious scrutiny.[6] The rising influence of Marxist and feminist theory, also predating *Writing Culture*, had gone along with a new concern for the nexus of culture, power, and history together with a more politicized anthropology.

Much about *Writing Culture* indeed bore the imprint of 1960s radicalism. The contributors were mostly baby boomers who had marched against the Vietnam War and been influenced by that era's countercultural currents. An antiracist, anticolonial sympathy for the subaltern ran through the book. What *Writing Culture* added to the mix were the new sensibilities of literary, poststructuralist, and postcolonial theory in various guises. The anthology's essays were by no means uniform in their agendas. Still, the citation of such otherwise disparate bedfellows as Derrida, Bakhtin, Baudrillard, Foucault, Frye, White, Barthes, and Said marked the growing interest in the politics of discourse, language, and representation that was to define so much inquiry in anthropology and related fields to the twentieth century's close and into the new century. As Clifford (this volume) observes in hindsight, *Writing Culture* occupied a "transitional moment," somewhere between the agendas and interests of the late 1960s and those of the fin de siècle.

Especially irksome to some critics was the new concern for reflexivity and representation. Treating ethnography not as a transparent record of other realities so much as a genre of writing with its own conventions, tropes, gaps, and silences was little more than self-indulgent navel gazing in one quite common view. And then there was the anthology's tilt to a postmodern, if one may be excused the hollowed-out word, skepticism about neat explanation and model building as against a more mobile, open-ended view of culture and society as a terrain of hybridization, disjuncture, and heteroglossia. Not only old school positivists found such tendencies objectionable and worse. Censorious criticism also came from the left, especially Marxist and feminist scholars. The Marxian-minded Nicole Polier and William Roseberry, for example, lamented that *Writing Culture* strayed too far from the ostensibly solid ground of political economy into the treacherous badlands of a depoliticized, la-la-land culturalism.[7] Feminists objected, reasonably enough, to there being only one woman, Mary Pratt, among *Writing Culture*'s nine contributors; they also faulted Clifford and Marcus for failing to acknowledge feminist genealogies of ethnographic experimentation and textual theorization.[8] To the harshest critics, the postmodern turn of the 1980s was a step backward, a rear-guard action that threatened to undercut hopes for a transformed anthropology. Many would have been pleased enough to see *Writing Culture* consigned to Eminem's waiting trash can without further ceremony.

———————

All the controversy only increased interest in *Writing Culture*. The book was a touchstone, even inspiration for its admirers, especially among a younger generation then coming up through the ranks. As John Jackson Jr. (this volume) remembers it, *Writing Culture* seemed to give us "license . . . for thinking unabashedly" about the craft of ethnography and, more broadly, the state of anthropology as a whole. The verve, intelligence, and originality of the contributions only added to the sense of something very different from the usual plodding academic anthology. *Writing Culture* found readers in literature, history, visual studies, and other fields, and beyond the United States. (It has been translated into Mandarin and four other languages.) Several hundred Google Scholar citations is one modern measure of an influential academic text; *Writing Culture* has been cited 8,638 times and counting.

This volume's opening essays furnish new ways to think about *Writing Culture* and the already almost exotically different times to which it belonged. If the book was bright and shiny in its moment, all of us—even the brainy kids in the class like the *Writing Culture* contributors—find ourselves dated by time's passing sooner or later. We are left, as Clifford puts it (this volume), "feeling historical." A master historicizer (and, it is sometimes forgotten, a historian and not an anthropologist by training), Clifford points to the enormous planetary transformations since *Writing Culture*'s publication: the cold war's end; the Internet and its consequences, overhyped and not; intensifying global interconnections and disjunctures; and too many more developments to name. Those changes make it impossible any longer, at least for Clifford, to maintain a tone of "confident, knowing critique." Instead Clifford wonders at a new world whose multiple centers, massive inequalities, and ever more unsustainable ecology make so precarious the future of the planet itself, not to mention that of our humble discipline.

It's the dizzying journey from then to now that preoccupies Michael Fischer in his essay. He offers reflections about anthropology and the world at three moments: 1984 (the year *Writing Culture* was actually compiled), 1999, and 2013. Along the way Fischer, an original *Writing Culture* contributor and intellectual whirling dervish, probes the cultural politics of fast-changing Asian cites, Iranian film, Bihari folk music, and more. He is unwilling to emplot his account through tropes of either progress or decline, underscoring instead that the "arrow of time does not move uniformly." He does see a role still for anthropology. Our "jeweler-eye craftsmanship in teasing out the refractions of everyday life," he insists, can sometimes "upset the echo-chamber master narratives, or aggregating voice, of politicians, political scientists, economists, and the mass media."

There's much else to be said about *Writing Culture*'s place in our disciplinary trajectory. A leading house historian of anthropology, Richard Handler, sets the postmodern turn of the 1980s within the field's changing sociology. Anthropology was a modest family affair back in the early days of Boas and his students. A few hundred people was a good annual meeting turnout. By contrast, anthropology expanded rapidly in American higher education's post–World War II boom. "We have grown," the field's doyenne, Margaret Mead, already wrote in 1973, "into a group of tremendous milling crowds, meeting in large hotels where there are so many sessions that people do well to find their colleagues who are interested in their same specialty." Those who now lament our "overspecialization," as Handler (this volume) notes, ignore that growth, with its accompanying fragmentation and diversification, is an expectable "function of normal science in a bureaucratized world." But these plural pathways do undercut the simple disciplinary periodizations that we like to invent to tidy up history's messiness. A closer look back at the 1980s—and Handler rereads the 1982 *Annual Review of Anthropology* to this end—recalls how much else was going on back then. The turn to reflexivity and representation headlined by *Writing Culture*, as strong as its imprint across the field, was hardly the only game in town. Some new developments proved dead ends; others, and Handler cites the example of the emerging interest in the anthropology of Europe, proved to have disciplinary legs of their own.

––––––––––

But what about anthropology now? The bulk of the essays here use *Writing Culture* as a launching point for thinking about the discipline today. One main concern revolves around that most canonical disciplinary mainstay, fieldwork. It's not exactly evident, besides out of habit and perhaps some science envy, why we still use this peculiar term that makes our research sound like a biology expedition to count baboons in a game preserve.[9] Nor, as various critics have noted, is it ever clear just where "the field" begins or ends in a shrunken world where nothing now stands, or perhaps ever has, more than a few degrees of separation from anything else.[10] All this said, the premise that fieldwork is our distinguishing bedrock remains as powerful as ever a century now since its original mythical charter in Malinowski's sweaty, disgruntled, libidinous Trobriand tenting. Most undergraduate as well as graduate anthropology programs have some required methods course. Others beyond the discipline, and sometimes the university, have even been poaching fieldwork to their own ends. It enjoys a certain fashionability among market researchers, political strategists, global health specialists, and other lost souls searching for something beyond the census numbers and online questionnaires.

Just what we learn in the field is not always so obvious. We assume that knowledge accrues in proportion to time spent in a place. But is this always so? Michael Taussig (this volume) points out that "first impressions are generally more vivid than subsequent ones." If you believe Malcolm Gladwell's best-selling *Blink*, then snap judgments may be more trustworthy than what we think we have learned after much study. We ourselves in our ethnographies like to tell self-deprecating fieldwork tales about confidence shattered—about the interview, encounter, or faux pas that forced us to see how our original assumptions were all wrong. These tales function to assure readers and ourselves that we really did gain some real insight in the end. (And, personally, I think you do learn more from sustained ethnographic engagement than any snap judgment or, for that matter, running algorithms on survey data from the safe remove of your university office.) In reality, of course, we're always partial prisoners of the ways we've been trained to see, no matter how much we want to flatter ourselves on our open-mindedness. What anthropologists "discover" in the field inevitably refracts, often mirrors, the discipline's agendas of the moment—"resistance" when that fascinated us, "governmentality" in its window, and so forth. Our newer tendency to emphasize that what we have learned is always fragmentary and incomplete—and shadowed by what Juan Obarrio, channeling Derrida, terms an unknowable "remainder"—is itself an overdetermined product of chastened post–*Writing Culture* sensibilities with a dash of newer high-theory complaint about the supposed tyranny of order.[11] Our fieldwork is always caught somewhere in between all too predictable discoveries and moments of something like genuine learning and sometimes even revelation. The trouble is that we're not always able to tell just which is which.

Kamala Visweswaran considers fieldwork's perils and possibilities in her contribution. An influential interlocutor in debates around feminist ethnography, Visweswaran relates how researching that most terrible of categories, genocide, has led her to see how "the field itself, . . . and our perception of it, shifts over time." If her work began with Hindus killing Muslims in Gujarat, it then took her elsewhere in South Asia, and then "inevitably back home," to Hurricane Katrina's devastation and the Iraq war. She coins "fieldnoting" by way of counseling mindfulness to the changing contexts of our efforts to decipher the world. Thus Visweswaran, on returning to this country, found her thinking going in new directions in reaction to the mainstream media's peculiar 24/7 brew of sensationalism, shallowness, and silence about some forms of human suffering. Her fieldnoting does not necessarily mean writing anything down. It does entail trying to remain alert to the forces both personal and not that so often change our own sense of what matters across a research project's long life.

We also face many new questions about fieldwork. Take, for example, the fact that multilocale research to track life in an interconnected world has become virtual orthodoxy by now. How do we pull this off without becoming spread so thin as to lose the intimacy of sustained ethnographic engagement that remains fieldwork's highest promise in the first place? And what does it mean for our fieldwork that so many of us now seem to be "natives" or at least "halfies" to the cultures we study, as opposed to an older day's proverbial outsiders? If fieldwork, as Sherry Ortner once defined it, is "the attempt to view other systems from the ground level," then what for that matter is the "ground" anymore?[12] After all, this age of cloud computing, the satellite, and so much traffic between the real and the simulated can make it unclear just where reality's terra firma begins, or, if Baudrillard had it right, whether any such thing exists any longer or perhaps ever did. How, more concretely, does one do the ethnography of Internet chat rooms, social media, or dotcom dating?[13] And what about new collaborative projects and other such experimental forms of research design?[14] There's never any shortage of things to discuss in those research methods classes.

The problem of writing lay, as the title had it, at the core of *Writing Culture*. Almost three decades later the poetics and politics of ethnography continue to be matters of much disciplinary discussion, and sometimes disagreement. As with fieldwork, the very word *ethnography* is clunky and dated, like a balky old power mower that works just well enough for us to keep on using it in spite of ourselves. Do any of us really imagine that what we write is about the "ethos" of those we study: the spirit of a *Volk*, that unfortunate Herderian fiction for dividing us humans into nations and peoples as if we had little else but anatomy in common? As Marcus underscores, the *graph* in *ethnography* has its own dimensions of anachronism. After all, the very idea of writing, at least anything more than a text or tweet, can seem old-fashioned now in the age of multimedia, streaming video and the avalanche of other digitized communication. It's a challenge to sell books at all nowadays, as any publisher will lament, other than the latest from some self-help guru, a famous movie star or politician's autobiography, or, of course, that celebrity chef's newest cookbook.

Growingly blurred boundaries of genre and expertise have made everything even trickier. As evidenced in wildly successful books like Anne Fadiman's *The Spirit Catches You and You Fall Down* and Katherine Boo's *Behind the Beautiful Forevers*, some journalists and other creative class writers have become, for lack of a better word, more "anthropological."[15] Much like us, they will go off somewhere, immerse themselves in local life in something akin to fieldwork, and then report back about what they've witnessed. We may have our quibbles with these books, but, unfortunately for us, they are often very well written and garner the reviews in the *New York Times*, radio and Internet attention, and big readerships that anthropologists seldom do. They sometimes end up on our syllabi, replacing writing by our colleagues. For that matter, you can now, as Fischer (this volume) underscores, find fiction that illuminates matters of culture and politics as well as or sometimes better than we do. What better book, for example, about colonialism's complexities than Amitav Ghosh's *Sea of Poppies* (though one would like to think that his anthropology training has something to do with that)? Or about contemporary Native American experience than almost anything by the Coeur D'Alene writer Sherman Alexie? And then there's the whole genre of memoirs by West African child soldiers, Latin American indigenous activists, and many more. Here postcolonials have their own say as opposed to being ventriloquized by the anthropologist. We had something of a monopoly, in the old days, over writing about people in out-of-the-way places. Now we don't have much of a franchise in anything at all.

Sales figures make the point in a cold way. An ethnography's typical print run is a thousand copies, tiny by trade press standards; the book is deemed successful if it sells all those. The only time we do much better is not because anyone chooses to read our books but through classroom adoptions, a form of forced consumption. As for our journal articles, they circulate among other graduate students and faculty with an interest in the topic, seldom farther. There's been experimentation aplenty with ethnographic form in the post–*Writing Culture* age, and for that matter before that. And lately there has been much talk about public anthropology to reach beyond the academy.[16] None of this seems to have much widened our readership. In the department of excuse making, we sometimes say that our books don't do well because they're too complex. This seems a dubious argument. After all, the likes of Boo, Ghosh, and Alexie produce nuanced work that still sells in big numbers. One also hears it said, as if we deserved a pat for daring truth-telling, that we don't have more readers because the politics of what we write is too radical for the mainstream. This isn't very plausible either. Being something other than an apologist for the status quo hasn't kept other intellectuals as varied in their views as Noam Chomsky, Judith Butler, Fredric Jameson, Leo Strauss, and Allan Bloom from gaining healthy readerships. Our sales shortcomings have more to do with other factors. We tend not to be very good storytellers, partly because we have no real training in this particular skill (and perhaps because we'd be novelists in the first place if we had much writing talent). We employ specialized trade jargon, sometimes more to sound smart than because it's really necessary to communicate our ideas. And then there's the increased competition in the crowded creative nonfiction market.

For all this, ethnography remains very much alive and even well in its modest way. Part of this has to do with the sociology of the profession. As Jurassic a medium as print may be, the journal article and the book remain the gold standard for hiring and promotion. We do hear ritualized talk from college administrators about reworking standards to value more highly teaching, filmmaking, community activism, and other work. And Fischer has described the emergence of so-called third spaces like studios, archives, and installations, many of them enabled by new technologies of various kinds.[17] Even so, it's still just about impossible to get tenure at a major research university—and sometimes also at liberal arts colleges—if you haven't published a book. That book is supposed to be an ethnography, with the collected essays, textbooks, mystery novels, and theory manifestos saved for later. As for university and other academic presses, they know that anthropology will not fix their own precarious bottom line, but ethnographies often do better than, say, the unfortunate likes of classical studies and French history. If anything, anthropology lists have grown in recent years (and Duke University Press is a noteworthy example). Ethnography, in short, is not an endangered genre no matter that we already seem to be moving toward reading books of all kinds more often on screens than on paper. While we might wish to reach bigger readerships, it's also true enough that sales is only one index of value. A need remains for the up-close, deeply engaged yet theoretically savvy view of things that good ethnography can provide as against the scary superficiality of so much sound-bite punditry and willed ignorance about the world.

It's actually an exciting time for ethnography in many ways. Like the study of kinship, spirituality and religion, or even play, we've seen the reinvigoration of traditional areas of ethnographic investigation from altogether new angles. Then again, the freeing of anthropology from its obsession with the primitive has allowed for the development of whole new areas of study: science and technology, of course, and yet also finance, bureaucracy, humanitarianism, environmental politics, sports, social media, and many other, often overlapping endeavors. There's historical ethnography that traces far-reaching patterns of flux and interconnection across centuries. And, be it African immigration to Norway or the Israeli Army's use of social media, we have much writing now about the new—yet another sea change for a discipline that didn't always pay much attention to history, change, or invention at all.[18] Marcus (this volume), ever the astute and sometimes visionary trend-spotter, suggests that "the temporality of emergence, of the contemporary (as the just past and the near future) defines as much if not more the mise-en-scène of many ethnographic projects today than the traditional distinctive space or site."

A number of this volume's essays take up the question of ethnographic writing for these new times. Kathleen Stewart asks (this volume) with characteristic inventiveness whether we can ever step "outside the cold comfort zone of recognizing only self-identical objects." According to Stewart, the very attempt requires a "reattuning" so as to "register the tactility and significance of something coming into form through an assemblage of affects, routes, conditions, sensibilities, and habits." Her own concern lies in the problem of precarity from her New England hometown, a Texas swimming hole, and the American road to her mother's decline. It's a question, as Stewart puts it, of trying to evoke "how things are hanging together or falling apart." She points to *Writing Culture*'s role in helping to clear "a field for an attention to emergent forms." Her own experimentation with timbre, form, and style has made its mark across anthropology and beyond. The line between anthropology, autobiography, poetry, theory, and observation blurs, sometimes melts away, in Stewart's essay here, as in so much of her other writing.

The ethnography of precariousness also concerns Anne Allison in her contribution. Allison wrote her first book, a feminist anthropology classic, about a Tokyo club where businessmen went to be fawned over by sexy young hostesses. As she describes it, *Nightwork* was still partly in the single-locale ethnographic tradition, albeit one very different from the picturesque rural villages of an older Japanese anthropology. There is surely even now sometimes a place for ethnography focused on a single site. But Allison's desire to decipher the post-bubble Japanese predicament led her to research that was "scattered rather than schematic and driven more by a sensing." She found that precarity itself, whether among Tokyo seniors or refugees from Fukushima's flooded radioactive devastation, proved often "beyond words" and to "def[y] groundedness" by its very elusive ubiquity. The resulting mobile ethnography of her moving essay here works through the vignette, the snapshot, and the chance encounter to evoke a Japan that juxtaposes the pain of unrealized longing against brave yet scattered attempts to fashion new forms of human connection.

That anthropologists can write, now, about Kyoto suicide prevention centers and Las Vegas strip malls measures the discipline's reinvention of itself to studying just about anything. But what about those ethnographers still working in the far-flung corners of the Third World that so obsessed anthropology in an earlier era? Africa, of course, ranked high among those archetypal areas, and no topic was more canonical than the investigation of African kinship systems. In his contribution Charles Piot returns to this sacred old subject but in the new post–cold war context of the scramble for exit visas and the hope for a better life abroad. Here Piot, a leading anthropologist of West Africa, shows how the U.S. visa lottery has led entrepreneurial Togolese to develop a creative cottage industry in fake marriages and invented relatives. In some ways, as he shows, the flexible, improvisational quality of fictive consular kinship politics is of a piece with everyday kin relations in Togo. But Piot also underscores its dimensions of newness, among other things the role of staged marriage videos and DNA testing surprises in the mix. If anthropology once helped to invent the fiction of unchanging primitive traditions, it's the opposite now. Like other Africanist anthropologists in more recent decades, Piot wants us to understand that life is everywhere in motion. He notes that the strangeness of visa lottery fakery is all too familiar in an age of product piracy, Wall Street Ponzi schemes, and the trampled border between the real and the fake. All of us, he insists, "traffic in nontransparent or compromised identities these days."

Writing Culture aimed to denaturalize ethnography by opening to scrutiny its history, politics, and conventions. Even now, however, an enduring disciplinary habit remains to presume a divide between field notes, typically unpublished, and the resulting ethnography, the great fetish of the finished book. Michael Taussig (this volume), who has set such a high-wire standard for original writing and thought across his career, wonders "if anthropology has sold itself short in conforming to the idea that its main vehicle of expression is an academic book or a journal article." He speaks in praise of the humble field notebook (no matter that it may nowadays be a tablet or laptop). Our notebook, Taussig suggests, "captures ephemeral realities, the check and bluff of life" in ways that our more formal published ethnography sometimes fails to do. It may indeed be the promise of the new collaborative multimedia formats—an instance of anthropology's emerging third spaces—to allow for other ways of doing things. To take just one example, the Asthma Files project, developed by Kim Fortun and Mike Fortun, brings together stray commentary, blog posts, articles, and more by anthropologists, epidemiologists, policy makers, and patients themselves. It crosses old boundaries of expertise, genre, and format through open threads of exchange and debate that stand in contrast to the printed book's dimensions of irrevocability and closure.

No longer does ethnography even focus only on our domineering species, as it did a few decades ago. We now have multispecies and cyborg brands of inquiry that seek to show for a fiction any ontology that would imagine the human, the animals, and the machine as separate spheres of being in the first place. Here dogs, magnetic resonance imaging, chickens, space rockets, and genetically engineered mice become the objects of a post-anthropocentric anthropology that probes the history and politics of our entanglements with other life forms. In his contribution Hugh Raffles, that rare anthropologist who has also had notable success as a trade author, presents us with a historical, cross-cultural exercise in the ethnography of stone. This requires radically reimagining scale and depth to grope our way back into the telluric reaches of geologic time. "In its stillness and its resonance," Raffles writes, stone "pulls us vertiginously into this vastness." The pocked sea rock he finds on an Oregon beach provincializes human existence in its juxtaposition to our relative newcomerness to planetary history and the ever more real possibility that we myopic, destructive beings will not even be around that much longer.

"We don't need a lot more anthropologists in the state," Florida's governor Rick Scott told reporters a few years ago, as if we were just a grade above cockroaches or some other household pest. The attempted retooling of higher education to align with the supposed necessities of cost cutting, job training, and market principles has put the liberal arts as a whole on the defensive. A proud anti-intellectualism, of course, is nothing new in America, and the Culture Wars demonology that paints anthropology, English, and other departments as nests of evil, politically correct drones still flourishes in conservative and other circles. These less than fuzzy feelings about us have now been hitched to the postfordist business model that makes such a mantra of downsizing, depoliticizing, outsourcing, and computerizing everything possible. The dearth of stable tenure-track positions has created a whole large class of subemployed adjuncts who suffer through bad pay, the slights of second-class university citizenship, and a demoralizing uncertainty about their future prospects. No wonder the defenders of anthropology and the other liberal arts have rushed to the barricades with statements, conferences, and reports to rebut the latest attacks.

Our modest field has managed to hang on in any event. There's little growth in anthropology or across the humanities. Here at Duke we graduate about twenty-five majors a year, as compared with several hundred in neuroscience and a small army in economics. It's the business, medical, law, and engineering schools that build the fancy big new glass buildings at universities everywhere. Yet the numbers of anthropology majors, Ph.D. students, and faculty have not declined but have grown some over the past decade. For better or worse, too, the promise of ethnography's more intimate understanding has attracted new patrons: corporations wanting better information about how to design and sell their products and, controversially, an American military seeking to learn more about the "human terrain" where it fights. The U.S. government and Microsoft are now reportedly the two biggest employers of anthropologists.[19] Scott, the unfriendly Florida governor, helped in 2009 to abolish the anthropology major at Florida State University. It has since been resuscitated there as against dark predictions that what happened in Tallahassee augured the shuttering of anthropology departments nationwide.

Why do we defend anthropology, besides the small matter of its being our chosen career? We tell prospective majors that the discipline will give them a valuable perspective on matters like diversity and multiculturalism, race and gender, globalization, and much more. That's all true enough; so are the clichés about the benefits of a liberal arts education. As to our political leanings, it's also true that one is more likely to run across an anteater in a shopping mall than a Republican anthropologist. It might not be a bad thing for us to have some greater diversity of political opinion within the ranks, or at least more than just the present span from left of center to some version of far left. But most of us do not try to sway students to any particular view, and it's not as if the warriors of the right wing don't get plenty of hearing in this benighted America of Rush Limbaugh and Fox News. If we really were hatching some sinister subversive plot against motherhood and apple pie, I'm not sure their defenders would have much to worry about anyway. Our modest numbers, shrunken departmental budgets, and proclivity for yoga, organic produce, and Priuses do not make for a very fearsome strike force.

Anthropologists cannot always agree on much anyway. Every field features what the feminist theorist Robyn Wiegman terms "object dramas," namely one or more key concepts that define, fixate, and vex that particular discipline.[20] The concept of culture has, clearly, been a prime drama object in anthropology. There have been endless attempts to pin it down once and for all, and, of course, they always fail. *Writing Culture* belonged to a moment of critique of the very idea of culture for seeming to suggest that a changing, interconnected world divides into fixed, bounded, homogeneous units, including calls to "write against" it.[21] Some of us tend now to avoid the noun for these problematic associations and yet continue to use the adjective cultural, which is really just a semantic evasion. Other anthropologists still speak about "American culture," "Japanese culture," or "Hopi culture" in more traditional fashion. There are always, meanwhile, new permutations of very old debates about the relationship between culture, economy, and society, however they may be defined. Much scholarship now also tracks the social life of the culture concept, namely its circulation beyond anthropology into fierce, sometimes bloody struggles over migration, nationhood, heritage, education, and the politics of exclusion and belonging. It's perhaps unsurprising that the lack of consensus would be so pronounced in a field whose ultimate objects of study, people, are so very different, contradictory, and changeable in the first place.

Anthropologists have always wanted to imagine a moral mission to their enterprise. For all the familiar and sometimes justified latter-day criticism, the likes of Boas, Mead, and Benedict and, across the Atlantic, Evans-Pritchard and Malinowski saw their would-be scientific findings in the laboratory of faraway cultures as countering stereotypes of primitive backwardness, at times even offering models for the West's own improvement. Their scholarship, more than we sometimes credit, advanced the then quite novel causes of racial equality and cross-cultural understanding. But the upheavals of the late 1960s and 1970s brought a more aggressively politicized style of being an anthropologist. As questioning of the very ideology of scientific objectivity found reinforcement in currents of feminist, poststructuralist, and postcolonial theory, calls sounded for an "activist," "militant," "barefoot," or, more recently, "public" or "anarchist" anthropology. Decoding racial, gendered, sexual, national, or capitalist formations of inequality became the biggest disciplinary fulcrum. By the end of the twentieth century it sometimes seemed as if every ethnography had politics or at least power in its title. Anthropologists, according to the new ethnographic self-fashioning, almost always positioned themselves in implicit or explicit alignment with the marginalized, the excluded, and the oppressed. Both our theoretical lenses and the objects of inquiry may have changed, all the way from resistance and social movements in the 1980s to neoliberalism, citizenship, and sovereignty at this century's beginning and, more recently, precarity and the politics of affect and hope. But the idea that anthropology can or even, as the more policing would have it, must contribute to the struggle against injustice remains powerful in our disciplinary ethos.

Kim Fortun makes a strong case for anthropology's potential contribution in her essay. A role remains, Fortun believes, for critiquing the actually existing order of things. Her own fine ethnography of the Bhopal disaster was a compelling examination of the intertwined stories of victims, lawyers, Union Carbide executives, and environmental activists in the aftermath of that outsized late industrial tragedy. Now, however, Fortun wants us to recognize that ethnography may also be a means for eliciting "the future anterior," a "space of creativity, where something surprising, something new to all emerges." This means designing forms of research that makes "hesitations and shifts" into an opening for generating "something that could not be said, could not be brought together before." Here the product of an ethnographer's labors may be a website, a digital archive, or perhaps a series of conversations, and not necessarily a more traditional ethnography at all. The multimedia, cross-professional, transnational Asthma Files project exemplifies just such an endeavor. Fortun cites as well recent ethnographic efforts to bring together convenience store chain executives, industrial designers, and locavore critics of the farm-industrial system to reconsider the politics and economy of food. The larger hope, she concludes, is for ethnography that "becomes creative—setting language games in motion, provoking different orderings of things, having patience for what we cannot yet imagine."

In her essay Danilyn Rutherford also advocates a retooled anthropology. Rutherford, who finds inspiration in David Hume's concepts of circumstance and sympathy, coins the label *kinky empiricism* to describe her agenda. This would entail a supple yet conjoined commitment to the empirical and the ethical that eschews the false guarantees of analytical closure much less moral certitude. Well known for her own first-class scholarship about Indonesia and Papua New Guinea, Rutherford remains alert to ambiguity and contradiction in good *Writing Culture* fashion. But she, no more than Fortun, does not wish to wallow in what David Chioni Moore calls "anthro(a) pology" for our disciplinary shortcomings.[22] "Even though we are aware of the partiality of our truths," she paraphrases Hume, "we still must act." Her essay makes its own strong case for an anthropology that might matter for the better in a dangerous, divided world.

Our scramble for the would-be moral and political high ground has shaped major disciplinary developments in the long shadow of the 1960s. Among the most notable has been claiming expertise over what Joel Robbins terms the "suffering slot."[23] Here the anthropologist brings back stories of pain, violence, and misery to throw into relief the world's terrifying injustices. This merging of ethnographic witnessing, moral crusade, and social analysis has been pressed by some of the era's most influential anthropologists, among them Nancy Scheper-Hughes, Veena Das, and, the closest thing we have to a celebrity, Paul Farmer.[24] The resulting work can sometimes, through little fault of its own, play into the condescending old conceit that poor, brown-skinned people can be rescued only by enlightened Westerners, an ideology recycled yet again in elements of the student humanitarianism boom of recent years. But this anthropology's embrace of responsibility for the suffering slot very self-consciously reverses the old-school disciplinary tendency to ignore the human costs of war, conquest, and poverty. Even as Boas and his students in America dedicated themselves to salvaging a record

of supposedly vanishing native traditions, they did little, as so many critics have noted by now, to document white colonialism's devastation, much
less try to stop it. Alfred Kroeber, who led the UC Berkeley department for
almost half a century, once was asked why he never wrote about the brutal
treatment of the Yurok, the California tribe among whom he most often
worked. He replied that he "could not stand all of the tears."[25] Whatever
the limitations to the anthropology of suffering, it's surely a good thing that
we now feel some obligation to not ignore the travails of our fellow human
beings (and I'm delighted myself to see so admirable a figure as Farmer become an undergraduate campus hero).

Still other ways of trying to make anthropology matter have developed.
Consider the genre of what might be termed exposé ethnography. Here the
anthropologist scrutinizes troubling American institutions—supermax prisons,
car culture, big pharmaceutical companies, military bases.[26] In this instance of
blurred boundaries, we edge onto journalism's turf and into a muckraking
anthropology that would have America face some of its own by turns stupid,
cruel, and self-destructive habits. Of late too we have seen growing interest in
what Arturo Escobar terms the *pluriverse*, namely in alternative models of life
and ontology to dominant Western models.[27] This scholarship is novel in its
varied inspirations and expansive ambitions, a role for anthropology in making visible and even designing a whole new plan for an imperiled planet. At
least in its strong interest in indigenous lifeways, the turn to the pluriverse also
bears continuities with the older tradition of what Fischer and Marcus called
"anthropology as cultural critique" and its strategy of using the example of
an elsewhere to rethink our own society (the hoary classic being, of course,
Mead's *Coming of Age in Samoa*, the best-selling anthropology book ever).[28]
Thus, for example, Marisol de la Cadena introduces the concept of "indigenous cosmopolitics" to suggest how some native ways of thinking challenge
or, at least, in Isabelle Stenger's terms, "slow down" the orthodox Western
worldview that divides nature and culture, magic and science, religion and
politics.[29] Here the anthropologist once more seeks to save us from ourselves
by opening our eyes to other ways of seeing the world (and with the attendant
perils of recycling shopworn essentialisms about native peoples as the guard-
ians of all that was lost in the West's fall into modernity).[30]

Digitality obviously brings a whole new, unanticipated set of factors into the
equation. In the *Writing Culture* era most anthropologists still prepared their
manuscripts on that now obsolete inscription device, the typewriter. None of us
had yet heard of email and the Internet, much less had any premonition about

how they would rule our lives. Jackson's essay explores how the digital "re-wires anthropological possibility" for better and worse. Now when we teach, we use blogs and online course material platforms and sometimes offer whole classes through the Internet; we access articles and books at a click, as against those many trips into the library stacks in an earlier day; and even those of us who have worked in faraway places, Peru in my case, now find that the "field" no longer seems far away at all in the age of Skype, Facebook, and the instant message. As much a cultural as a technological revolution, the cyberization of anthropology has brought different habits, rhythms, and sensibilities, among them the prototypical time-space compression of postfordist times. Now, as we know too well, an undergraduate can instantly email his complaint about an exam grade's supposed unfairness instead of cooling his heels until office hours. Graduate students keep abreast of the latest publications and grants and the progress of their peers through the Internet's glutted communications net-works. (One wonders what role the sense of always measuring and being mea-sured, not to mention the perennially bad job market, plays in so much anxiety and depression in anthropology doctoral programs.) The foreshortening effect of digitality, the sharp-sighted Jackson suggests, also brings new monitoring and accountability. He wonders about members of the African Hebrew Isra-elites of Jerusalem, the religious sect he has studied, watching and perhaps objecting to a talk he gave about them at Stanford University, now archived as a webcast. The Internet, Jackson concludes, "humbl[es] the ethnographer's aspirations for a kind of a one-sided voyeurism." No longer do anthropologists enjoy the undemocratic luxury of saying whatever they please about "their" people without having to worry about anyone talking back.

The great widening of anthropology's gaze introduces still other quanda-ries. So much has the field turned from its former fixation on the primitive that more anthropology dissertations appear every year about the United States than any other country. Much ethnography, in the older disciplinary tradition of documenting Otherness, remains focused on what Micaela di Leonardo calls "exotics at home"—the homeless, the imprisoned, the addicted, the migrant.[31] But that's by no means always true now with the anthropology of finance, biotechnology, advertising, law, and other research that puts the more privileged under anthropology's microscope. Funding for anthropol-ogy dissertation research stateside is still sometimes in scarce supply. (For example, the SSRC and Fulbright support only international projects.) It can also be hard for anthropologists of the United States to get hired, at least in an anthropology department (and this because most departments already have faculty researching topics in this country thanks to that familiar blow-back trajectory where middle-aged, tenured anthropologists, for family and other reasons, leave their original Third World research sites for new projects closer to home). Then again one wonders if we might (already?) have gone too far toward bringing anthropology back home. If the discipline is really to be the study of human life everywhere, it surely behooves us to stay spread out. We do not, after all, want to play along with the parochial narcissism of an America that would like to imagine itself the center of the cosmos. There's a place, I'd say a need, for a discipline that insists on a genuinely global perspective. The matter of coverage and focus looks different, of course, from the standpoint of other anthropology traditions—say, the French or growing Chinese, Indian, or Brazilian ones. What counts as the field, home, and away have their own distinctive history in these places, each with its own questions about just what ought to be the distribution of disciplinary attention.

––––––––––––

It's hard to tell where anthropology may be heading next. The discipline sometimes feels like a wacky grab bag of diverging concerns and agendas in the first place. Our four subfields are outrageously different in their history, foci, and the skills they demand. If the arrangement were not our real-life Boasian inheritance, it would have taken some LSD-tripping university administrator to dream up housing in the same department the likes of biological anthropologists, real scientists with labs and microscopes, and we humanities-oriented culturals (whose natural sciences expertise, or mine at least, quite often does not go much beyond watching the occasional Discovery Channel special on the search for the Abominable Snowman).[32] Cultural anthropology alone remains a crazy quilt with its countless AAA subsections. We work in very different conditions, from community colleges to four-year liberal arts colleges and universities, public to private institutions, not to mention outside the academy. We bring our own particular, sometimes idiosyncratic tool kits of theory and method to every new research project. Those milling meetings crowds show no more sign than ever of rallying to the banner of any single topic, methodology, or grand unifying paradigm. (And, when held in more bewitching cities like New Orleans, the assembled anthropologists spend less time at the panels than in nightclubs and bars anyway.)

But neither does the field seem about to dissolve anytime soon. We anthropologists, or at least the culturals, do have some things more or less in common: a history, habits, and shared reference points. The venerable liberal arts structure, of which we are a relatively entrenched part, shows some considerable staying power. Nor does anthropology's penchant for what Clifford Geertz once termed "epistemological hypochondria" keep us from enjoying still a certain appeal to other fields—literary scholars turning to ethnography to get beyond the text; historians looking for ways to squeeze culture from the archives.[33] A few anthropologists now even hold influential positions, among them the chancellorship at a major university and the World Bank presidency. We might seem to be threatened by the latest shiny, well-funded, much-ballyhooed brands of inquiry: brain imaging, evolutionary psychology, genomics and epigenetics, behavioral economics, and various brands of Big Data and the tyranny of the algorithm. Perhaps they will unlock human behavior's secrets, thereby rendering obsolete our interpretive sensibilities as well as our belief in fieldwork's essential merits. But I doubt it. How to understand the world seems more likely to remain an area of contestation in which the weight of nature and nurture, the relative merits of quantitative and qualitative research, and so many other primordial debates assume new forms without any final resolution.

I do think the mantra of complexity and contingency has run its course. The insistence in *Writing Culture* on multiplicity, heterogeneity, and the limits of metanarratives was novel in its moment, and yet is now an annoying ethnographic cliché. Lately, in contrast, we've seen big interest in big books like David Graeber's *Debt* and Michael Hardt and Antonio Negri's *Empire* trilogy that do not shy from big claims about the world. (Interestingly these tomes, perhaps because they promise big answers, have sold surprisingly well despite or perhaps partly because of their unapologetic academese.) The older, ritualized call for a so-called biocultural synthesis, which seldom used to go anywhere beyond the occasional conferences and obscure edited volume, has found some new traction at anthropology's intersection with the booming neurosciences.[34] Then too we have the phenomenon of what might be termed posttheoretical ethnography that, while informed by high-tech debates about textuality and the politics of representation, keeps its visible theoretical and citational apparatus to a minimum.[35] The trajectory of theory in anthropology obeys its own predictable laws: some new orthodoxy's ascendancy and then the usual Oedipal counterreaction against it; the swing of fashionability's pendulum between lumping, building grand generalizing models, and splitting, the questioning of monological claims as many in the *Writing Culture* generation did; and, of course, the search for truly or purportedly understudied new topics for investigation (as, for example, in the increased interest in infrastructure, or the current sound studies boomlet.)[36] All the recent thinking about a political ecology of things that insists on the conjoinedness of life and matter is only the latest thread of inquiry spun from theory's twirling wheel.[37] Our pathways sometimes lead us to surprising and truly fresh insights, and other times just into dead ends.

I suspect that the question of what difference we might make in the world will also continue to occupy us. The culture of twenty-first-century anthropology is still very much flavored by activism and social critique, and, happily enough in my opinion, we remain a default doctoral studies choice for twentysomethings of the kind who organize anti-sweatshop campaigns, answer phones at the rape crisis center, volunteer with an African AIDS clinic, and lean otherwise to doing left-oriented, politically minded good. I do not myself especially like the labels of "activist" or "public" anthropology, with their somewhat flat, confining, and self-righteous ring. For that matter it's not always evident just what the righteous moral pathway may be in an age when good intentions do not always have their expected consequences (as the grow- ing anthropology of humanitarianism would have us remember), and larger hopes for mobilization affix themselves to such impossibly vague subjects as the "multitude" and the "99 percent."[38] At the same time we know that apathy and its twin traveler, cynicism, are hardly an adequate moral alternative in a world so in need of compassion and change. Many anthropologists, whether or not seeing themselves as activists, continue searching for their own ways to cul- tivate human kindness and social justice in their writing, teaching, and research- ing. (In this volume they range from Allison's "volunteering observation" after the Fukushima tsunami to Piot's courtroom testimony for Togolese asylum seekers.) That search surely can, should, and will continue in the years ahead.

Any attempt at more ambitious forecasting of anthropology's future is likely a losing proposition. I'm not sure we even have as much control over disciplinary directions as we might like to imagine. As often as not the grand transformations of anthropology have answered to history's bigger gravita- tional forces: the Boasian repudiation of Victorian Social Darwinism tied to Progressive-era reformism; the 1960s social movements at home and decolo- nization abroad propelling anthropology's reinvention in its present more politicized, postprimitive, postcolonial shape. If anthropology has been in a bit of a holding pattern in these most recent decades, then surely whatever outsized global developments await us will transform the field once more in one way or another. The growing disciplinary attention to climate change (the anthropocene? . . . the "capitalocene"?) responds to the mounting evidence for the bigheaded foolishness of our wild modern dream of unchecked planetary development. What if we do commit species suicide in a sooty toxic cloud? A third world war breaks out when some crazy leader's forefinger strays to the nuclear button? Or, if one prefers to indulge in utopianism's pleasures, we manage to find our way somehow to a better, more just planet? The ship of anthropology, if it stays afloat, may not look for so much longer anything like it does today.

We bob along for now in a dark dirty sea far from any sheltering shore.

Acknowledgments

We dedicate this volume to Ken Wissoker, a treasured friend and visionary editor who has done so much to promote anthropology in his years at Duke University Press. For comments on this introduction, I am grateful to Anne Allison, Charles Piot, Kamala Visweswaran, Katya Wesolowski, and members of our Cultural Anthropology Department at Duke University who gave feedback at a work-in-progress group session. Piot had the original idea for the *Writing Culture* twenty-fifth-anniversary conference out of which this volume grew; he and Allison, as editors of *Cultural Anthropology*, sponsored the event itself with support from the Cultural Anthropology Department and John Hope Franklin Humanities Institute at Duke. Can Evren provided key editorial assistance. Jade Brooks, Susan Albury, and the all-star team at Duke University Press did their usual marvelous job in getting the book into publication.

Notes

1 This comes from Eminem's track "Cinderella Man" (2010), lyrics available at http://www.azlyrics.com/lyrics/eminem/cinderellaman.html.

2 Some of the essays in this volume were first presented at the Writing Culture at 25 conference at Duke University, September 30–October 1, 2011, and later became part of a special issue of *Cultural Anthropology*, which I also edited. These pieces appear here in revised form. Allison, Fischer, Handler, Piot, and Visweswaran wrote their chapters especially for this volume, and, as with my introduction, they are published now for the first time.

3 On the San Francisco BDSM scene, see Weiss, *Techniques of Pleasure*. Jones, *Trade of the Tricks* explores magic in France; Edmonds, *Pretty Modern* looks at plastic surgery in Brazil.

4 On the challenges for women of color, see Navarro et al., "Sitting at the Kitchen Table."

5 The term *epistemic murk* comes, famously, from Taussig, *Shamanism, Colonialism, and the Wild Man*, xiii.

6 Hymes, *Reinventing Anthropology*; Asad, *Anthropology and the Colonial Encounter*.

7 Polier and Roseberry, "Triste Tropes." See also Sangren, "Rhetoric and the Authority of Ethnography."

8 See, for example, Mascia-Lee et al., "The Postmodern Turn"; Behar and Gordon, *Women Writing Culture*.

9 As to terminology, it should be said that other terms have their own limitations. Dwelling science is too precious; deep hanging out is too flip. The suggestion box is open.

10 Gupta and Ferguson, *Culture, Power, Place* remains among the best discussions of these dilemmas.

11 Obarrio, "Postshamanism."

12 Ortner, "Theory in Anthropology Since the Sixties," 143.

13 See Boellstorf et al., *Ethnography and Virtual Worlds*, for more on the ethnography of virtual worlds.

14 Lassiter, *The Chicago Guide to Collaborative Ethnography* contains a good discussion of collaborative ethnography; Field, *Abalone Tales*, is a fine example of a collaborative ethnography.

15 The genre blurring has also occurred with film. Just as creative nonfiction has encroached on ethnography's turf, many documentary filmmakers have grown more "anthropological" in approach. The border between documentary and ethnographic film has become very porous, with visual anthropologists like Lucien Taylor making films like *Sweetgrass* (2010), shown at documentary film festivals, and, conversely, skilled documentarians producing very "ethnographic" work, including about themes like native life in the Amazon that would once have been the province of ethnographic film. Some new documentaries, interestingly, also take up themes of reflexivity and the politics of representation in ways that reflect debates in anthropology about these same issues—for example, Elizabeth Barret's *Stranger with a Camera* (2000) and a dramatic film, the charming Norwegian *Kitchen Stories* (2003).

16 Borofsky, *Why a Public Anthropology?*

17 Fischer, *Emergent Forms of Life*.

18 Kuntsma and Stein, in *Another War Zone*, write about the Israeli Army and social media; McIntosh, in "Before and After," about African immigration to Norway and the history of anti-immigrant sentiment there.

19 See Graeme Wood on corporate anthropology, or what he terms "Anthropology Inc.," *Atlantic*, February 20, 2013, http://www.theatlantic.com/magazine/archive/2013/03/anthropology-inc/309218/. Albro, "Anthropology and the Military" gives an overview of the debate around anthropology's involvement in "human terrain" research for the military.

20 Wiegman, *Object Lessons*.

21 Abu-Lughod, "Writing against Culture."

22 Moore, "Anthropology Is Dead."

23 Robbins, "Beyond the Suffering Subject."

24 For more on Farmer, see *Mountains beyond Mountains*, Tracy Kidder's Pulitzer Prize–winning book about him.

25 For more on Kroeber, see Buckley, " 'The Pitiful History of Little Events' "; and Starn, *Ishi's Brain*.

26 On supermax prisons, see Rhodes, *Total Confinement*; on car culture, Lutz and Fernandez, *Carjacked*; on the U.S. military base in Diego Garcia, Vine, *Island of Shame*; on big pharmaceutical companies, Dumit, *Picturing Personhood*.

27 Escobar, "Sustainability."

28 The phrase *anthropology as cultural critique* comes from the title of Marcus and Fischer's 1999 book. Gupta and Ferguson, in their introduction to *Anthropological Locations*, raise a set of useful warnings about this strategy's traditional deployment of us/them dichotomies that can efface intertwined global histories.

29 De la Cadena, "Indigenous Cosmopolitics in the Andes." I should add that the sharp-sighted De la Cadena is fully aware of the perils of romanticization I raise below.

30 I discuss some of the problems around politics of indigeneity as well as anthropology's peculiar relationship with Native America in Starn, "Here Come the Anthros (Again)." See also De la Cadena and Starn, *Indigenous Experience Today*.

31 Di Leonardo, *Exotics at Home*.

32 I am not myself, for all this, necessarily against the four-field model, with arguments on both sides; for the case against it, see Yanagisako and Segal, *Unwrapping the Sacred Bundle*. Lewis, in *In Defense of Anthropology*, offers a defense, albeit a somewhat tendentious one, of the four-field tradition.

33 Geertz, *Works and Lives*, 71.

34 See Rose and Abi-Rachelle, *Neuro*, for the case for the relevance of the neurosciences to the human sciences in general.

35 Kernaghan's *Coca's Gone* is a fine example of the genre I am calling posttheoretical ethnography.

36 The new interest in sound grows partly from ethnomusicology, yet with other influences. A classic text is Feld's *Sound and Sentiment*. A fascinating, more recent exemplar is Novak's *Japanoise*.

37 Bennett's *Vibrant Matter: A Political Ecology of Things* is a key text, and I take my phrasing here from the subtitle of her fascinating book.

38 On humanitarianism's paradoxes, see Redfield's fine recent book on Doctors without Borders, *Life in Crisis*.

CHAPTER 1

Feeling Historical

James Clifford

———————————

Twenty-five years after *Writing Culture*. What was that moment? Where are we now? The conjunctures. And a story to connect them.

Telling history in medias res, historicizing while standing on the historical banana peel. One thing is certain: you will be proven wrong, or at best, passé.

I'd like to say from the start that I'm uncomfortable with statements like those I've heard recently: "*Writing Culture* transformed ethnography" or "*Writing Culture* was a game changer." Transformations were occurring. Games were changing. But *Writing Culture* was part of the changes, not their cause—however avant-garde we may have felt at the time.

Writing Culture registered, very imperfectly, what now seem to have been historic forces for change: anticolonial and feminist, to mention only the two that I stressed in my introduction. There were plenty of others. The book's gaps, its "exclusions," have been amply explored: race, class, gender, sexuality. And where is visual culture? What about film, so important in the reconfiguration of ethnographic practice? Isaac Julien's *Territories* was screened in 1984, the year of the Santa Fe seminar. And Faye Ginsburg recently reminded me of Jean Rouch, a neglected inspiration. Where are technology, communications media—structuring forces that today loom so large?

The fact that the book was widely read, that it was debated and made sense in contexts beyond anthropology at least shows its embeddedness in the historical moment. Its originality? At best, you get to be six months ahead of the zeitgeist.

This is how our project looks to me a quarter-century later. The retrospection I offer here is very much a song of experience, not of innocence. My own writing (I won't speak for the others) now seems innocent in its tone of confident, knowing critique—a voice so irritating to many of *Writing Culture*'s detractors.

Today I feel embarrassed by that voice. I also wish I could reclaim some of its confidence.

Let me begin again, with another return to *Writing Culture*, a recent French translation of my introduction, "Vérités partielles, vérités partials" (2011). The translation, with a preface, was the work of a doctoral candidate I've never met: Emir Mahieddin. I was asked for a short afterword. I'll use it as the starting point for my expanded reflections here.

Reading one's own words in translation is always an experience of estrangement. One sees, hears oneself from a distance—another person in a different time. And of course any translation, however faithful, is something new, a performance for unimagined audiences. What could *Writing Culture* possibly mean, what work might it do, for French readers (or for any readers) in 2011? In his astute introduction Mahieddin suggests that *Writing Culture* and, more important, the intense debates that followed its appearance twenty-five years ago, have attained a kind of "classic" status. No longer a succès de scandale, the book can perhaps be read for what it actually says.

In the United States when "postmodernism" was so urgently resisted, the barbarians at the gates were associated with "French theory." Simultaneously in France "le postmodernisme Américain" was being held at arm's length. But of course the zeitgeist didn't respect national borders. Many of the trends associated with postmodernism had their own French trajectories in the work of Jean Jamin, Jeanne Favret-Saada, Jean Bazin, Marc Augé, and Alban Bensa, to name just a few prominent anthropological examples. I might also mention Bruno Latour and François Hartog. The interdisciplinary openness of *l'Homme* under Jamin's editorship seems very much in the critical, experimental spirit of *Writing Culture*. And yet, as Mahieddin notes, there has been resistance, a sustained suspicion of intellectual movements that were pervasive across the Atlantic and the English Channel: cultural studies, feminist theory, various neo-Marxisms, critical studies of race and ethnicity. Ten years ago a quick trip on the *Eurostar* from London to Paris took one into a different intellectual universe. In the bookstores, where were the topics that filled the British shelves? Where was race? Gender? Deconstruction? One looked in vain for Stuart Hall, Fredric Jameson, Donna Haraway, Paul Gilroy, Judith Butler, or their local equivalents. Today the situation seems to be changing, the general attitude less insular, certainly among younger scholars. Perhaps *Writing Culture* will have its delayed moment in France. Perhaps.

———————

As I read *Writing Culture* now—my own words especially—I feel most profoundly their historicity, their distance. They belong to another world. There is no entry for *globalization* in the book's index. No *Internet*, no *neoliberal*, no *postcolonial*. A *wiki*? For us, back then, it might have been some kind of *djinn* or spirit! Writing was, well, writing—a matter of pen and paper. Today it's not hard to imagine the cover photograph of *Writing Culture* with Stephen Tyler furiously texting and his bemused "informant" absorbed in a cell-phone call.

So much has changed in these twenty-five years. How can the changes be understood? What historical narratives make sense of them? In retrospect I have come to believe that a profound shift of power relations and discursive locations was going on, and still is. Call it, for short, the decentering of the West. The discipline of anthropology has been an inextricable part of this decentering, and so have its critiques, books like *Writing Culture*. I hasten to add that decentering doesn't mean abolition, defeat, disappearance, or transcendence of "the West"—that still-potent zone of power. But a change, uneven and incomplete, has been under way. The ground has shifted under our feet.

A conversation from the early 1970s comes to mind. I was a doctoral student doing research work at the London School of Economics in the Malinowski papers, and one day outside the library I found myself chatting about the history of his discipline with Raymond Firth, the great anthropologist of Tikopia. Firth had been a student and colleague of Malinowski. He shook his head over attempts to connect anthropological research with colonial power, in particular the important book edited by Talal Asad, *Anthropology and the Colonial Encounter* (1973). Without minimizing the issue, Firth thought the relations between anthropology and empire were more complex than some of the critics were suggesting. He shook his head in a mixture of pretended and real confusion. What happened? "Not so long ago we were radicals. We thought of ourselves as gadflies and reformers, advocates for the value of indigenous cultures, defenders of our people. Now, all of a sudden, we're handmaidens of empire!"

This is what it's like to feel historical. The marking of colonialism as a "period" (a span of time with a possible ending) came suddenly to Euro-American liberal scholars, at least those who noticed the changes. Who would have predicted in the early 1950s that within a decade most of the colonies ruled by France and Britain would be formally independent? Feeling historical can be like a rug pulled out: a gestalt change perhaps, or a sense of sudden relocation, of being seen from some previously hidden perspective. For Euro-American anthropology, the experience of a hostile identification as a Western science, a purveyor of partial truths, has been a troubling, alienating, but ultimately enriching process. The same learning opportunity challenged many scholars of my generation with respect to gender and race.

In retrospect I locate *Writing Culture*'s intervention within a larger, postwar narrative of political and cultural shifts. To explain the changes and the perspective I bring to them I will need to explore my personal experience, like Firth's, of being repositioned. The relevant slice of history just happens to coincide with my own lifetime. Perhaps the critics who insisted that postmodern reflexivity could only lead to solipsism were right after all!

Born in 1945, I grew up in New York City and Vermont. This was the peace of the victors: the cold war standoff and a sustained, U.S.-led economic boom. My fundamental sense of reality—what actually existed and was possible— would be formed in circumstances of unprecedented material prosperity and security. Of course, my generation experienced recurring fears of nuclear annihilation. But because disarmament was not around the corner, we learned, on a daily basis, to live with "the balance of terror." In other respects the world seemed stable and expansive, at least for white, middle-class North Americans. We would never lack resources. Wars were fought elsewhere. The lines of geopolitical antagonism were clearly drawn, manageable.

New York City during the 1950s felt like the center of the world. North American power and influence were concentrated in downtown Manhattan. A subway ride took you to the United Nations, Wall Street, the Museum of Modern Art, or avant-garde Greenwich Village. The dramatic decolonizing movements of the postwar period arrived belatedly in the form of civil rights, the Vietnam debacle, and a growing receptiveness to cultural alternatives. My critical thinking would be nurtured by radical art and the politics of diversity. Its sources were dada and surrealism, cross-cultural anthropology, music, and popular culture. New historical actors—women, excluded racial and social groups—were making claims for justice and recognition. I saw academic work as inseparable from wider challenges to societal norms and cultural authority. The moment brought a new openness in intellectual, political, and cultural life. To mention only the U.S. university, the ethnocentric, male-dominated English department of the 1950s now seems like a kind of bad dream. The moment also produced exclusivist identity politics, hedonistic subcultures, and forms of managed multiculturalism. The language of diversity could mask persistent inequalities. My own writing never escaped the liberal pretense of "making space" for marginal perspectives. Yet despite these limitations, the politics of cultural critique, of experimentation and inclusion were serious responses to an ongoing, irreversible displacement.

When I was thirty-three I moved from the North Atlantic to the edge of the Pacific, from one global ocean and world center to another. For a time I was a diasporic New Yorker, living out on a periphery, the West Coast. But little by little the presence of Asia, the long history of North-South movements in the Americas, and influences from culturally rich Island Pacific worlds made themselves felt. I was living in a decentered, dynamic world of contacts. The whole idea of the West as a kind of historical headquarters stopped making sense.

Moreover in northern California I could clearly see that the decentering at work was not just an outcome of postwar decolonizing energies and contestations during the global 1960s. These forces had made, and were still making, a difference. But the shift was also the work of newly flexible and mobile forms of capitalism. I was caught up in two unfinished, postwar historical forces working in tension and synergy: decolonization and globalization. Santa Cruz, California, my home after 1978, epitomized this doubleness. A 1960s enclave of countercultural, antiauthority visionaries, the town was also a bedroom community for the high-tech world of Silicon Valley. This was the "Pacific Rim" of massive capital flows, Asian Tigers, and labor migrations. I also lived on a *frontera*, a place in the uncontrolled, expanding borderland linking Latin America with the United States and Canada. In the northern half of Santa Cruz County: a university and town government strongly identified with multicultural, feminist, environmentalist, anti-imperial agendas. In the southern half of the county: a population of Mexican and Latino immigrant workers, a long history of labor struggles, and the growing power of agribusiness. I began to think of the present historical moment as a contradictory, inescapably ambivalent conjuncture: simultaneously post- and neocolonial. My writing in the 1990s grappled with this recognition that the energies of decolonization and globalization were historically entangled—sometimes tightly, sometimes loosely or in struggle.

California felt less like the U.S. West Coast and more like a crossing of multiple unfinished histories. My book *Routes* (1997) reflects this sense of dislocation. Its final chapter, "Fort Ross Meditation," took me north to Alaska and another *frontera* region, Beringia. Fort Ross, just up the coast from San Francisco, was an outpost of the Russian fur-trading empire, its labor force composed of Aleut (or Alutiiq, as they now call themselves) sea otter hunters. I would follow the legacy of these mobile natives in contemporary Alaskan identity politics. (This is in my current book, *Returns*.) The Fort Ross contact zone also led me to a deeper concern with the histories of indigenous California, a topic I've pursued through the open-ended story of "Ishi," the state's most famous Indian. Teaching in Santa Cruz also opened contacts with South Asia and the Island Pacific through the graduate students who studied in the University of California, Santa Cruz's interdisciplinary history of consciousness program. Academic travelers, they identified themselves as "postcolonial" or "indigenous." Some would remain to teach in the United States; others went home. Circulation and contact continue. These younger scholars' clear sense of working within—while resisting and looking beyond—a Euro-American world of ideas and institutions intensified my own sense of being displaced, a "late-Western" subject. I also felt myself recruited to their projects.

———————

A deepened awareness of geopolitical (dis)location empowers and limits my historical perspective in ways I can only begin to grasp. Developments after 2000 are even less susceptible to narration than the post-1960s decades. It is impossible to say with certainty what comes next. A few things, at least, seem evident: The United States, newly vulnerable, is no longer an uncontested global leader. Its military surge following 9/11 proved unsustainable—a spasmodic reaction to secular, irreversible changes. There will doubtless be further adventures, but U.S. global hegemony is no longer a credible project. It is countered economically by Asia and Europe; by Islam as only the most visible among non-Western globalizing ideologies; by resistance to neoliberalism in Latin America and elsewhere; by financial instability and uncontrollable markets; by the volatile, uneven spread of predatory forms of capitalist accumulation; by rising inequality, scarcity, and instability worldwide; by deepening ecological limits and competition for resources; and by the internal fragmentation and fiscal emergency of more and more nation-states. The signs of systemic crisis and transition are everywhere—crisis without resolution, transition without destination. In the 1980s Margaret Thatcher could famously declare, "TINA: There Is No Alternative." In the early 1990s Francis Fukuyama, with a straight face, announced "the end of history." Today everyone knows there are many alternatives, for better and worse.

Where does *Writing Culture* fit in this history that I've been painting with a broom? Conceived in the early 1980s it can be understood as either a late 1960s or an early 1990s work. The book's critical energy, its reforming zeal, and its sense of (neo)colonization as the principal locus of power relations signal a 1960s genealogy. But one need only contrast it with a precursor, Dell Hymes's influential collection from 1972, *Reinventing Anthropology*, to see the changes. *Writing Culture* is distinctly post-1960s in style and emphasis, especially in its concern with discursive determination, its assumption that forms of representation actively constitute subjects in relations of power. The world it expresses is more that of Foucault than of Fanon. Or perhaps I should say more late Foucault than early Fanon.

As the 1960s waned and neoliberalism took hold, visions of revolution were replaced by cultural and intellectual tactics of subversion or critique. By the 1980s frontal resistance to a mobile and inventive hegemony seemed useless. We were in a Gramscian "war of position." What could not be overthrown might at least be undermined, transgressed, opened up. For many intellectuals working inside Euro-American centers of power this meant supporting "diversity" in both epistemological and sociocultural registers. Space could be cleared for discrepant senses of the real; positions could be staked out for struggles that could only be imagined. Dominant forms of authority and common sense could be criticized, theoretically disassembled. *Writing Culture*, with its rejection of monological authority and commitment to experimentation, made sense in this conjuncture.

I see *Writing Culture* as occupying a transitional moment—late 1960s to early 1990s—in the larger history of the past half-century. And I understand this postwar history as the interaction of two distinct but entwined historical processes: decolonization and globalization. Neither process is linear or guaranteed. Both are contradictory and open-ended. Both have worked to decenter the West, to "provincialize Europe," in Dipesh Chakrabarty's words. This is an unfinished but irreversible project. Decolonization and globalization have been historically linked during the past sixty years, but their roots are different, and so may be their futures. *Writing Culture* reacted—with insight and blindness—to profound shifts in global culture and society. It is very much a work of its time. Yet it seems to be having a second life in the present conjuncture. Experiments in ethnography abound, as Kim Fortun makes clear in her visionary preface to a recent "relaunch" of the book by the University of California Press. What new uses are being found for the critical tools in this book from a former world? *On verra ça.*

Rereading *Writing Culture*, I'm struck by how much less "historical" we felt back then. The book does not float in metacritique, as some critics have claimed. It is very much oriented toward practice. But its explicit historicizing seems relatively thin. One encounters talk of the "world system" (more or less in Immanuel Wallerstein's terms). And the power of colonial legacies shows up a lot (in chapters by Renato Rosaldo, Mary Pratt, Talal Asad, and me). George Marcus grapples directly with political economy—with the ethnographic problem of representing "the system." Writing about Paul Willis, he notes, a bit wistfully, that at least Marxists can assume a fully worked out, recognizable theory of the whole. For Marcus, however, large-scale political, economic, cultural articulations pose a genuine problem of representation—a problem now more acute than ever.

Paul Rabinow attempts to historicize the book's undertaking from a place of critique on the edge of its regime of truth. He finds symptoms of "postmodernism," relying on an early version of Fredric Jameson's influential work on the cultural logic of capitalism's latest stage. This historical perspective, to be developed by Jameson and, later, David Harvey, was only just emerging, and it was still quite ethnocentric—grounded in Europe and North America with little sense of different historicities or even of global governmentality. (In this latter arena Rabinow, like the rest of us, would soon be on a rapid learning curve.)

Michael M. J. Fischer's contribution grapples with historical emergence. He surveys diverse forms of ethnic autobiography, taking the pulse of what had not yet come to be called "identity politics." The "postmodern arts of memory" he invokes as models for reflexive ethnographic writing take decidedly post-1960s forms: nonessentialist, relational, "inter-referential." Far from a vision of containment, or taxonomic multiculturalism, Fischer discovers uncontrollable energy, a spilling out of categories. *Postmodern*, in his usage, denotes sites of invention and excess. Yet he still feels able to round it all up in a generalizing, authoritative way, a mode that would get him into trouble with ethnically identified critics.

A good deal of *Writing Culture* now seems like the "critique" Bruno Latour thinks has painted itself into corners.[1] We often operate within ready-made diagnostics of power: colonial, institutional, hegemonic. Overall the book's contributors show little sense of their epistemological embeddedness, their precarious historicity. Looking back at my own writing, I notice the certainty of its uncertainty, its confident critical tone. Partial truths are picked apart. But there are in the book few "situated observers," as Renato Rosaldo would later name the displaced social scientist. There is "provincialization" of the West, to be sure . . . but only up to a point. Our province remained the decentered center of the world. No doubt Michel-Rolph Trouillot saw something like this when he wrote about the "timidity" of *Writing Culture*'s critiques.

For us, feeling displaced was exciting, not scary. Perhaps this best sums up the distance I feel today from the book's conjuncture.

Let me say another few words about decolonization and globalization from my shaky perch in the new millennium. I've said that the historical changes I've lived through are aligned by these two historical forces.

Globalization is not, or not simply, "the capitalist world system." It is of course capitalist . . . and more. I hold on to the much-abused word as a sign of excess, a name of the evolving world of connectivities we can't represent. Globalization in this sense is obviously not the 1990s version—"the end of history," "the flat earth." Nor is it the universal enemy—José Bové tilting against McDonald's, the Battle of Seattle. Globalization is the multidirectional, unrepresentable sum of "material/semiotic" relations (as Donna Haraway might put it). It's not simply a continuation of imperial dominion by other, more flexible means, as critics on the left are likely to observe. It's more than that. You can't say imperialism from below, but you can say globalization from below, or from the edge. *Globalization*, for me, is a place-holding name for an articulated, polycentric totality. Multiple zeitgeists. A bush, or tangle, or historicities.

Likewise for *decolonization*. This denotes a historical process, not an event—not the national liberations of the 1950s and 1960s that were initially successful, then co-opted. Decolonization names a recurring history—blocked, diverted, continually reinvented. The energies once bundled in phrases like *the Third World* or *national liberation* are still with us. They reemerge in unexpected sites and forms: *indigeneity* (all those people once destined to disappear), *the Arab Spring* (whatever that turns out to be).

There is something genuinely hopeful in the surprises that history can be counted on to deliver. We can certainly take heart from the failures of the dominant systems we resisted (and became, in the process, dependent on). We can be grateful for the inability of hegemonic common sense to subsume alternatives, to round up, to account for everyone. What new identities, alliances, social struggles, and modes of conviviality are emerging?

This hopeful, or at least exciting, feeling of historical possibility is inseparable, at least for me, from another emotion, something I didn't experience twenty-five years ago: the visceral awareness of a "given" world suddenly gone. The ground shifting, for better and for worse. Serious questions about our grandchildren's future. Feeling historical.

This is not about terror. The terrorist, a scapegoat, is a symptomatic condensation of instabilities that are deep and world changing.

The vulnerability to political violence and economic insecurity that many of us feel today is intensified by ecological threats that can no longer be managed or exported. What happens when the supplies run out, when the resource wars get really desperate? Of course this feeling of exposure is a version of what most people in the world have always known.

The certainty of having lived in a First World bubble of security that is no more. Good riddance to that. And now?

Twenty-five years after *Writing Culture*: the excitement, the fear of being in the real.

Note

1 Latour, "Why Critique Has Run out of Steam."

CHAPTER 2

The Legacies of *Writing Culture*
and the Near Future of the
Ethnographic Form: A Sketch
George E. Marcus

The *Writing Culture* "moment" really began for me with the arrival of a visitor to our department at Rice in 1980 (we were collectively discussing, I recall, orality and writing in the production of ethnography), with his (Harvard book) bag full of books. The visitor was James Clifford, and he presented an early version of his essay "On Ethnographic Authority" as he passed around valuables—exemplars (I recall most memorably, Jeanne Favret-Saada's *Deadly Words*)—of what was to become the reflexive turn of experiment and all of its variants in "writing culture."

What is the equivalent of such a bag of books in thinking about legacies of *Writing Culture* today?

Writing Culture was an ambitious and much needed critique of anthropology by means of literary therapy applied to its primary genre form.[1] Issues of politics, the claims of anthropological knowledge, and what exactly is transacted in fieldwork all became matters of experiment with a rather modest textual form that became richly overburdened for a time, and then settled into new conventions that accommodated rhetorics of argument, "doing" theory, and a general so-called reflexive turn. This legacy of experimenting with forms has now shifted to and blended with contemporary challenges to still mostly individualistic projects of ethnographic research in a more globally organized or, rather, arranged, world in which fieldwork must be constituted other than locally. Far from being matters of new method, about which anthropologists have been famously implicit and unspecific, these challenges are once again about the forms of knowledge but have now shifted from texts as reports from the field to the production of media (web texts, forms of collaborative thinking, articulations, concept work amid data or as data) within, or alongside, the field, as the latter has changed its character[2]—and modes of making them accessible to multiple constituencies, including the professional. Although the latter trend might be seen as mainly a result of spreading new information technologies—the vaunted digital revolution—it would be a mistake, without underestimating at all their significance, to miss the continuity of *Writing Culture*'s concerns with critique through experiments with (discursive) forms in the same impulses today to find ways, media, and modes that mesh ethnographic discourse itself within anthropology's reinventions of fieldwork as a process of inquiry.

So, in this reidentification of the concerns of *Writing Culture* in the present, I want to identify two tendencies:

1. There are shifts in the forms of scholarly communication, or at least in the ecology of the present expansion of digital possibilities, and their effects on the ethnographic genre of research and writing: the book remains important to ethnography, of course, but in a different ecology that favors "commons" of various sorts. Chris Kelty has written about this as the function of composition as a key form of ethnographic process based on its collaborative, collective grounds (drawn from the practices of crowdsourcing, open source and access, and the formation of recursive publics).[3] What does the book or its related productions (e.g., the scholarly article) out of the ethnographic process become within this ecology? Some of the exemplars of new forms that I will mention arise as a function of trying to situate ethnographic research today in this ecology and developing embedded, accessible expressions of it in the process.

2. To certain degrees, there has been an involution of form in the writing of ethnographic accounts, a certain settling in of theoretical influences as dictating writing practices—leading to a mannerist, or even a baroque form.[4] Notable ethnographic accounts are often marked by tendencies of excess in descriptive and theoretical ardor, and a desire to surprise by tropes of unusual juxtaposition. Less baroque forms of ethnography must find their richness, I argue, outside now established theoretical traditions of critical ethnographic writing, and the appeal of alternative forms of articulating thinking, ideas, and concepts inside or alongside the challenge of situating and managing the fieldwork process—in "third spaces," archives, studios, labs, "para-sites" and the like—lies in just that.

The discursive thinking produced in these forms along the way of field-work is not especially antitheoretical or overly pragmatist but is foremost open and sensitive to found perspectives as sources of its own ideas and its own language of commitment to argument or critique. The use of critical cultural theories from the 1980s and 1990s is a means of creating an often ancillary apparatus for a kind of found and direct concept work in designed spaces of experiment and intervention alongside the valued serendipity of fieldwork's movements and circuits (these could be, e.g., studios, installations, workshops, or simply seminars as or lateral to fieldwork). Most acutely the ethnographic process becomes transitive and recursive, in addition to being already deeply reflexive. Writing culture within this process moves from the field notebook (in anticipation of the eventual text) to certain accessible, if not public, forms of concept work and critique in the protracted, phased segments of many fieldwork projects today. It is experiments and attempts at these kinds of forms that I have been especially interested to examine today as a legacy of 1980s writing culture debates in their displacement within the terrain of anthropological inquiry that is conventionally categorized as "method."

The 1990s, the 2000s, and the Center for Ethnography at the University of California, Irvine

After the 1980s writing culture debates that put in play a paradigm of critique for anthropological research—from, say, the early to mid-1990s onward—anthropology in the United States had then to rethink itself, as did a number of other disciplines, in relation to the perception and reality of macro social changes that went under the rubric of *globalization*. As a discipline it had to work through knowledge economies, global projects of political economy, assemblages, or circulations to find its way to both its traditional and new subjects at the ethnographic scale (face-to-face, everyday) in which it is committed to work. This task was more than just recontextualizing or renarrating the scenes or locations where ethnography could be done. It meant literally moving in scapes or flows, reinventing the concept of the field, reproblematizing the traditional object of study and exploring new ones. This collective thinking was reflected at the time by a spate of resonant "trend" writing about the recalibration of the scale and meaning of the basic tropes of anthropological research method so as to set them in motion.[5]

The diverse and fascinating ways that the trends envisioned in the 1990s as the challenge of globalization to the previously more circumscribed ways of conceiving projects of ethnography have played out through the first decade of this century as problems of designing fieldwork and its practices in, through, and between complex institutional orders (e.g., Ong and Collier's *Global Assemblages* is, for me, an iconic text, among others like it, of the ethos of ethnographic research during this period). Conditions for ethnographic research glimpsed or evoked in the 1990s are now full-throttle trends of research practice, to be examined as experimental moves or improvisations project by project, as they are reported in ethnographic writing still dominated by critical theory, as they are evoked in the shifting terms of "tales of the field"—the particular kind of shop talk in which anthropologists like to indulge about their tradecraft, as they are taught in graduate mentoring, and, most important, as they are reflected in the alternative media and forms, notably collaborative, through which access to both fieldwork and its results in development is made available.

In broad brush I am particularly interested in projects that have to work through complex knowledge economies to shape their own anthropologically conceived objects of study, projects in which the balance has shifted from previously marked epistemological interest in defining ethnographic research questions by the intense examination of anthropologist-other intersubjectivity to a marked ontological interest in the problem of conceiving complex objects of study. (In this, anthropology's participation in science studies has been crucial in conditioning it more generally to working through knowledge economies to sites of everyday life.)[6] Commensurately the reflexive turn, instilled by 1980s critiques of ethnographic writing, has been overshadowed by a transitive (or alternatively, recursive) turn. Anthropologists move in circuits, assemblages, or among relations—as working metaphors for defining the field—and they move situated discourses that they accumulate in unusual configurations. This movement and posing of arguments out of the places where they are usually made, heard, and reacted to are distinctive acts of ethnographic fieldwork that are political, normative, and sometimes provocative in nature; deserve their own designed modalities accessible to readerships, audiences, and constituencies who consume ethnography as a form of knowledge. In this sense, indeed, ethnography has routinely become "circumstantially activist,"[7] not so much as a contingent effect of the unfolding of research as multisited but rather as central to its strategies of asking and pursuing questions among its constituencies, including and encompassing activists, social movements, jurists, humanitarian interventions, international organizations, and, for that matter, corporations, agencies, and labs as well, but always in the name of a distinctive tradition and form of disciplinary knowledge.

The visions and tropes of the 1990s have thus become plans, designs, and technologies for giving form to fieldwork in the present. The classic ethnographic textual form—even as amended since the 1980s and given its learned pleasures—is a very partial and increasingly inadequate means of composing the movements and contests of fieldwork, both naturalistic and contrived, collaborative and individualistic, that motivate it and on which it is intended to report. The alternative is middle-range forms of collaborative articulations in the course of inquiry that need, in turn, trials and experiment under the mantle of disciplinary recognition and authority that anthropology has to confer on the research that it engenders.

These developments are indeed under way, and my own vantage point to explore them is from within the Center for Ethnography that since its founding at the University of California, Irvine, in 2005 (www.ethnography .uci.edu) has been interested in studying the conditions of contemporary challenge to and enhancement of common understandings in disciplines (not just anthropology) that promote and value ethnographic inquiry—say, for example, at the time of the 1980s *Writing Culture* critique, as well as before and after, in the unfolding of projects of ethnographic research, whether pursued as the initiatory pedagogical dissertation project or as successive later projects in maturing research careers.

The following are six conditions that shape ethnographic projects today and to which the Center has paid special attention. In my own view such conditions are significant in encouraging experimentation with the discursive forms of collaborative thinking enmeshed within or alongside the pursuit of still largely individualistically conceived projects of fieldwork.

1. MOST PROMINENTLY, THE IMPERATIVE AND IMPULSE TO COLLABORATE

Collaboration has always been an ingrained dimension of fieldwork, more or less recognized. But today it is also an explicit ideology of and pervasive form for doing all sorts of business—scientific, corporate, infrastructural, and so forth. It is this imperative to collaborate built into sites and situations of ethnographic research that affects its deeply individualistic mode of production and stimulates it to revise its ethos of participant-observation toward forms of explicit but ambiguous collaborations, sometimes compelled, sometimes entered into as ethnographic strategy or opportunity. Collaboration is now doctrine in the worlds in which anthropologists move. Creations of alternative forms alongside and within fieldwork are in part explicit adaptations to this condition of doing research and in part much needed elaborations of the collaborative impulse that has always been in fieldwork projects. Collaboration is thus both a constraint in working through contemporary knowledge economies to topics, approaches, and attention to data that are distinctively anthropological in character and a desire of a research tradition that had long restrained collaborative impulses. This makes any set of working collaborative relations cutting across sites of fieldwork highly political and a challenge to traditional conceptions of the ethics of research.

2. DOUBLE AGENCY

Anthropology's thriving, distinctive culture of research, composed of a cluster of informal practices and standards, has an uncertain, often ill-fitting relationship to the demands and analytic languages-in-use of the larger institutional structures and ecologies of research in terms of which it must define and shape itself, for the sake of such quite tangible "goods" as research funding and disciplinary recognition and of public and academic conversations in which anthropology would like to count as participating. Its deeply regulative norms often conflict with the larger contexts in which it must be successful as a contemporary knowledge-producing discipline. At least part of the solidarity and identity of anthropologists today is based on a premise of their own disciplinary "cultural intimacy,"[8] a shared understanding that they are playing a game of doubleness, or fancifully of double-agent-cy, on the level of individual research project design and development. There is a sense of producing research for both "us" and "them" at the same time, in different registers. Every exploration of an alternative form evoked in this sketch is also a productive and more explicit exploration of this condition of double agency within or alongside the scenes of fieldwork as they unfold.[9]

3. RECEPTION AND GRANULAR PUBLICS WITHIN THE FRAMES OF FIELDWORK

The widespread call, at least in U.S. anthropology, for a public anthropology signals the intense interest of anthropologists in the responses to their work by the publics (or commons) of varying composition and scale that it is able to touch. These responses seem to matter more to many anthropologists, at

least affectively, than professional responses to their work. Some of the alternative forms in and alongside fieldwork that I am surveying accommodate
this desire and define challenges of design that address it. How can this interest in reception—as engagement with constituencies while the research is in
progress as an integral dimension of it—become a granular dimension of the
scale and process of a fieldwork project? This is not just a question of what the
subjects think of what the anthropologist has written about them but how
diverse responses to a project as it develops become part of its integral data
sets, and then the basis for professional reception and assessment of their own
products of knowledge by anthropologists themselves in a double, dialogical
process by which the results in progress of anthropological inquiry are both
public and authoritative knowledge. Folding receptions into anthropological research through alternative forms, such as the studio, the para-site, or
the dynamic archive, also responds to and "passes" for a kind of operative
imperative, like that to collaborate, in neoliberal institutional arrangements
and projects, to provide voice for "stakeholders." But in the studio or para-
site contexts of ethnography, this accommodation of reception in research
agendas themselves plays into anthropology's own longer standing critical
rationales and commitments. All of the forms that I evoke below explicitly
define publics or constituencies as a dimension of fieldwork itself.

4. INCOMPLETENESS AND SCALE

Ethnographies never have delivered literal holistic accounts of any of the social scales that they have represented, but the research that has produced ethnographies has been undertaken with satisfactory (or satisfying) imaginaries
of the broader social systemic contexts in which it operates (even doctrines
of "partial knowledge" provide, by deferred imagination, this systemic context for the intimate scale of ethnograph).[10] How to evoke and understand
broader scales in ethnographic research projects became more problematic
during the 1990s—not so much in the rhetoric of ethnographic writing as in
the planning and doing of ethnographic research—with multiple discussions
of "the global situation," on the one hand, and, on the other hand, with
the weighted shift from epistemological to ontological concerns in several
important arenas of ethnographic research (e.g., sciences studies, political
economy, development). With the failure or weakening of holistic systems
rhetorics that assist the defining of sites or circuits of ethnographic research,
incompleteness becomes a methodological postulate, even a theorem. How
a project in its intensive doing is incomplete not only becomes an interesting

question in itself but also a probe with which to establish paraethnographic connection with research subjects or counterparts who perhaps share an affinity with the ethnographer based on a dimension of variable speculation about agencies elsewhere, and an encompassing, contextualizing systemic scale. (I once conceived these relations of research as based on complicity rather than rapport.)[11] In any case a speculative imaginary of an ethnographic sort for how the everydayness of one's inquiry relates to the unseen everydayness of connected elsewheres becomes an important dimension of fieldwork that is motivated to create alternative forms to probe with others in the circuits of fieldwork this "theorem" of incompleteness within or alongside many ethnographic projects today.

5. THE TEMPORALITY OF EMERGENCE

Working on and in the temporality of emergence, of the contemporary (as the just past and the near future) defines as much if not more the mise-en-scène of many ethnographic projects today than the traditional distinctive space or site, with a definable past and a captured present. The present becoming the near future at least shapes a common orientation of ethnographer and subjects and provides the negotiable basis of mutual concept work—a shared, baseline imaginary for it—on which the collaborative experiments with form that I am evoking depend. Orientation to the emergent present thus produces the aesthetic satisfaction of surprise that in part drives ethnographic inquiry but also connects with the parallel aesthetics found among the intellectually more active of ethnography's subjects, as interlocutors and epistemic partners in research.

Kim Fortun in her chapter for this volume conceives of this distinctive temporality of ethnographic research in the contemporary as the "future anterior":

> Ethnography . . . can be designed to bring forth a future anterior that is not calculable from what we now know, a future that surprises. Ethnography thus becomes creative, producing something that didn't exist before. Something beyond codified expert formulas.
>
> The future is anteriorized when the past is folded into the way reality presents itself, setting up both the structures and the obligations of the future. . . . Toxics, like the future anterior, call on us to think about determinism but without the straightforward directives of teleology.

The temporality of emergence is thus a condition of the research situation and a feature of the material—the data as such—that ethnography collects, but more significantly, it is a component of the ways of thinking and analysis that the ethnographer and her subjects try out on each other as fieldwork proceeds. Eventually this temporality finds itself as a framing and analytic language in the writing of ethnographic texts, but much before that it is a key dimension of the way concepts and thinking emerge collaboratively and speculatively in the field.

6. THE APPEAL OF DESIGN AND THE STUDIO AS A LEGITIMATE FORM OF EXPERIMENTATION IN ASSOCIATION WITH FIELDWORK PROJECTS

Design practices have had great appeal in recent years across a number of practices in the human sciences that were reshaped by critical culture theories during the 1980s and 1990s especially. Bruno Latour has attractively dubbed design as "the cautious Prometheus"—evoking a kind of pragmatic, small-scale ethos and plan for the critical scholar as researcher with activist inflection in an era of phlegmatic left-liberal political imaginaries.[12] Design thus has within it associations with critique and critical practices yet thrives in formal relation to markets and commerce. Optimistically the appropriation of design methods, then, might give ethnography (to which designers have been drawn in their need to take users into account and in their own curiosities through "cultural probes") the affordance of the "mole" in "third spaces." This may be wishful thinking, but in terms of how fieldwork is conducted, it does offer the concept of the studio and its practices as a material means of experimenting with alternative forms within or alongside the serendipitous movements of ethnographers in fieldwork. The studio captures a micro public, or its representatives, evokes a scaled-down commons, while creating a literal space for broad, speculative, and explicit theoretical thinking and a culturally sensitive means to shape an unruly field or domain of research circulation. It can establish an authority for ethnographic inquiry, building on that existing for the design studio, where that of ethnography itself is more than usually constrained or barely recognized.[13]

Third Spaces and So Forth

Michael Fischer influentially posited during the early 2000s that anthropology "now operates in a set of third spaces" in which "anthropology's challenge is to develop translation and mediation tools for helping make visible the difference of interests, access, power, needs, desire, and philosophical perspective." He goes on to say that "these third spaces are terrains and topologies of analysis of cultural critique of ethical plateaus. They are dramaturgical processes, fields of action and deep plays of reason and emotion, compulsion and desire, meaning making and sensuality, paralogics and deep sense, social action and constraints of overpowering social forces."[14]

My sense is that many projects of ethnographic research roughly from the turn of the century forward are indeed operating in third spaces, but both of their own making and design as well as in those "found" and posited. So what are these third spaces literally? How have they been imagined, and sometimes literally produced, stage-managed, or forged out of the circuits and serendipitous movements that fieldwork projects define? For third spaces to be found, must they to some degree not be produced, elicited as domains of speculative thinking, alongside and increasingly defining situations of fieldwork? What are the varieties of such moves and inventions? How are they conceived, and what do they portend for anthropological knowledge?

Exemplars

These questions have come to be the intellectual spine—the orienting themes—of the Center for Ethnography at UCI, with a curiosity about the many projects that were then self-consciously emerging at its inauguration (in 2005) and becoming established arenas of anthropological research endeavor amid the networks, assemblages, knowledge economies, and complex institutional arrangements of global orders that had been the prominent subjects of the influential "trend" writing in anthropology during the 1990s that I mentioned and anthropology's early forays into sciences studies, as well as fascinations with critiques of neoliberalism, flows, circuits, ethnographic multisitedness, and so forth. Immersive fieldwork certainly has remained the ideology of ethnographic research in these arenas, but its ultimate results, its developing ideas and arguments are functions of different sorts of participation that pursue a line of thinking in the field, often collaborative and collective in nature, that requires not only documentation (in field notes and diaries, e.g., leading to the monograph) but also forms of elicitation, demonstration, and accessibility to publics and readerships in process. Thus in contemporary ethnographic projects, prototypes—working versions anticipatory of a result—have become in a sense more important productions than finished and rounded interpretative texts. But these productions need their forms, their spaces, their studios and media. It is the variety of such experiments in form that the Center has sought to follow, encourage, provide perspective on, and perhaps use to articulate the rudiments of a theory of such practices.

In terms of digital technology, the website, and its evolving capacities (e.g., the development of content management systems, of text-oriented websites, or blogs, like WordPress) to represent, communicate, and create opportunities for participation, has been the working medium for the development and communication of alternative forms embedded in or alongside the research process. The capacity, knowledge, and resources to support digital forms for ethnography are another matter—and a challenge. Yet the following exemplars all make use of such technology at different levels and stages of commitment. Overall they provide the means of continuing access during the life of a research project to experiments with the ethnographic form whether they are performed through such technology (as in some experiments in dynamic archiving) or through active staged interventions and studio events alongside fieldwork for which digital technology provides a means of continual reporting and engagement in relation to its granular, built publics along the way. What such forms, technologically assisted or not, provide access to is not so much data but the analytics and thinking of a research project in progress. They certainly do not trump as yet the conventional ethnographic text or book. Rather, at this juncture, they can provide an enframing ecology for it. But as both the performed events as forms and the technologies for discursive access to them develop, they do promise to be more than just supplementary to or enframing of the classic modes of writing culture.

In the spirit and within the limits of this sketch, I merely categorize, with brief descriptions and annotations, a sample of the projects that I have been following. I cite their own self-presenting websites and statements for consultation by the reader as a means of following them in their devised modes of anthropological scholarship that develop continuously and alongside the broader and encompassing projects and knowledge economies through which they constitute their research as fieldwork under the range of contemporary conditions that I described.

DYNAMIC ARCHIVING

Rather than mere repositories of data or accumulated scholarship, archives in the mode of ethnographic experimentation are active, animated, open-ended, multilevel, and transitive in authorings, genres, publics, commons, and internal relations, monitoring the shifting conditions of producing ethnographic research today. Among the exemplars that I am surveying they are the most fully alternative to the authoritative print genres of scholarly communication. Their conventional success depends on resources, investments, and patronage of the technologies through which they are created. In this way they are perhaps no different historically from, say, encyclopedias and cabinets of curiosity when they were in fashion. From the many such projects under way today morphing conventional disciplinary practices,[15] Mike and Kim Fortun's Asthma Files project is a work in progress that illustrates the considerable hurdles in actually producing a platform true to the project's considerable ambitions and vision, as well as providing a continuing in-depth conceptual, theoretical, and normative discussion of the project's imaginaries rooted in the ethnographic stuff of the world.

In such projects not just technological possibility but also curatorial practices become key to the construction, maintenance, and arguments-within-form of dynamic archiving, as contemporary "writing culture."[16]

STUDIOS, LABS, PARA-SITES

Studios and labs established in relation to particular fieldwork projects, collectively or individually pursued, have different durations, compositions and intellectual styles. They are often influenced by the working practices of a variety of design disciplines (e.g., architecture, graphics, product design, or design modalities in informatics and computer science, or theater arts and art-making movements like conceptual, performance, and installation art) or natural sciences that combine lab work with fieldwork.

A lab model is the Anthropological Research on the Contemporary (ARC; anthropos-lab.net), begun in the mid-2000s at Berkeley and that has gone through a number of changes.[17] It has evolved a distinctive sense of how collective lab work should develop alongside ongoing ethnographic research projects (the function of "concept work" that it defines for itself), and there are some interesting debates early in its history, and archived on its website, about alternative ways a lab or studio initiative might relate to existing ways of thinking about the conduct of fieldwork.[18] In its later iterations ARC reports on specific studio events in relation to particular fieldwork projects in progress.

A studio model is the para-site developed from the mid-2000s as well at the Center for Ethnography at UCI as a modality available to "first fieldwork" projects of dissertation research in progress that provides an opportunistic means of untying certain conceptual or relational knots that emerge during or after (in the postdoc period) such pedagogically monitored research. The scenes for such events are carefully thought through, designed, and even staged, and depending on its problems, and its politics, so to speak, brings together different constituencies to the research, including those in the field (informants, subjects, members of its publics) and those not (e.g., supervising, mentoring professors, fellow students, relevant experts).

Although the para-site concept of studio events alongside or within field-work was originally a pedagogical modality,[19] it has migrated into an element of thinking about ethnographic projects in maturing careers. However, para-site studio interventions were not meant to be part of the design or planning of fieldwork projects in their early stages but rather a resource or form in reserve, thought through as such and adapted to the conditions of doing ethnography today—especially with regard to the imperative and the impulse to collaborate, discussed previously. Para-sites are thus opportunistic and meant to reduce the abstraction of the theoretical processing of ethnographic data by pushing such processing into staged dialogic occasions of the ethnographic research process.[20]

PROJECTS WITHIN (OR ALONGSIDE) PROJECTS

An important category of projects of contemporary ethnographic research that create conditions for the kind of experimentation with forms, like the studio, lab, staged or designed intervention, or curated archive that I have been discussing, are those embedded within and usually funded and given assigned "space" by much more powerful, often international, and cross-institutional projects. These are ethnographic research functions within the leviathan, so to speak, the new assemblages, arrangements, and animating ideas of governing orders. Actually most ethnography today, no matter how local, occurs within or in relation to such regimes, the reflexive sides of which exercise increasing auditing scrutiny, itself of variable ethnographic interest of what it sponsors.[21] The condition of producing ethnography that gives rise to a critical function of the kind *Writing Culture* promoted within the craft of producing ethnographic discourse (in its textual genre, but now, as I argue, in fieldwork) is the sort of double agency that I mentioned. And these ethnographic projects within larger patron projects that negotiate different agendas epitomize this condition of double agency and perform it, so to speak, alongside forms that it produces, sponsors, or participates in: conferences, studios, seminars, planning meetings, and so forth.

Two such projects that I have followed with fascination are the Institute for Money, Technology and Financial Inclusion (http://www.imtfi.uci.edu/), conceived and directed by my colleague at UCI, Bill Maurer, and funded as a project of the Bill and Melinda Gates Foundation, and Paul Rabinow's term as director of the Ethics, Law, Social Implication component of a multiuniversity initiative (SynBERC) funded by the National Science Foundation to establish the emerging field of synthetic biology.[22] Together they provide an interesting and revealing comparative probe into projects that align (and contest) the purposes of critical ethnographic inquiry with those of megaprojects that define space and a certain domain of agency for the latter. Both projects define anthropological research and media as a contemporary legacy of writing culture within the clockwork of Weber's bureaucratic rationality or of Foucault's governmentality. They exhibit both the subtleties and the more overt politics of so doing, as well as the experiments with digital, conference, and workshop forms on which depends a sense of doing fieldwork while participating in the work of larger projects.

ENVOI

A post-modern ethnography is a cooperatively evolved text consisting of fragments of discourse intended to evoke in the minds of both reader and writer an emergent fantasy of a possible world of commonsense reality, and thus provoke an aesthetic integration that will have a therapeutic effect. It is, in a word, poetry—not in its textual form, but in its return to the original context and function of poetry, which by means of its performative break with everyday speech, evoked memories of the ethos of community and thereby provoked hearers to act ethically.
—Stephen A. Tyler, *Post-Modern Ethnography*

Notes

1 The task of the Santa Fe seminar from which these essays emerged was to introduce a literary consciousness to ethnographic practice by showing various ways in which ethnographies can be read and written. The question for the anthropologist is, then, how consequential this literary therapy should be. Does it merely add a new critical appreciation of ethnography, which one can take or leave in reading and writing ethnographic accounts, or does it clear the way for reconceptualizing anthropological careers and valorizing innovations

in strategies for projects that link fieldwork and writing? See Marcus, "After-word," 262.

2 Faubion and Marcus, *Doing Fieldwork Is Not What It Used to Be.*

3 Kelty, "Collaboration, Coordination, and Composition."

4 See Marcus, "Ethnography Two Decades after Writing Culture."

5 In U.S. anthropology, works such as Appadurai, *Modernity at Large*; Tsing, "The Global Situation"; Gupta and Ferguson, *Culture, Power, Place*; and Marcus, "Ethnography in/of the World System," among several others.

6 See especially Fischer, *Emergent Forms of Life and the Anthropological Voice* and *Anthropological Futures.*

7 See Marcus, "Ethnography in/of the World System."

8 See Herzfeld, *Cultural Intimacy.*

9 As Marilyn Strathern has said, based on her own forays into complex big science projects and redemptive of ethnography in those contexts, "Social anthropology has one trick up its sleeve: the deliberate attempt to generate more data than the investigator is aware of at the time of collection" (*Commons and Borderlands*, 6). This "more data," this surplus of interpretation and insight—more than subjects, clients, or a broad public perhaps desire or understand—is often the stuff that defines the double agency of fieldwork research. In the alternative, experimental forms emerging today this stuff finds expression and articulations that can morph, travel, and gain constituencies within the operations of fieldwork and beyond. The inevitable position of double agency today becomes, in studios, para-sites, lateral positionings, the basis for the composition of thinking forged in the field that can travel and articulate more broadly the "trick up anthropology's sleeve."

10 See Otto and Bubandt, *Experiments in Holism.*

11 Marcus, "The Uses of Complicity in the Changing Mise-en-Scène of Anthropological Fieldwork."

12 Latour, *A Cautious Prometheus?*

13 In evoking design as a kind of ground for the figure of innovation in the emergence of alongside practices, I have been cautioned about overenthusiasm for design practices (e.g., participatory design) and what they in fact do by anthropologists such as Lucy Suchman and Melissa Cefkin who have made their careers in working in regimes of design process. See Suchman, "Anthropological Relocations and the Limits of Design"; Cefkin, *Ethnography and the Corporate Encounter.* Also, in evoking design as an inspiration, I have sometimes been misunderstood as being mainly interested in how ethnography can work within and aid design and studio projects—a relationship that has long been established (especially in Scandinavia) and has continuing currency in a number of design fields, such as architecture and especially informatics (see Dourish and Bell, *Divining a Digital Future*). I am interested rather in what design thinking and process affords for projects of ethnographic research in

their own terms and conceptions. I am interested, then, not in ethnography folded into design but design folded into independently conceived projects of ethnography that often now develop collaborative commitments and modes of operation along the way. Design thinking inside ethnography anticipates perhaps such collaborations and provides spaces, framings, and a history of forms to develop them. Introducing design forms and thinking into or alongside field-work, still individualistic and naturalistic, in habit, stimulates trials of concept and value that otherwise await the process of writing culture in the conventional modes of scholarly production.

14 Fischer, *Emergent Forms of Life and the Anthropological Voice*, 3, 4.

15 For example, the Matsutake Worlds Research Group, whose website, mat-sutakeworlds.org, archives a continuing collaborative research endeavor that I began to follow as I was writing this essay. It has evolved from the influential writing of Anna Tsing in the 1990s and 2000s about doing ethnography in the "global situation," to the formation of the Matsutake Worlds Research Group among her students and associates as a collaborative project in its archival form online as ethnography in progress. See Matsutake Worlds Research Group, "A New Form of Collaboration in Cultural Anthropology."

16 Here is a summary of the project by its creators, drawn from their website: "The Asthma Files is an experimental, digital ethnography project structured to support collaboration among distributed, diversely focused researchers, and outreach to diverse audiences. . . . The Asthma Files operates on an open source platform that supports both the research process, and rapid, creative sharing of research results. As the project matures, there will be active outreach to various audiences, including scientists, health care providers, journalists, policy makers and people with asthma. . . . The Asthma Files maintains a continually expanding and evolving list of reasons the project is important. This list, in the substantive logics drawer of the archive, keeps all involved mindful of the historical conditions in which we work, and of the challenge of linking academic research in the social sciences and humanities to contemporary social problems. The Asthma Files also maintains a continually evolving list of design logics that shape how the research is imagined, carried out and represented. These logics are drawn from social, literary, and aesthetic theory. Curating a list of design logics allows theoretical ideas to animate without overdetermining The Asthma Files."

17 See Rabinow, *The Accompaniment*.

18 See also Marcus, "Collaborative Options and Pedagogical Experiment in Anthropological Research on Experts and Policy Processes."

19 The ethnocharrette is another variant on the studio event, besides the para-site, that is being developed, by Keith Murphy and myself, at the Center for Ethnography at UCI, specifically as a pedagogical modality for thinking through and remaking published ethnographies as prototypes for other forms

and formats. For reports on our first two ethnocharrettes, consult http://ethnocharrette.wordpress.com/.

20 Theatricality is an interesting source of stimulation in thinking about the conduct of para-sites, briefly explored in Deeb and Marcus, "Theatricality in Ethnography at the World Trade Organization."

21 Strathern, *Audit Cultures.*

22 See Rabinow, *The Accompaniment*; Rabinow and Bennett, *Designing for Human Practices.* Studio events in relation to this project are on the ARC website subsequent to Rabinow's controversial exiting of SynBERC.

CHAPTER 3

Between History and Coincidence:

Writing Culture in the *Annual Review*

of Anthropology, ca. 1982

Richard Handler

IN MEMORY OF GEORGE STOCKING

History

Suppose you are a historian of anthropology interviewing elders in the early twenty-first century about the progress of culture theory in relation to the development of American anthropology. I am your informant. You ask me to list books written during my lifetime having some form of the word *culture* in the title and that I consider to have been professionally influential. I respond with this list:

> Raymond Williams, *Culture and Society* (1958)
> Jules Henry, *Culture against Man* (1963)
> David Schneider, *American Kinship: A Cultural Account* (1968)
> George Stocking, *Race, Culture, and Evolution* (1968)
> Clifford Geertz, *The Interpretation of Cultures* (1973)
> Roy Wagner, *The Invention of Culture* (1975)
> Marshall Sahlins, *Culture and Practical Reason* (1976)
> George Marcus and James Clifford, editors, *Writing Culture* (1986)
> George Marcus and Michael Fischer, *Anthropology as Cultural Critique* (1986)
> James Clifford, *The Predicament of Culture* (1988)

I can tell you a story to justify this list; I have told it before.[1] Moreover other people have told similar stories. In fact it is a fairly well agreed upon historical narrative.[2] When George Marcus and James Clifford reported in the pages of *Current Anthropology* on the conference out of which *Writing Culture* was to come, they gave a thumbnail sketch of "a specific situation of uncertainty and potential change" facing anthropologists at that time:

At least since the early 1960s, internal critiques of traditional anthropology have developed along three fronts. A diverse confessional and analytic literature on fieldwork experience has served to demystify the "method" of participant observation. New theoretical paradigms, largely inspired by postwar French and German philosophy, are challenging the conceptual models of culture and society under which professional social scientists have operated since the turn of the century. And the critique of colonialism in recent decades has made anthropologists aware of the ways their discipline has been implicated in particular historical milieus and of how politicized in world historical terms the contexts of their work and their subjects' lives have always been.[3]

A few years later George Stocking, the doyen of historians of anthropology, provided a six-page version of the same story as part of an essay attempting to "delimit" anthropology and thereby to sketch the "boundaries of a boundless discipline."[4] Stocking proceeded by periodizing the discipline over the twentieth century, narrating the emergence, out of "multifarious origins," of anthropology's turn-of-the-twentieth-century "contingent unity," its growth during a "classical period" (1920–60), and its postcolonial, postmodern crisis.

Stocking's account of the crisis is an expanded version of Marcus and Clifford's paragraph. In Stocking's telling the crisis is precipitated by the end of colonialism, the rise of American imperialism, the Vietnam War, and "the countercultural and political resistance of young people in advanced capitalist countries." For anthropologists, positioned "astride the boundaries between Europeans and non-Europeans," the crisis was multidimensional: "substantive, ideological, methodological, epistemological, theoretical, demographic, institutional."[5] The publication of Dell Hymes's edited volume *Reinventing Anthropology* (1972) was an important moment of the crisis, its contributors articulating many key themes:

Deemphasizing the study of exotic "others" at the periphery, anthropology should focus more on disempowered social categories of the center. Augmenting the traditional orientation downward toward the powerless, it would also "study up" toward the groups that wielded power. . . . Ideologically, it would move beyond the liberal posture of relativistic tolerance toward one of radical engagement in the struggles of the powerless against the holders of power. Methodologically and epistemologically, it would reject the positivistic assumption that cultures or cultural behavior could be observed as "objects" in the external world and, instead, would recognize the essential reflexivity of participant observation and the inherently problematic character of the knowledge generated by the ethnographic process.[6]

With respect to epistemology and methods, Stocking specifically noted the importance of the "crisis of representation," citing *Writing Culture* as well as Marcus and Michael Fischer's *Anthropology as Cultural Critique* and Clifford Geertz's essay on "blurred genres."[7]

In graduate school in the mid-1970s I was a student of Stocking and of David Schneider.[8] As a graduate student I wrote a master's thesis on kinship in Jane Austen's novels, a research paper (for a Stocking seminar) on Edward Sapir's literary work, and a doctoral thesis on Quebecois nationalism.[9] It took me six years of postdoctoral work to transform the thesis into a book.[10] During that time the emerging work of Marcus and Clifford spoke, I felt, directly to me, helping me to reflect on my Quebec materials and reshape the thesis in theoretically engaging terms.[11]

Having brought to published fruition the work that I began as a graduate student and taken up a post at the University of Virginia, by the mid-1990s I began telling the story of culture theory and cultural crisis in American anthropology in the following way.

As an undergraduate at Columbia University from 1968 to 1972 I studied anthropology at a place where Boasian cultural anthropology, French and British structuralism, cultural ecology, and Marxism were all in play and vigorously debated. My most memorable undergraduate teacher was Robert Murphy, and while I did not fully understand his theoretical magnum opus of that time, *The Dialectics of Social Life* (1971), I could hear his skeptical, compassionate voice in the prose. He told us once in our senior-year seminar that he wrote *Dialectics* in order to publish a book that ended with the words *fuck you*, which it did:

> This brings us to a final negation of Durkheim. Ritual and the sacred do not express the solidarity of the social group nor do they symbolize the constraint of its norms upon the individual. Rather, they bridge the contradiction between norm and action and mediate the alienation of man from his fellow man. . . . It is thus of consummate importance that rebels against the social order find little response to their verbal challenges to God and capitalism, the two great values of American culture, but can

drive their elders into a frenzy by flagrant breaches of manners. As if to illustrate the ultimate absurdity of social life, in 1964, a handful of young students were able to reduce the entire state of California to hysteria by walking about the Berkeley campus with signs stating in bold letters: "FUCK YOU."[12]

When I arrived at Chicago in September 1973 I found that Murphy was held in high esteem by my teachers there, but they disagreed with his attempt to split the difference between culture and practice. Our first graduate core course was taught by Sahlins, whose lectures were published three years later as *Culture and Practical Reason*. Although Geertz was no longer there, the cultural anthropologists of the department saw themselves as the center (worldwide, I suppose) for cultural or symbolic anthropology. We students knew we had to come to terms with Marxian materialism and various kinds of practice theory, but in our curriculum symbols-and-meanings anthropology held center stage. George Stocking's work brought Boasian anthropology to life for us, and Barney Cohn was working on the materials that would be so important to the anthropology of colonialism of the 1980s.[13]

When I went to Quebec in 1976 for a three-month stint of preliminary fieldwork, I had vague ideas about a "cultural account" of life there,[14] but I quickly learned that nationalism was the only game in town. Studying nationalism, I found, required revising the culture theory I knew. The natives were busy using something like an anthropological theory of culture to promote an identity and a political agenda. I came to realize I needed not a theory of culture but a theory of a theory of culture, not to construct a cultural account but to write ethnographically about the politics of culture. The ways anthropologists and nationalists invented culture, for their own purposes, became my theoretical conundrum, and since "invention" was at issue, writing about that conundrum was doubly problematic. Engaged already, through my work on Austen and Sapir, with the question of the relationship of anthropology and literature, I found the writings of Marcus, Clifford, Fischer, and others to be revelatory. I felt I'd been groping on my own toward the work they were doing. Reading their work, and that of the contributors to *Writing Culture*, connected me to a community of like-minded scholars and gave me models to try out.

My trajectory, then, went from culture theory through the politics of culture to the invention of culture and writing culture. Clifford's poignant statement in the introduction to *The Predicament of Culture* seemed to distill the meaning of the disciplinary history I felt I'd lived: "Culture is a deeply compromised idea I cannot yet do without."[15] Ten years later I wrote that anthropologists didn't really "do" culture theory anymore.[16] It seemed to me by then that we'd made theoretical peace with the epistemological issues of "the crisis," if not with the political issues of the world. I understood, I thought, our recent disciplinary history. And yet . . .

Coincidence

Commenting on the republication of *Reinventing Anthropology*, Hymes remarked, "We sometimes reduce the past to a linear sequence, slotting people into it one after the other. That is to be oblivious to how the past was for those who lived it, to what to them seemed open and possible."[17] Following Hymes's insight, I must admit that while the list of books above is chronologically arranged, it represents neither my personal story nor the history of the discipline. For one thing, the chronological order of the publications is not the order in which I read them. I discovered Henry's angry, funny ethnography of the United States long after I'd read most of the other works. His critique of American society can easily be seen as a precursor of the repatriated anthropology championed by Marcus and Fischer and of various strains in the cultural studies world as well.[18] But most anthropologists today would not include *Culture against Man* on their list; most have probably never heard of it.

Indeed we can seriously ask whether any two anthropologists' lists would coincide. As Margaret Mead noted at the time of the original publication of *Reinventing Anthropology*:

> When I asked 80 colleagues, variously selected from many areas and lines of association, to name the five most important books of the last 5 years, only four books were mentioned more than twice. . . . The interpretation that one informant placed on it, that nothing of very much importance has really happened in the last 5 years, is simply inaccurate. A great deal has happened, but no consensus can be reached, because of the extraordinary diversity within the subject.[19]

Let us reflect a bit on the idea of "diversity within the subject." Despite the categorical hegemony (in the public imagination) of disciplinary labels, most disciplines in the contemporary academy are interdisciplinary. Disciplines have been precipitated out of complex histories in which organizational units (departments) housing more or less closely related enterprises became locally institutionalized, more or less securely, in universities. At the same time, these disciplines became nationally and even internationally institutionalized as professional associations, and over time such associations, encompassing smaller groups spawned by subfields, have become associations of associations. With its four-field fetish, U.S. anthropology is more explicitly interdisciplinary than most disciplines. While there are both negative and positive takes on the four fields,[20] it seems fair to say that despite its internal diversity (if not fragmentation), anthropology's institutional staying power can be attributed in part to its ability to appeal to a range of audiences and granting agencies *across* the science/humanities divide.

What this means in practice, however, is that since the early 1950s American anthropology has become an institutional home for many people who don't talk to each other and perhaps can't even understand each other's professional jargons. As Stocking noted, Boas did not expect the anthropology of the future to be populated by people who would be expert in more than one or perhaps two of the subfields.[21] Whether he foresaw the exponential demographic growth of the field after World War II is unknown, but looking back in 1973 Mead found it "astonishing": "From a tiny scholarly group that could easily be fitted into a couple of buses, and most of whom knew each other, we have grown into a group of tremendous, anonymous milling crowds, meeting at large hotels where there are so many sessions that people do well to find those of their colleagues who are interested in the same specialty."[22] Surveying the same disciplinary transformation, Cora Du Bois wrote of her surprise at realizing, after the war, that the close-knit anthropology community she had known in her graduate student days at Berkeley during the 1930s had become "at best . . . an aggregate of isolates, at worst of self-seeking careerists."[23]

An aggregate of isolates and *anonymous milling crowds*: these are paradigmatic terms to describe modern mass societies, and anyone who has attended the annual meeting of the American Anthropological Association (AAA), between Mead's last years and the present moment (2013) knows that such terms are apt. The association today has thirty-eight subsections and more than eleven thousand members, and it sponsors twenty-two scholarly journals and is about to absorb the Society for Economic Anthropology.[24] It is a bureaucratically organized, functionally segmented professional association. More generally it is what Alexis de Tocqueville called a civic association.

Tocqueville famously maintained that such associations (we can also call them interest groups) are structurally essential to mass egalitarian societies. In such societies, he argued, individualism is a dominant cultural value, but since all individuals are defined as equal, any one of them is weak, insignificant, lost in the crowd. Lacking leaders of ascribed status central to the structure of aristocratic societies like those of feudal Europe, citizens of democracies had to band together to accomplish social endeavors:

> Wherever at the head of some new undertaking you see . . . a man of rank in England, in the United States you will be sure to find an association. I met with several kinds of associations in America of which I confess I had no previous notion; and I have often admired the extreme skill with which the inhabitants of the United States succeed in proposing a common object for the exertions of a great many men and inducing them voluntarily to pursue it.[25]

In these associations people are united in pursuit of a common interest. But it is important to realize that the social ties linking members of an interest group are thin, not thick: they are single-stranded, defined narrowly in terms of one common interest. Other aspects of members' lives remain irrelevant for purposes of the group. Tocqueville argued that interest groups had to be "numerous" in order to "have any power," but this meant that outside the group its membership would be "scattered," each individual isolated from the others, "detained in the place of his domicile by the narrowness of his income or by the small unremitting exertions by which he earns it."[26] This peculiar combination of association and isolation leads, among other things, to the anonymous milling crowds of the AAA annual meeting, where six thousand people united by a professional identity, but little else, come together for a frenzied few days of intense mutual activity that occurs, paradoxically, among strangers.

But of course there are meetings within the meeting: these mass annual gatherings of anthropologist-strangers provide the setting for more specialized or personalized relationships that play out among myriad professional subgroups, networks, and small bands of close friends. I have often returned home from the annual meeting with a clear sense of its key themes and metaphors and, extrapolating from those, with a vague sense of "where the discipline is going." But I usually have a cautionary afterthought, in which I ask myself: Did the archaeologists, the biological anthropologists, the linguists, the Africanists, the Sinologists, the applied anthropologists, the medical anthropologists—did any of them abstract the same meaning of the meeting? Indeed did they even attend the same meeting?

If, then, "the meeting" and "the association" and the discipline itself are Dumontian collections of individuals,[27] people with a presumptive shared professional identity but perhaps far less in common than membership in the same organization suggests, it may well be that one's experienced sense of the ongoing development or history of the discipline is at best partial and at worst highly idiosyncratic. To be able to move, analytically, from the messy phenomenology of the anonymous milling crowd to the neat abstraction of a historical narrative, we need a bridging concept. Such a concept will help us understand the history or histories that might emerge when, at a succession of annual meetings, *particular* collections of anthropologists, most of whom are personally unknown to one another, were brought together. We need, in short, a theoretically worked-up notion of coincidence.

We understand *coincidence* to mean simultaneous occurrence in space and time and, more particularly, a "concurrence of events" or of people "having no apparent causal connection" (*OED*). In the case of anthropologists co-occurring, as it were, at the meetings, if we parse the causality behind their presence, as Evans-Pritchard parsed Zande notions of causality in relation to witchcraft, we would have to say that membership in the anthropological profession "caused" each of them to attend the meetings.[28] But we would have to go on to cite multiple other causes to account for each person's scholarly and professional aims in attending the meeting, and for the specific events, social relations, and activities in which each engaged while there.

Thus the biographical trajectories of individual anthropologists coinciding at the annual meetings are motivated by, or put together from, a much greater variety of "influences," "forces," or "causes" than any bird's-eye disciplinary history could ever include. Moreover the coincidences that occur to people in mass society are not solely coincidental; rather, underpinned by the modern architecture of objectified, homogeneous space and time,[29] they are staged in a certain way. Anthropologists, members of an academic discipline and of a professional association, plot their attendance at the annual meeting many months in advance, coordinating their trip to the meeting with their teaching schedules and their personal lives, not to mention airline schedules and hotel reservations. The details of the meeting itself (city, venue, coordinating committee) are plotted years in advance by the AAA professional staff. Thus does it happen that an aggregate of self-seeking, careerist isolates can converge for a few days in the same spot for an apparently Durkheimian moment of collective effervescence—however differently it may be experienced and interpreted by the thousands of attendees. Bureaucracy, the modern machine that coordinates our time and space, runs the show, or at least sets the stage.

The professional publication is a bureaucratically managed meeting of another kind, and like the meeting, it coincidentally brings together apparently unconnected anthropologist-authors, according to a production schedule. Outside the ritual moment of the meeting, scholarly disciplines are largely held together literarily by professional publications.[30] These are our newspapers, and newspapers are central to sociality in mass societies, as Tocqueville, writing long before Benedict Anderson,[31] described. "Lost amid the crowd," Tocqueville wrote, American citizens "cannot see and do not know where to find one another. A newspaper then takes up the notion or the feeling that had occurred simultaneously, but singly, to each of them. All are then immediately guided towards this beacon; and these wandering minds, which had long sought each other in darkness, at length meet and unite." There is "a necessary connection," he concluded, between associations and newspapers: a newspaper is "an association that is composed of its habitual readers."[32]

Updating Tocqueville to account for scientific specialization, we should perhaps say that a disciplinary serial publication is an association supported by its subscribers, but subscribers are not necessarily habitual readers. While anthropologists may subscribe (often passively, as a "benefit" of membership in the professional association) to *Anthropology News* or *American Anthropologist*, few of us habitually read those publications; that is, few of us read them cover to cover. Indeed many of us don't read the general anthropological publications at all, paying attention solely to the specialized journals covering our particular interests. From the outside the general publications (so-called flagship journals) may seem to represent, and therefore stand for, the discipline, but insiders may see them as little more than coincidental collections of individual voices and essays that have little relationship among them.

Coincidental collections might seem to defy history making. To construct a narrative of disciplinary history—to tell the story of *Writing Culture*—the standard method is to read diachronically, looking for at least an implicit sequential account of motivation, causality, or influence. The historian strings together texts on a timeline, constructing, as I did at the outset, a list of important texts that represent the progress of the discipline or a trend within it. But if we want instead to say something about openness and multiple possibilities, as Hymes enjoined us to do, then perhaps we should read synchronically, that is, read *across* the discipline, seeking disparate senses of anthropology at a particular moment.

To experiment with such a method, I will review several essays from the 1982 issue of the *Annual Review of Anthropology*. I chose *Annual Review*, and this particular volume, for two reasons: first, it was the place of publication of Marcus and Cushman's essay "Ethnographies as Texts," a seminal work of the writing culture moment; second, *Annual Review* was designed to provide coverage across all areas of anthropology, and more important, the very notion of an annual review implies a discipline in time, specifically a discipline progressing through history. In brief, reading *Annual Review* conveys a sense of different scholars' quite different understandings of disciplinary history at a single moment of time. As we shall see, these authors, coincidentally gathered together in the pages of a volume of a serial publication, probably would not have seen themselves making the same history as their fellow travelers.

Annual Review began life in 1959 as the *Biennial Review of Anthropology*, a publication created to cope with the postwar disciplinary growth of anthropology. Its editor, Bernard Siegal, noted in his opening remarks of the first volume, "The output of anthropological writing has become so great that even specialists find it next to impossible to keep abreast of all the relevant literature in their own fields." As part of an effort of "stock-taking," *Biennial Review* would be a "regular series" summarizing "the more noteworthy papers and monographs" of a particular "anthropological field" in the "two or three years prior" to the publication of each volume.[33]

Siegal listed five fields to be covered: "social and cultural change, physical anthropology, linguistics, social organization, and the psychological dimensions of culture."[34] But he noted that such a categorization of anthropology's subfields might very well change in future volumes. It did, and it didn't. Reviewing the tables of contents between 1959 and 1982 (the *Biennial Review* became the *Annual Review* in 1972), we can see that American anthropology's four-field approach remained the dominant organizing device. Even so the list of topical specialties within each of the four fields, the relationship of such specialties to regional or geographic specialties, and the relationship of topical fields in anthropology to related work outside the discipline—all these problems of categorization occupied the editorial board, which tended to rationalize its decisions in each volume's foreword. But even as the editors tried to justify their choice and presentation of topics, they recognized (1) that particular topics waxed and waned in importance, and that consequently (2) editorial categorizing schemes would change over time and finally (3) that to some extent the contents of a given volume depended on "the availability of authors who are sufficiently qualified and sufficiently altruistic to attempt reviews."[35] In sum, in a rather cheerful way the editors provided a running commentary about their belief in the scientific progress of a unified discipline even as they described their not altogether successful attempts to corral knowledge making in the field within a set of stable categories.

Other Scribes, Other Stories

In 1972, when the *Biennial Review* became the *Annual Review*, Stephen Tyler became one of the editors. One of the contributors to *Writing Culture* (indeed the subject of its cover photo), Tyler was a colleague of George Marcus and Dick Cushman at Rice University. Marcus noted that Tyler had been "a particularly important stimulus for [him]" in the work that led to the 1982 essay "Ethnographies as Texts." That paper was also "inspired" by a course Marcus cotaught with Cushman, Classics in Ethnography.[36] Tyler suggested that Marcus work up the material for publication in the *Annual Review*; with help from Cushman, Marcus did.[37]

Marcus and Cushman approached the topic of ethnographies as texts within the rhetorical conventions of the *Annual Review* and following a scheme of historical stages similar to that of Stocking. They surveyed recent experiments in and analyses of ethnographic writing, and they presented those writings as evidence for the emergence of a new stage or moment in the progress of the discipline. (Their new stage corresponds to Stocking's "crisis" period.) They analyzed ways the new writings were "disturbing the tacit consensus" about fieldwork, ethnographic writing, and the relationship of both to theoretical progress in the discipline. As they saw it, the tacit consensus held sway over "the last 60 years," a period dominated by "Anglo-American ethnographic realism." (This is Stocking's "classical period.") Marcus and Cushman suggested that experimental ethnographic writing was at once a theoretical development "indigenous to anthropology" and a response of anthropologists to a changing world: "The future . . . is in ethnographies that are based on very different notions about how cultural distinctions should be defined and textually represented in a contemporary world unlike that previously, which at least plausibly offered closed systems—tribes, peoples—as subjects through which ethnographic realism historically developed."[38]

In their final sentences they framed their review as a discussion necessary for anthropology's larger "goal of constructing systematic knowledge of other cultures."[39] Indeed, as the essays in the present volume show, "the future" of anthropology after 1982, and after the writing culture moment more generally, has included the development of an experimental research tradition that has melded differently sited (compared to work of the classic period) fieldwork with differently reported, differently written results.

We are back, then, to the historical narrative with which I began this essay. But if we turn to other essays in the 1982 volume of *Annual Review*, what sorts of stories will we find? That volume contains thirteen essays, including one in archaeology, three in biological anthropology, one in "regional anthropology," seven in cultural-social anthropology, and a reflective piece by an elder statesman. Here I will consider, by way of example, three of them.

AN ELDER'S TALE

Beginning in 1973 *Annual Review* featured an opening article by a distinguished elder reflecting on his or her career: Margaret Mead (1973), Fred Eggan (1974), Raymond Firth (1975), Wilton Krogman (1976), Carleton Coon (1977), Meyer Fortes (1978), Grahame Clark (1979), Cora Du Bois (1980), and Ralph Beals (1982).[40] Beals thus became one of Marcus and Cushman's coincidental fellow travelers in 1982.

President of the AAA in 1950, Beals (1901–85) studied anthropology as an undergraduate and a graduate student at Berkeley, beginning in 1922 and receiving his Ph.D. in 1932. Although Stephen Murray, in a thumbnail biography, saw Beals as "a Boasian anti-theory descriptivist,"[41] his *Annual Review* essay is a straightforward statement of an anthropological philosophy as well as an evaluation of the discipline's future. Beals conducted fieldwork in California and then in Mexico. For a time during the Depression he worked for the National Park Service before securing an appointment at UCLA to teach anthropology in the psychology department.[42] His professional career ran from the community of graduate students and professors at Berkeley in the 1920s, through the lean years of the Depression, then World War II—the "golden age" when "everyone," including other academics and government agencies, "discovered" anthropology[43]—and on to his postwar work developing anthropology at UCLA and nationally, through the AAA and various research councils.

Murray described Beals as "an active force in building up UCLA from a satellite of Berkeley into a major university."[44] In his essay Beals considered at length the expansion and professionalization of anthropology starting in World War II. His "Washington experience" during the war made him "sympathetic" to applied anthropology, especially in relationship to government agencies and funding organizations, and this in turn led him to be concerned about "the lack of any organized voice for anthropology." Thus he played a role in the reorganization of the AAA in 1947, but "35 years later" he found himself "not so sure of [its] benefits" since it "placed much of its control in the hands of nonprofessionals." Beals was even more ambivalent about the uses of applied anthropology: "It is now more evident than it once was that much of applied anthropology involves manipulating people. While this can be interpreted as being 'for their own good,' it is questionable whether such actions are for the good of the subjects or for the good of the administering agencies." Anthropologists, he concluded, "owe much to the people they study," and they often have "deep attachments" to them. But he was no longer "confident" that he knew "what is for the benefit of the people [he was] studying."[45]

Looking back Beals defended the Boasian culture concept and claimed that in the earlier part of his career, he and his colleagues were not nearly as naïve theoretically as they were being made out to be (in 1982): "We talked unabashedly about what culture did and did not do without shame for our apparent reification. Culture we used as a shorthand and we knew very well that only human beings really acted." In their field studies he and his colleagues recognized that the communities they studied were neither geographically nor historically isolated. Thus they "were concerned with the relations of groups studied with their neighbors," and they rejected "the idea that any tribal or subtribal culture, however many unique features it might have, could be viewed as an isolated system functioning in a vacuum." They knew, in sum, that anthropology "requires a concept of cultural change."[46]

Looking ahead Beals felt that culture change was still a critical topic for anthropologists, although he wanted to disentangle it from acculturation studies, which, in his view, were too psychologically oriented. He thought that new work in ecology, economic anthropology, and urban anthropology held promise and that such subfields were to be distinguished from the "passing fads" that "overspecialization" breeds. Above all he maintained his allegiance to the culture concept: "Today, culture seems to be 'old hat' and is even rejected by some younger anthropologists as a vague . . . concept." Refusing to apologize for the term, Beals concluded, "Culture to me is the indefinable concept that mediates between the biological world and the social behaviors of human species. It is the common denominator that links our rapidly expanding fields of specialization." Thus the culture concept would allow anthropologists to balance disciplinary expansion—specialization and overspecialization—and disciplinary coherence and guarantee a future for the discipline. "It may be that anthropology is destined to fly apart. I do not think so, but I am prepared to be wrong."[47]

THE DEVELOPMENT OF DEVELOPMENT ANTHROPOLOGY

Allan Hoben's review (1982) of anthropological participation in development work is a mildly triumphalist or progressive narrative of the emergence of a new disciplinary subspecialty. Hoben structured his narrative in terms of three decades of postwar development work: the 1950s, 1960s, and 1970s. Anthropologists, who had willingly participated in government-sponsored war work, did not sustain a presence in the growing postwar development industry. Hoben argued that they were limited both by their own theoretical focus on timeless, well-integrated local cultures and by the dominant development paradigm of the 1950s and 1960s, the main tenets of which—the superiority of Western rationality, the universality of Western economic history, and the importance of industrial "take-off"—were anathema to anthropologists. While some anthropologists were recruited into development work in the 1950s, mainly as specialists on local traditional cultures, by 1970 most had left the field, attracted away by the growth of academic opportunities in the *Sputnik* era and also repelled in light of their field's growing anticolonial consciousness.

Hoben also pointed out that anthropologists were not skilled at analyzing bureaucratic politics and, more generally, that they had not yet come to realize that the government bureaucracies out of which development projects emerged were themselves cultural and social worlds worthy of study. But from the mid-1970s on, development agencies began to pay more attention to poverty, bottom-up development, and community participation, following the lead of Robert McNamara, president of the World Bank.[48] There was a role for anthropologists in the new context, but they had to learn how to function both as analysts and as bureaucrats in situations where conflicting agendas and fast-changing political fashions made it difficult to carry out the kind of long-term research that anthropologists favor. According to Hoben, anthropologists gradually rose to "the challenge of using their professional perspective to analyze and respond to the bureaucratic environ-ment in which they work as 'participant observers.' "[49]

Moreover when anthropologists began returning to development work in the 1980s, they had learned "to transcend the naïve negativism" that had earned them the reputation, among other development professionals, as "hy-percritical Cassandras who made too few constructive suggestions." They did this through fine-grained empirical work that allowed them to puncture bureaucrats' (and economists') myths about either the irrationality or the excessive rationality of peasants ("the peasant as an economic maximizer"); through "comparative studies" pointing to "emergent lessons and recurrent issues that are invariant to regional differences"; and finally through "behav-iorally oriented" work that "can analyze patterned behavior of many kinds as the result of choices made within a specified social, historical, ecological, and economic setting."[50]

In Hoben's analysis there had been real theoretical progress between the 1950s and 1980s, as American anthropologists abandoned their too exclusive focus on local cultural patterning, learned to use "quantitative analysis of be-havior patterns" in concert with "local institutional analysis characteristic of British social anthropology," and at the same time, influenced by "neo-Marx-ist and other political economic approaches," reconnected their research on specific sites to world-historical trends. The result was that by the early 1980s anthropologists had much to contribute to the development field. The "new development anthropology," Hoben thought, could "improve program planning and project design" not only by providing good data and analysis of field situations but by "illuminating the organization, interests, and strategies of local elites and bureaucrats at all levels." Here was an example of what we might, a few years later, have called an at least partially repatriated anthropol-ogy. For Hoben, it was clearly a case of a subdiscipline, development anthro-pology, that was destined to "continue to mature" in ways that would "prove mutually beneficial for both development and anthropology."[51]

THE REGION MAKES THE SUBSPECIALTY MAKES THE REGION

David Gilmore's essay "Anthropology of the Mediterranean Area" walks a fine line between delineating, in positivist terms, a "Mediterranean area" and reviewing the growth of a literature that argues for the existence of such an area and for a subdiscipline devoted to it. He seems to have been doing both, self-consciously. At the outset he asserted that "an anthropology *of* the

Mediterranean area" (as opposed to research done *in* the area) "which includes both Christian and Muslim sides is both new and controversial." He reviewed works of the prior thirty years that had "demonstrated important underlying similarities between north and south" sufficient to posit "Mediterranean unity." And he claimed that such work had led "many anthropologists" to accept "the idea of a Mediterranean specialty." The goal of his review essay, then, was "to determine the criteria by which a 'Mediterranean' area may be demarcated geographically and culturally," and then to assess "recent research on the common themes which contribute to the concept of a Mediterranean unity."[52]

If his introductory remarks waver between a focus on the region as such and on the existence of a scholarly project to study it, the following discussion focuses squarely on real-world features that had been offered as evidence for regional unity. Gilmore reviewed geographic and environmental configurations; cultural features ("a bundle of sociocultural traits"); "cultural contradictions" that "reflect . . . some underlying dialectic"; historical connections forged out of centuries of trade and migration; and shared features of political economy. "Each dimension," he concluded, "is a necessary but not sufficient criterion for defining the Mediterranean construct." But he thought that the "unity" of the region "emerges . . . from an analysis of the unique concurrence of all these multiple factors."[53]

In the remainder of the essay Gilmore reviewed the most recent work on the area, carried out, in many cases, by scholars who had become more aware of their participation in a regional subspecialty. He concluded, as he began, by intertwining a discussion of the region and one of the subdisciplines devoted to its study:

> An anthropology of the Mediterranean region has grown to the point where it may now be considered a legitimate subspecialty. . . . If it has not quite come of age, it is at least a vigorous adolescent waiting for a professional *rite de passage* to pass into healthy adulthood. It still needs much parenting: we need to know more conclusively what the continuities really are that make north and south more than simply adjacent culture zones sharing a similar environment. This will require less insularity and provincialism among all the workers in this region.[54]

Personification is here used to stake a claim concerning the subdiscipline, not the region itself, but in Gilmore's vision, the future of the subdiscipline will be assured by research that shows ever more convincingly that the region is more than a figment of the scholarly imagination.

Twenty-five Years

It is reasonable to claim that all these anthropologist-authors, writing at the same time (ca. 1982), would have seen themselves participating in different histories of anthropology or different anthropological traditions. They would have differed in their understandings of the relationship of the culture concept to the state or progress of anthropology as a discipline, the ontological reality of culture areas or regions, the appropriateness of various research methods, and the role of anthropology in the wider society. Had I included *Annual Review* essays by archaeologists and biological anthropologists, we would have found an even wider range of intellectual and disciplinary orientations.

It is also reasonable to imagine, however, that Beals, Hoben, Gilmore, and Marcus and Cushman could have talked to each other, despite their disagreements. Beals engaged the critique of cultural reification generated by (among others) the writing culture folks. Hoben joined Beals in a constructively critical response to applied anthropology, and both authors recognized that political economy and world-systems theory spoke directly to their own anthropological projects. Gilmore balanced his assertions about Mediterranean unity with an awareness of the scholarly construction of geographic regions. And all these authors reaffirmed a commitment to anthropology's comparative approach to worldwide cultural diversity.

But beyond theoretical and methodological trends that can be shown to add up to a coherent history of anthropology, or that can be used to demonstrate the opposite (a discipline flying apart, in Beals's phrase), we can attend to bureaucratic-organizational features that would seem to keep most American anthropologists in line, attending the same meetings, publishing in the same journals. Four years after Gilmore, Hoben, Beals, and Marcus and Cushman published their essays, *Writing Culture* was published. In the same year the Society for the Anthropology of Europe was founded, with Gilmore among its organizers.[55] The present volume has emerged from a conference marking the twenty-fifth anniversary of *Writing Culture*. At the time of this writing, the Society's website featured a "25th Anniversary Retrospective Page." Given our base-10 counting system and our conception of homogeneous time, the twenty-fifth anniversary is considered a milestone: a quarter of a century, as we say. Beals titled his *Annual Review* essay "Fifty

Years in Anthropology," but in the first paragraph he wondered whether "60 years" was the more appropriate quantity of time. Hoben sketched the history of development anthropology with the decade as the significant temporal unit. Like Gilmore, he forecast a healthy future for a subdiscipline, and the elder, Beals, was still willing to bet on the future of the discipline, anthropology. Marcus and Cushman too saw a future for anthropology, one emerging from the crisis that had generated the writing culture experiment.

For practicing anthropologists, the creation and institutionalization of new subfields is a normal result of professional work. When one is building one's career by establishing a new field, a new discourse, a new jargon, there is little time to worry about most of the rest of the discipline. With a bit of luck one's innovation can be commemorated twenty-five years later and even rejected as "old hat" by the next generation. The ongoing "overspecialization" of anthropology that alarms us as we become elders and leads us to remember differing histories of our discipline is a function of normal science in a bureaucratized world. Thus the coincidence of six thousand anthropologists at the annual meeting of the American Anthropological Association presents a challenge to historians of anthropology that may require us to learn something about a different subfield: the sociology of the professions. Perhaps the diachronic succession of meetings, utterances, and publications that we draw on to compose a history of anthropology can be viewed, synchronically, as the repetitive eruptions of an underlying, unchanging structure. To give the final word to Tocqueville: "American society is animated because men and things are always changing, but it is monotonous because all these changes are alike."[56]

Notes

1 See Handler, "Interpreting the Predicament of Culture Today."
2 But see Rutherford, this volume, for an alternative narrative.
3 Marcus and Clifford, *The Making of Ethnographic Texts*, 267.
4 Stocking, *Delimiting Anthropology*, 303–29.
5 Stocking, *Delimiting Anthropology*, 320.
6 Hymes, *Reinventing Anthropology*, 321.
7 Geertz, "Blurred Genres."
8 I also learned a great deal from Bernard Cohn, Meyer Fortes (who was a guest instructor in 1973), Marshall Sahlins, and Michael Silverstein. After graduating I maintained collegial relations with all these mentors, but I remained closest, personally and professionally, to Schneider and Stocking, whom I retrospectively adopted as "my teachers."

9 My master's thesis was eventually incorporated in Handler and Segal, *Jane Austen and the Fiction of Culture*. My paper on Sapir was published in the first number of Stocking's *History of Anthropology* series. See Handler, "The Dainty and the Hungry Man."

10 Handler, *Nationalism and the Politics of Culture in Quebec*.

11 Marcus, "Rhetoric and the Ethnographic Genre in Anthropological Research"; Marcus and Cushman, "Ethnographies as Texts"; Clifford, "On Ethnographic Surrealism" and "On Ethnographic Authority."

12 Murphy, *The Dialectics of Social Life*, 243–44.

13 Cohn, *An Anthropologist among the Historians and Other Essays*.

14 Schneider, *American Kinship*.

15 Clifford, *The Predicament of Culture*, 10.

16 Handler, "Interpreting the Predicament of Culture Today," 77.

17 Hymes, *Reinventing Anthropology*, vii.

18 Handler, "Critics against Culture," 154–85.

19 Mead, "Changing Styles of Anthropological Work," 9.

20 For a negative take, see Segal and Yanagisako, *Unwrapping the Sacred Bundle*. For a positive, see McKinnon and Silverman, *Complexities*.

21 Stocking, *Delimiting Anthropology*, 308.

22 Mead, "Changing Styles of Anthropological Work," 1.

23 Du Bois, "Some Anthropological Hindsights," 4.

24 Mullings, "President's 2012 Report to the Membership," 24.

25 Tocqueville, *Democracy in America*, 114–15.

26 Tocqueville, *Democracy in America*, 120.

27 Dumont, *From Mandeville to Marx*, 47–60.

28 Evans-Pritchard, *Witchcraft, Oracles and Magic among the Azande*.

29 Anderson, *Imagined Communities*, 22–36; Whorf, *Language, Thought, and Reality*, 134–59.

30 Goffman, *Stigma*, 25. In what ways the ongoing shift to online publication will change the sociality of professional associations is a topic well beyond the scope of this essay.

31 Anderson, *Imagined Communities*.

32 Tocqueville, *Democracy in America*, 119–22.

33 Siegal, "Foreword," v.

34 Siegal, "Foreword," v.

35 Siegal and Beals, "Foreword," v.

36 Marcus, "Rhetoric and the Ethnographic Genre in Anthropological Research," 507.

37 Marcus, personal communication.

38 Marcus and Cushman, "Ethnographies as Texts," 65, 27, 60, 64–65.

39 Marcus and Cushman, "Ethnographies as Texts," 66.

40 Mead, "Changing Styles of Anthropological Work"; Eggan, "Among the Anthropologists"; Firth, "An Appraisal of Modern Social Anthropology"; Krog-

man, "Fifty Years of Physical Anthropology"; Coon, "Overview"; Fortes, "An Anthropologist's Apprenticeship"; Clark, "Anthropology and Human Diversity"; Du Bois, "Some Anthropological Hindsights"; Beals, "Fifty Years in Anthropology." There was no such essay in the 1981 volume, and of those listed, only Clark's was not autobiographical.

41 Murray, "Ralph Beals," 136.

42 Murray, "Ralph Beals," 134; Beals, "Fifty Years in Anthropology," 6–11.

43 Beals, "Fifty Years in Anthropology," 12.

44 Murray, "Ralph Beals," 135.

45 Beals, "Fifty Years in Anthropology," 14, 15, 16.

46 Beals, "Fifty Years in Anthropology," 5, 7.

47 Beals, "Fifty Years in Anthropology," 20, 2, 21.

48 Hoben, "Anthropologists and Development," 357; Rist, *The History of Development*, 159–62.

49 Hoben, "Anthropologists and Development," 362.

50 Hoben, "Anthropologists and Development," 362, 354, 368, 365, 351.

51 Hoben, "Anthropologists and Development," 368–69, 369, 370. Thirty years after Hoben wrote, development anthropologists remain similarly optimistic (see Venkatesan and Yarrow, *Differentiating Development*), but not all of them would consider the progress Hoben foresaw to have been achieved in the intervening years. In particular the participatory, bottom-up approach that was gaining traction in the 1980s had, some now think, been pretty thoroughly co-opted by bureaucratic routines (see Kothari, "Authority and Expertise"). Commenting on her work in a local government reform program in Tanzania in the 1990s, Maia Green concluded that "the openness of anthropology" gives it "a certain epistemological advantage over other forms of knowledge when it comes to addressing the unanticipated. But these attributes . . . render it difficult to corral. . . . Being hence impossible to implement because of its vagueness and fluidity, anthropological knowledge resists application to templates and grids. It is this attribute . . . that makes it so importantly 'useless' in terms of its utility to other disciplines" ("Framing and Escaping," 53–54).

52 Gilmore, "Anthropology of the Mediterranean Area," 175, 176.

53 Gilmore, "Anthropology of the Mediterranean Area," 178, 180–81, 184.

54 Gilmore, "Anthropology of the Mediterranean Area," 199.

55 Rogers, "Notes from the President," 1.

56 Tocqueville, *Democracy in America*, 239.

CHAPTER 4

Time, Camera, and the
(Digital) Pen: Writing Culture
Operating Systems 1.0–3.0
Michael M. J. Fischer

Ethnicity, like race and like the genome, in its double-stranded biological and cultural twists is often a maguffin, the elusive, often specialized-knowledge object of everybody's search and self-construction (despite outbreaks and pandemics of stereotyping and othering). It is as well a Hitchcockian time stamp for an essay in *Writing Culture* a quarter century ago.[1] In these tumultuous twenty-five years, writing culture has gone through at least three versions, or time warps, psychodynamics, and writing technologies: pen, camera, digitization. Writing culture and *Cultural Anthropology* (the journal) have also gone through shifts in building porosities, first with the humanities, then the media, and lately emergent biological and ecological sensibilities. In the following pages I attempt to capture with "pen" (or laptop), for a sedimented print world, the magic pad or 4-D triangulations of historical discourses, operating systems, and sociocultural con-texts.

My own contribution to *Writing Culture*, "The Postmodern Arts of Memory," turned out to be one of a trio of essays on ethnicity, torn religions, and science articulated through monologic, double-voiced, and triangulated autobiographic genre perspectives.[2] It explored female and male ethnic *identities* that can assert themselves without bidding or conscious desire and that over a life or a text are fused from their multiple sources into a singular voice. These were grounded in a particular historical moment of American life and served as uneasy fit, and thus critique, for the three-generation model of immigration and assimilation of earlier anthropological models of Americanization. The finding of a voice expressed itself in varied narrative forms: the talk stories from fragments and silences of parental or community pasts; bilingual or multilingual *intereferences*;[3] psychodynamics and dialogics of working through and acting out emotional truths through a telling to another; diversions and subversions of humor; and the polysemy and ambi-valences of poetry. For the exploration of modern *torn religions* I looked to *double-voiced* or *stereoscopic* biographies of transitional religious figures by modern transitional figures whose psychodynamically powerful interpretations of the former served as screens for their own and their communities' irresolvable double-bind commitments. And for *technoscientific imaginaries* I looked to the formal homologies of the ways female and male scientists narrate and give meaning to their autobiographical trajectories and to their disciplines' trajectories via *triangulations* with multiple powerful, often conflictual others (mentors, rivals, collaborators).[4]

In this chapter I follow up on these narrative and anthropological threads with three sets of time-stamped reflections. I draw upon often extra-departmental networks and collaborative circles I have had the good fortune to be part of and the work of students I have attempted to encourage to contribute to collective projects of generalized exchange.[5] Each section uses films, theater, photos, and digital media from Indian, Iranian, Chinese, and American parallel worlds to evoke mood, tense, or temporality as well as reminders of changing technological, environmental, and sociopolitical horizons. An emergent thread traces the growth of a new biological and ecological cultural sensibility, one that explores the increasingly fine granularity shifts from disciplinary societies to more diffuse but more pervasive ones of code and variants of neoliberalisms identified by Foucault and Deleuze.[6] Throughout, anthropological voices (there are many more) are evoked to help articulate these shifting sensibilities. Ethnographic and anthropological jeweler-eye craftsmanship in teasing out the refractions of everyday life can often upset the echo-chamber master narratives, or aggregating voice, of politicians, political scientists, economists, and the mass media.

1984. Operating Systems 1.0: Times out of Joint, Camera out of Focus, and Pens Running out of Ink

Hello, I am Macintosh. It sure is great to get out of that bag.
Unaccustomed as I am to public speaking, I'd like to share with you a maxim I thought up the first time I met an IBM mainframe: NEVER TRUST A COMPUTER YOU CAN'T LIFT.
—The 1984 launch video
(http://www.youtube.com/watch?v=2B-XwPjn9YY)

Now fear an IBM dominated and controlled future. They are increasingly and desperately turning back to Apple as the only force that can insure their future freedom (laughter, applause). . . . Will Big Blue dominate the entire computer industry (no!), the entire information age (no!). Was George Orwell right about 1984?

—October 23, 1983 Apple annual sales meeting in Hawaii

(http://www.youtube.com/watch?v=JTVDWGtf9m4; http://www.youtube.com/watch?v=GeWnlrcdwPI)

Looking at photographs of middle-class lives in the 1950s–1970s in places like Iran can produce time-warp shocks. The women and men look so modern, so much more so than the "retro" veils and three-day-growth beards of the 1980–2000s. Or perhaps it is a class inversion, with the arrival in the nouveau riche and new middle classes of recently urbanized members of what once were less privileged strata, often along with their modernized evangelical religious sensibilities—as if deploying Max Weber's modalities of upward social mobility and sense of cultural distinction, updated with grass-roots organizing, smartphones, social media, and megachurches. *Retro* is a fashion term, not a return but a referencing, an intereference (à la Serres) interfering with, deferring to alternative modernities, insisting on different values and valuations, calling on different enunciatory communities, mustering often considerable political weight. California-style ranch houses in Ahwaz (Iran) and the Helmand Valley (Afghanistan) in 1984 were perhaps enclaves, but the steel frame and glass-and-concrete townhouse developments in Yazd and Qum were similar to prefab housing elsewhere in the world. Once accustomed to the aftereffects of the Islamic Revolution, such as increasing black veiling of women in the Arab, Turkish, as well as Iranian worlds, along with, importantly, increasing employment of women in the labor force, the gaily colored and stylish hijab of Indonesian and Malay women, affixed and decorated with eye-catching silver pins, can be disconcerting, a crossing of codes.

The arrow of time does not move uniformly, as elites and development pundits of modernization and modernity at large with their finance-scapes and biopolitical markets sometimes allowed themselves to think. Indeed time-warp shocks and times out of joint reverberate across many temporal expectations and false dawns for whole populations or parts of them. Descartes, watching the Vatican's imposition of public dogma on Galileo in 1633 for political control reasons (rather than scientific or truth ones), defensively tempered his own claims, recognizing that the movement of history was not necessarily on his side or that of Renaissance mercantile and capitalist bourgeoisies who believed in science, the ability to under-stand and control the world, and who tried to consolidate power through parliaments and law courts.[7] A wonderful cartoon by the Armenian anthro-pologist Levon Abrahamian shows a globe being thrown at a fleeing Galileo with the caption "The world is round, but not in this case," as a commentary on ethnic-nationalist claims in bloody wars as the cold war receded, de-spite the misplaced or aspirational common sense that essentializing ethnic and nationalist claims should be things of the past in a globalized world.[8] The women's movement in German social democratic politics in the early twentieth century and the Rosie the Riveter generation of female workers in the U.S. World War II defense industries similarly found themselves pushed back into domestic subaltern positions.[9] Already in the nineteenth century Friedrich Engels had described industrialization as an initial rise of women's status and employment, followed by pushing women back into the domestic sphere, offloading the costs of labor reproduction from capital onto a famil-ial division of labor, with employed women and children being paid less.[10] Antonio Negri uses the analogy of Descartes to restage the limitations of the hopes of the autonomist workers social movement in northern Italy during the 1970s "second industrial divide" of small-batch, high-tech, flexible ma-chinist shops attempting to share control of the means of production in an economy of flexible accumulation. He renews the analogy in his postscript to the 2007 English translation as a comment on the limits to the hopes of the "multitude" against globalized capital such as the Zapatista revolt, the Se-attle protests, the movement of the World Social Forum, and most recently Occupy Wall Street movements (for which the anthropologist Jeff Juris has become an early ethnographer and analyst).[11]

Operating Systems 1.0 of the 1984 era were transitional, upsetting to cul-tural norms, but mostly still optimistic. They crossed the membranes of first and second natures (the natural environment and the man-made environ-ment) and were only beginning the crossings of third and fourth natures (reworking human nature inside out, using companion species as tools for positive consciousness of living with diversity).[12] The recombinant DNA moratorium of 1975 and its gradual lifting were still fresh in both fear and promise, one of the first great public culture debates of the emerging bio-technology era (to be followed by debates over genetically modified crops, stem cell research, and so on).[13]

The *Writing Culture* essays written in 1984 (published in 1986) were con-temporaneous with the year of "You will see why 1984 won't be like 1984" from the famous Ridley Scott ad for the Macintosh computer, aired during the Super Bowl on January 22, 1984, with a woman hammer thrower smashing the Orwellian screen. The launch of the Mac two days later ends with Alice (of Alice in Wonderland, and of Alice and Bob, the canonic names in computer science scenarios) standing on a chess board. Ten years later the World Wide Web Consortium was founded at MIT, and the acceleration of a new digital world operating system began, with its early utopian hopes captured in the Grateful Dead songwriter John Perry Barlow's "A Declaration of the Independence of Cyberspace" (1999).[14] Various strands of the communication media began to converge, interoperate, miniaturize, and become invisible, leading to a phase shift, a worlding of cyberspace in how we think about time, place, and theory.[15] The discursive and cultural infrastructure of the world was changing. In 1984 Sony and Philips introduced the first commercial CD players (which my wife and I missed, having spent much of the year in India and returned thinking CDs were still certificates of deposit).

Transitions were not just happening in the West. In 1984 China's Fifth Generation filmmakers exploded onto the international scene with the release of *Yellow Earth* by the director Chen Kaige and the cinematographer Zhang Yimou. Zhang would have a string of successes in film, opera, light shows, and the globally viewed opening and closing extravaganzas of the 2008 Beijing Olympics. Richard Havis says of *Yellow Earth* that it was the first Chinese film "at least since the 1949 Communist Liberation, to tell a story through images rather than dialog."[16] In any case, the Fifth Generation became known for its stunning cinematographic tableaux of Chinese history opening allegorical spaces for criticism and critique that could not be made (as easily yet) verbally or in print. By the early 2000s the Internet and social media would be the tools of the *demos* to circumvent print censorship and create public pressure and new accountability against discriminatory labor laws and ill treatment of migrants and for biosecurity in epidemics such as SARS (2002–3), H5N1 (2009), and H7N9 (2013).[17]

Yellow Earth signals moments of cultural phase shifts in style and sensibility. Its story, set in 1939 as the Chinese Communist Party (CCP) and Kuomintan are allied against the invading Japanese, and before the postwar victory of the Chinese Communist Revolution, ends with a village rain dance on the dried-up land and failed crops. The fourteen-year-old girl forced to marry an older man so her dowry can be used to pay for her mother's funeral and brother's engagement has drowned in the Yellow River as she attempted to flee and join the CCP forces to fight for a new world. The soldier sent, quasi-ethnographically, from the CCP propaganda unit into Kuomintan territory to collect peasant folk songs, to rewrite them with communist lyrics, to raise the morale of CCP peasant troops, is now a pretext looking back across the Yellow River of time, across the Great Famine and the destructive Cultural Revolution, and forward to a less tradition and ideology straitjacketed future. The contrast could not be greater: by 1998, with Zubin Mehta conducting, Zhang would direct a lavish production of Puccini's *Turandot* first in Florence and then in Beijing; the film *The Making of Turandot at the Forbidden City* (1999) explores the differences of "work practices" across cultural presuppositions, for instance, about lighting effects, while at the same time celebrating the renewed global interactions after the cold war.

In a parallel way 1984 in Iran marks the shift of Iran's two leading filmmakers and their colleagues toward what would become in the 1990s another international cinema sensation, like the Fifth Generation films of China in the 1980s, as the cynosure of attention. Mohsen Makhmalbaf in 1984 made his last propaganda-style film (*Fleeing from Evil to God*) and began to experiment with docudrama (*Boycott*, 1985; *A Moment of Innocence*, 1996, both drawing from his arrest as a youth for stabbing a policeman) and increasingly incisive social commentaries on Iranian society after the Iran-Iraq War (The *Peddler*, 1987; *The Cyclist*, 1989; *Marriage of the Blessed*, 1989). The last in particular would use the device of a shell-shocked war photographer's camera, as it clicked, working as a shifter back and forth between revolutionary promises and betrayals. Likewise Abbas Kiarostami turned from his shorts and trilogy of parable films using children's perspectives (*Where Is the Friend's Home*, 1987; *The Key*, 1987; *Homework*, 1989) to his films of indirection, eliciting thoughts about social changes in the fabric of social life. *Close Up* (1990) is a meditation on filmic judgment, the use of both close-up and wide-angled cameras, diegetically the former for the courtroom and the latter for things that cannot be introduced in court. The Koker trilogy on an earthquake near Tehran (*Life and Nothing More*, 1991; *Journey to the Land of the Traveller*, 1993; *Through the Olive Trees*, 1994) likewise is more than a portrayal of disruption, loss, and reconstruction, involving the actors both in their diegetic and extradiegetic lives (looking for an actor from a previous film; watching the unfolding of a socially impossible love). *The Taste of Cherry* (1997) and *The Wind Will Carry Us* (1999) stage different strata of society in relation to questions of responsibility, the ability to retrieve another from alienation or acts of self-destruction and suicide, and the intrusiveness of the filmic, ethnographic eye of Tehranis (and foreigners) into villagers' elaborate cultural socialities, conflicts, and ritual tools of repair or boundary policing. "The wind will carry us" is a line from the poet Forough Farrokhzad, a kind of Susan Sontag modernist free-thinker and filmmaker (of a leper boarding school with its own deep allegorical resonances). *The Wind Will Carry Us* also hilariously and allegorically has the filmmaker within the film constantly running up the village's highest hill to try to catch the signal from Tehran for his mobile phone. In *Taste of Cherry*, set amid construction sites, unfinished daily social rituals such as tea drinking, an ambiguous (unsuccessful) suicide, and alternative filmic and video endings, remain unfinished as if a commentary on Iranian projects that can never be finished.

The unfinishing, sometimes undoing of modernity took other turns as well, especially in Ahmedabad, India, where my wife and I spent much of 1984, where I did fieldwork with the Jain community, notationally focusing on mercantile communities (Jains and Parsis) turned industrialists negotiating between their own communal moralities and those of their labor forces from other communities. It was a year of three shattering upheavals: (1) the assassination of Indira Gandhi four months after her decision to attack the Sikh Golden Temple in Amritsar, killing the separatist Jarnail Singh Bhindranwale and his followers, and the communal violence against Sikhs that followed; (2) the Bhopal disaster, an icon of the series of industrial disaster denials and citizen epidemiology and mobilizations from Minimata (Japan) and Love Canal (New York) to Woburn (Massachusetts) and Fukushima (Japan); and (3) the eruption of caste-linked riots in Ahmedabad over affirmative action or caste-reservation access to medical and engineering education, foreshadowing the parallel worlds of economic growth and some of the worst communal violence in India since Partition that would occur in 1992 with the destruction of the Babri Masjid in Ayodhya after a BJP campaign of *yatra*s (religious processions), and again in 2002 beginning in Ahmedabad after the Sabarmati Express train with Hindu pilgrims from Ayodhya was burned and riots spread across Gujarat state. The BJP chief minister Narendra Modi was alleged to have used communal tensions repeatedly for political advantage and in 2013 was slated to head the BJP slate for prime minister.

These events transformed much of the anthropology, cultural studies, comparative literature, and other social research in India. There was a turn (as in the ethnographic and contemporary turn in Chinese and Iranian films) to the workings of everyday life, media of persuasion, spaces of new interaction among castes, and the creation of new public spheres, consumer consciousness, self-help organizations, and civil society organizations.[18]

Already in 1984 India was spawning a growing consumer movement, supported by the wildly popular television show *Rajini*, in which every week for half an hour an ordinary housewife would go out into the world to battle for consumer rights. In the next six years India would liberalize its economy and become a leading member of the rising BRIC (Brazil, Russia, India, China) players in the global economy, with information technology leading the way, not only as back office and call center support in a twenty-four-hour global business world but also as a source for transforming public planning through geographical information systems and through modeling public services on information flows, pioneered by such socially as well as technologically innovative companies as Infosys.[19] Not all changes are registered macroscopically; among the most important vehicles of visual suasion in the campaign leading up to the 1992 destruction of the Babri Masjid was the dissemination throughout the visual field of small stickers with the image of Ram or his signs, a tactic that would again prove effective in the 2009 presidential elections in Iran, when green ribbons produced a Green Wave.[20]

While *Writing Culture* is still firmly set in anthropology's print age, by the 1990s and the decade of *Late Editions* anthropology was writing under the anxiety of the digital but before the digital age fully set in.[21] The decade of the 1990s is one of accelerating transitions as the world emerged from cold war divisions, undoing and redoing societies of discipline with those of code. For instance, Hong Kong returned to China in 1997 under a one-state two-systems arrangement, with a war of influence affecting both.

Changes at the political surface index only roughly the changes underfoot that anthropology is so good at revealing. The year 1989, the two-hundredth anniversary of the French Revolution, saw the Velvet Revolution in Prague and election of Vaclav Havel; the Polish government holding talks with Solidarity and a gradual transition to democratic governance; the dismantling by Hungary of the border fence with Austria and introduction of multiparty democracy; the withdrawal of Soviet troops from Afghanistan, and of Cuba from Angola; the largest labor strike (coal miners in Siberia) in Russia since the 1920s; the resignation of Rajiv Gandhi after his Congress Party lost half its seats; the first Brazilian presidential election in twenty-nine years and the first post-Suharto Indonesian one.

The year 1989 also saw Khomeini's fatwa against Salman Rushdie for publishing *Satanic Verses* (1988), a story of migration, and elevating of well-known hadith stories into the global commons rather than keeping them within the world of the *umma*, a story that would be replayed in updated media circuits with boomeranging cartoons fifteen years later.[22] Signaled in these communicative shifts of cultural texture are cosmopolitical intereferences, acknowledgments, and resistances. They are cultural transformations from eighteenth-century Habermasian public spheres to twentieth-century Public Culture, always already structured by the culture industries (broadcasting and "creative" advertising to mass audiences), increasingly, if partially, reworked by digital many-to-many messaging. One spoke in the 1990s hesitatingly of "new global orders"—environmental effects of industrial production, for which climate change would become a diffuse figure of speech; financial crises mediated by "structured instruments" such as derivatives, for which *neoliberalism* became a diffuse figure of speech; and transnational media productions, for which CNN and Al Jazeera became temporary tokens, while underneath anime, video games, J-pop and K-pop (Japanese and Korean popular culture) homesteaded new knowledge economies. These would become terrains for innovative ethnographic work.[23]

1999. Operating Systems 2.0: From IT, Genom, and Genome to Omics and Neurons

The content of the global movement which ever since the [1999] Seattle revolt has occupied and (redefined) the public sphere is nothing less than human nature. The latter constitutes both the arena of struggle and its stake.
—Paolo Virno, "Natural-Historical Diagrams"

The shift toward biocapitalism and its alternative sociopolitical-legal forms in the aftermath of the 1980 Bayh-Dole Act and *Chakrabarty* Supreme Court decision in the United States has been the subject of increasing anthropological attention.[24] While in the late twentieth century much attention was focused on reproductive technologies, in the twenty-first century the focus has shifted to a broader series of biotechnologies, from genomics (both agricultural and biomedical) to the coming era of the brain and neuroscience research along with its ethical, legal, and social armatures and its possibilities for alternative pathways.[25] In a nice turn of phrase, the Italian philosopher Paolo Virno, building on Derrida's prescient essay "The Aforementioned So-called Human Genome," speaks of *natural-historical diagrams* "in which human praxis is applied in the most direct and systematic way to the ensemble of requirements that make praxis human. The stake: those who struggle against the mantraps placed on the paths of migrants or against copyright [and patent] on scientific research raise the question of the different socio-political expression that could be given, here and now."[26]

The millennium shift from gene and *genom* to *genome* (like Abram to Abraham in the Hebrew Bible) and on to multiple "omics" signals a shift toward more fundamental worlds of exploration into third and fourth natures.[27] It pushes further also, perhaps, the difference registered by the titles of Johannes Fabian's two books, *Time and the Other* and *Out of Our Minds*, both recalibrations of nineteenth- and early twentieth-century anthropology, the one via rhetorical creations of sequentialized parallel (or local) worlds, the other acknowledging the role of psychotropic altered states of mind in the encounters across local worlds (facilitated by drugs or not) and millennium shifts to renewed research on the brain and neuroscience.

The turn of a millennium is one of those loops in "second" or man-made "nature" (2000 C.E., a merely common era–defined millennium), like the spaghetti coils of highways traversing modern Asian cities, that accrues symbolic meaning, initially arbitrarily, but then takes on a force of its own. In 2000 this was beautifully instantiated in the apocalyptic Y2K scare, in which it was feared that mission-critical computer systems might fail because their legacy codes had only two digits for the year and might mistake 2001 for 1901. Planes could drop out of the sky; emergency rooms might lose power. Computer programmers made good money for a short time providing patches and fixes.[28]

By the new millennium, after a twenty-year incubation, the anthropology of science, technology, and society (STS) had emerged alongside, broadening the purview of, British social studies of science, French actor network theory, the social studies of technology, and the social history of science. Four features distinguish the anthropology of STS: (1) a detailed interest in the sciences and technologies themselves in contrast to cherry-picking cultural metaphors; (2) a global perspective, not just an account from Western Europe and North America; (3) strategic multilocale or multisited ethnographic access to complex distributed processes such as the global chemical industry or global clinical trials; and (4) a concern with the powerful aesthetics of imaginaries and explorations via bioart, literature, film, and drama of the possibilities of democratizing science, exploring the ramifying effects of technologies, and charting the emotional and psychic investments of both. The task of translating legacy knowledges into public futures draws on four kinds of genealogies: test drives and libidinal drives, protocols and networks, landscapes or ethical plateaus, and reknitting global moieties split by the cold war.[29]

The anthropology of science and technology has produced an impressive body of studies emerging from subservience to the older, merely constructivist forms of STS. The Duke University Press book series *Experimental Futures: Technological Lives, Scientific Arts, Anthropological Voices* provides one venue for exploring the expanded horizons of the anthropology of science and technology, in contrast to neighboring fields more focused on traditional academic philosophy of science debates largely formulated in the early twentieth century.

A broader venue can be seen in the topics of recent anthropology of science and technology books and dissertations, which include (nonexhaustively) evidence law and the incorporation or exclusion of visual media (handwriting, fingerprints, PET scans, video animation) from the courtroom;[30] e-documents in a culture of cryptography;[31] interpretive meanings of visualizing, amplifying, or proliferation technologies such as medical scans, tissue culture technologies, and clinical diagnoses;[32] open software as sociopolitical infrastructure, e-governance in Latin America and e-kiosks in India;[33] e-tools for collaborative work at a distance, and its failures;[34] Taiwanese biostatisticians as providers of bridging tools for global clinical trials, a case of a nonrecognized country using expertise to be a player;[35] biological citizenship after disaster, bioethnic conscription in disease studies, and bioavailability as biopolitics;[36] surgical training of muscular as well as cognitive memory, pharmaceutical marketing and objective self-fashioning through drugs, and turning of selves into clinical subjects;[37] forms of biocapitalism under different national agendas;[38] identity contradictions and psychoses mediated by organ transplantation for patients and physicians in Turkey and moral rejection of organ transplantation in Egypt;[39] transmission of structural biology through bodily performance;[40] race and the marketing of medicine, genomics, and diversity;[41] product design and safety law;[42] nuclear safety;[43] executive coaching;[44] psychiatry, depression, and negotiating different class- and religion-linked public health discourses in Iran;[45] epidemic and transgenerational addiction as a technoculture of affect;[46] computational artificial life and American folk kinship idioms, deep-water marine biology and logics of ancestry, microbiopolitics of bacteria and cheese;[47] climate change vernaculars in Canadian First Nations, U.S. evangelicals, corporate green audits, climate scientists in the public sphere, climate science under different national agendas;[48] biological crafts from do-it-yourself biologies and geometric modeling with yarns and plastics to molecular gastronomy and synthetic biology; citizen epidemiology, gas fracking, and endocrine disruptors;[49] "smart" electricity market making by engineers and traders in contrast to economists, digital mapmaking in contests between First Nations, mining geologists, and forest ecologists.[50]

Two films of the year 1999–2000, again drawing on different parallel, partially local, Chinese and Iranian worlds may serve to mark a subtle yet profound shift in cultural consciousness parallel to the shift registered in the anthropology of science and technology "in which human praxis is applied in the most direct and systematic way to the ensemble of requirements that make praxis human,"[51] or in a more anthropological term, as the subtitle of our book series puts it, attention to "technological lives, scientific arts, and anthropological voices."

Ning Ying's *I Love Beijing* (retitled *The Warmth of Summer* after censors feared the title would be understood as sarcasm, itself a dynamic feature of the metastases of proleptic and preemptive meanings) is the third of her Beijing trilogy tracking three generations of Beijing residents in China after Deng Xiaoping. Her extraordinary documentary *Railroad of Hope* (2002), interviewing people on the move West of agricultural labor migrants from Sichuan to the cotton fields of Xinjian, and her seven shorts for UNESCO (*In Our Own Words*, 2001) on child and women trafficking, on an HIV/AIDS prevention outreach by Buddhist monks, on a center for Shanghai street children, and on a migrant worker's child, illustrate the turn (also taken up by the Sixth Generation filmmakers). This turn chronicles social issues in more direct, often first-person accounts and realist reportage than was possible a decade earlier. Ning, a former assistant director on Bertolucci's 1987 *The Last Emperor*, trained both in Beijing's Film Academy and in Italy, has emerged as a distinctive voice among the Fifth Generation Chinese filmmakers. She deploys an ethnographic and almost Kiarostami-like gaze on the three generations. *For Fun* (1993) shows a group of retired senior citizens who gather to play and sing arias from their favorite Beijing operas, a popular pastime one can still see on the streets today in many Chinese cities. A story line is gently formed around the deference given a former doorman at the Grand Beijing Opera House, who gradually takes on an increasingly dictatorial air but does get the group recognition and a performance, until it dissolves under the stress. The film ends as the people begin again to come together. The retired doorman sits and listens from around the corner and then slowly walks back. *On the Beat* (1995) deals with the middle-aged during a campaign against allegedly rabid street dogs, a bureaucratic comedy amid the tearing down of old *houtong* neighborhoods. *I Love Beijing* (2000) turns to the displaced youth, a twenty-something taxi driver who is getting divorced and dates, in turn, a migrant waitress from northeast China, a popular radio show host, a professor's daughter and primary school teacher, and finally a peasant from the countryside, whom he ends up marrying. His journey of comic hard-learned realism is figured (in the original script) by having him first driving a Toyota Crown Salon and ending up in a beat-up yellow mini-van. Extradiegetic reality intervenes: these two cars were already hard to find in fast-changing Beijing by the time filming began. More recently Ning has scripted the cult film *Perpetual Motion* (2005), in which well-known figures in Beijing play fictional characters satirizing their own social types (described in delicious detail by Gina Marchetti).[52]

Ning's work and that of the Sixth Generation filmmakers—such as Jia Zhangke's short documentaries that are studies for his urban-social problem feature films, such as *Unknown Pleasures* (2002) and the documentary *In Public* (2001), shot in the coal mining town of Datong, and *Still Life* (2006) and the documentary *Dong* (2006), shot in Fengjie, one of the cities marked for flooding by the Three Gorges Dam—in this sense is not unlike some of the films by Iranians at the same time. One thinks of the anthropologist-filmmaker Ziba Mir-Hosseini's *Divorce Iranian Style* (1998) and *Runaway* (2001, both with Kim Longinotto). One thinks of Rakhshan Bani-Etemad's powerful film *Under the Skin of the City* (2001) on a woman textile worker with an invalid husband, her own occupationally caused asthma, a daughter's abusive husband causing the daughter to run away to prostitution, and her eldest son's failed efforts to go to Japan to earn more money, capped by footage of a woman candidate for political office making arguments that would be taken up again in a documentary on women running for political office (*Our Times*, 2002). Bani-Etemad also has done a documentary on a shelter for women (*Angels of the House of the Sun*, 2009). Like the documentary *Divorce Iranian Style* and a full ethnography on divorce courts and the politics of women's rights by Arzoo Osanloo,[53] Reza Mir-Karimi's feature film *Under the Moonlight* (2001) presents a nuanced picture of a seminary student on a picaresque journey among the homeless who teach him about mutual care and the way religion might fit into life in a different way than his fellow seminarians might imagine in their scholastic studies.

These films parallel the ethnographic and anthropological craft of detailing the unintended consequences and differential refractions to policy initiatives, "ethnographic pebbles in the way of theory,"[54] ethnography producing more reality-tested and grounded theory, upsetting the echo-chamber master narratives that pass from aggregation (abstracting, algorithmizing, modeling, simplifying from the data) to imperative (policy implementation backed by temporary money and jobs). Recognizing this failing, the World Bank is beginning to contract with anthropologists to ground-truth the work of its staff and its economist contractors, who often can't see or access the ground through the distancing abstraction and sophistication of their statistical methods and the blindness of needing to attend to only what is measurable.[55]

A very different kind of refraction of everyday life sometimes caught most powerfully on film accesses another contemporary anthropological preoccupation: social trauma and repair, mental health and PTSD from Peru to Aceh.[56] Two such films are Ebrahim Hatamikia's *Red Ribbons* (2000) and the anthropologist Robert Lemelson's *40 Years of Silence* (2009). These films explore the psychic aftereffects of violence and war and complement new anthropological work on health care systems after AIDS and increasing patient demands for rights to care from Brazil to Botswana.[57] In *Red Ribbons* a lone war veteran lives underground and obsessively removes land mines, placing red ribbons to warn of areas not yet cleared; a woman suffering from false pregnancy hysteria returns to the ruins of her home in this mined area and red-ribboned desert land; and a recluse Afghan migrant guards a graveyard of armored tanks, including one buried like a turtle (inhabiting both the land of the living and the underworld). Each lives in his and her own world of delusional reality, communicating with the others through emotional miscues and needs. The Lemelson film follows a number of village characters (this time all too real) and their memories and psychological disturbances stemming from the massacres of 1965 in Indonesia.

War-induced PTSD, however, is not the only cause of disturbances of the brain, and mental health anthropologists were central to the 1996 *Global Burden of Disease Study* (sponsored by the World Bank and the World Health Organization),[58] which, to the shock and disbelief of many health policy practitioners, identified neuropsychiatric diseases as the leading cause of global disease burden, with enormous costs to national economies as well as to the affected individuals and their caregivers. This was measured by not just premature mortality normalized against expected life spans but also healthy years of life lost to disability. These occur in early life (e.g., autism), in young adult life (schizophrenia, usually diagnosed in late teens to early thirties, just when families have made their maximum investment in education), and at the end of life (neurodegenerative disorders), as well as depression at many stages of life. The pharmaceutical industry, however, is shutting down its neuroscience research, leaving governments worried about especially rapidly aging populations. Thus because of the need to plan for increasing burdens of disease as well as because rapidly emerging new technologies—neuroimaging, brain stimulation, brain-computer interfaces, stem cell therapy—promise an engine of economic growth, neuroscience has become one of the hot new priorities of government investment, and the twenty-first century is said to become a century of the brain as the twentieth was of the gene.[59]

2013. *Changes under Foot, Playing the Scales, Remending the Silk Roads*

Images became live. . . . There is less of the protest art . . . more of the practical . . . new media beyond activism. . . . Although the Iranian government controls the Internet and threatens to close down the connection to the outside world, digital culture is expanding. . . . *Lawful intercept technology* . . . activists were still still trying to gather cases where Nokia[-Siemens] intercept technology had led to . . . imprisonment . . . [and] death. . . . If this case advances in court in favor of activists, . . . Nokia intercept technology could become unlawful.
—Mazyar Lotfalian, "Aestheticized Politics, Visual Culture and Emergent Forms of Digital Practice" (2012)

I think words operate like musical notes that the eyeball hears. "Cloud Atlas" is the name of a piece of music by the Japanese composer Toshi Ichiyanagi, who was Yoko Ono's first husband.
—David Mitchell, author of *Cloud Atlas* and *The Thousand Autumns of Jacob de Zoet*

Already descriptions of events are chronicled faster, better, cheaper, and out of control on YouTube. If you wish, you can hear and see "the rhythmic beat of the [Iranian] revolution" in a series of YouTube videos, shifting some of the referencing of writing culture from library to audiovisual instant access.[60] One of the images that instantly went viral and "live" is the death of Neda Agha-Soltan, shot on the streets of Tehran in 2009. Lotfalian's "images become live" points to the flourishing of digitally mediated collaborative art beyond the event and out of the control of authorities who wished to deny and reframe what everyone saw.

When Agha-Soltan's dying went live, the image multiplied. It was enhanced, abstracted, schematized, collaged into multiplying semiotic messages, and otherwise moved hand to hand, keyboard to keyboard, up the use and value chain as a multivalent signifier, symbol, and allegory. The artists and transmitters, professional and casual, who created socialities with the cell-phone-captured video are people in whom Lotfalian is interested as enlivening the image beyond simple representation, remaking public culture vital and anew. Similarly Orkideh Behrouzan draws attention to the Persian digital blogosphere as a dynamically functioning *affective* space where the 1360s (1980s) generation for the first time can recognize itself, recalling generational experiences that now turn out to be not just individual traumas, as they were experienced at the time, but cultural subjectivations that can be processed and worked through with one another.[61] Experience can, through call and response, posting and commenting, affirming and contesting, be transmuted from alienation and passivity into new active sociocultural life.

For the moment (like Galileo and Descartes), the activists are losing in court cases under the Alien Tort Act: two Iranian plaintiffs sued Nokia-Siemens Networks, and several Chinese citizens have signed onto a case against Cisco, both cases alleging that use of intercept technology by the Iranian and Chinese governments have violated their and others' human rights and have led to torture and death. The U.S. Supreme Court on April 17, 2013, dismissed Esther Kiobel's suit against Royal Dutch Shell Petroleum in the 1995 torture and execution of her husband in Port Harcourt, Nigeria on jurisdictional grounds that there was not sufficient "touch and concern" or "sufficient force" on U.S. soil. A number of international lawyers, however, observe that this decision goes against the trend of providing some international accountability and a venue for victims of abuses in places where suits cannot be brought in domestic courts.[62]

The argument for international accountability of suppliers in the information technology industry seems not unlike that used by the Coalition for Environmentally Responsible Economies (CERES), founded in 1989, the year of the *Exxon Valdez* oil spill. CERES proposed principles first named Valdez and then named CERES Principles. As described in Candis Callison's ethnography of different, not always mutually understood vernaculars of concern about climate change, by getting Fortune 500 companies to sign on to green sustainability audits, advocates and the public can gradually hold these companies to more and then more stringent sustainable practices.[63] Water governance struggles over tweaking local and international regulations and models of use rights and the common good, with networks to share experiences of particular local experiments around the globe, have also become the site of ethnographies of iterative efforts to make the results come out in ethically acceptable ways.[64] Similar struggles perhaps can be seen in the evolution of how some patient advocacy groups are trying to move beyond fundraising into the scientific discovery enterprise and in Brazil the judicialization of constitutionally guaranteed rights to health care.[65] The creation of web tools for database creation to track the environmental and health damage of shale gas "fracking" across the United States changes the nature of both public culture and ethnography.[66]

In all these and other circumstances of the new millennium, anthropological fieldwork and writing culture is not, as they say, what it used to be.[67] Nor is it always where it is expected to be, as in the growth of anthropologists hired by Fortune 500 companies to rethink work practices or user responsiveness, and by the World Bank to ground-truth anomalies in the work of their staff and their contractors.[68] Where ethnography, anthropology, and writing culture is most useful is not necessarily the on-the-ground and local worlds alone, but rather the ability to play up and down the entire scale from ground to theory, policy to reality, and across globalized, distributed, or value-chain accumulated processes from locus to locus (defined both by geography and by professional and lay occupation in those processes), and increasingly across comparative genomic species boundaries to what is biologically conserved across species and what has mutated, generating diversity or restriction. Attention to what Ulrike Felt calls "archaeologies of [sociopolitical] engagement" can identify also multiscalar loci and historical openings where alternative imaginaries and policies to those of master narratives of progress and risk management led by expert and economic lobbies can be envisioned and alternative technological futures promoted, "an approach to innovation governance which [gives] space to pondering over benefits for society and the 'public good' [rather than] limiting their frames of reference to narrow economic benefits or issues of direct risks."[69]

In the picture of the world in 2013, a frequent sight, for instance, is of students at the National University of Singapore holding textbooks open with one hand, the other checking their teacher's archived video lectures on their smartphones. Truth lies in the triangulation between constantly updated lectures as research updates the science and canonic platforms of knowledge codified in more slowly updated textbooks. Truth lies in the shifting of heads between smartphone, textbook, and colleague at the next table, sharing, correcting, testing, reconstructing, and forging new paths, skills, and understandings. These students, as they turn their heads back and forth, and cycling through their phones from lectures to chat and back, are looking into the sociocultural and technological infrastructures of new globalizing universities, and they do so with humor, social critique, and a sense of new possibilities. At Tembusu College at the National University a collaborative student-painted mural adorns a classroom building hallway with rebus puns: A book titled *All About Me* replaces the head (Facebook) of a lad seated cross-legged, thumbs up. A girl presses the *send* button on her iPhone and the trap doors of her skull open, releasing a bird (bird brain?). The bird is chased by a large grinning figure (Roald Dahl's Friendly Big Giant) with a butterfly net, logos of Facebook, LinkedIn, and other commercial icons on his chest, seeking to capture the desires released for resale to marketers. The bird flies toward a barefoot girl in tank top and jeans with a camera for a head who, holding up her hand, signals "Hi." Nearby a fish-headed figure, standing next to a tombstone labeled "RIP Meg Aupload 2005–2012," with a fishing pole goes phishing for passwords into the skull of a bespectacled figure walking with a cane, perhaps to upload the terabytes of previous generations' knowledge. A wind-blown tourist couple with cameras float above a ghostly woman's head with Microsoft icon eyes, while a detached hand tosses an open-jawed, eye-popping head, and a conveyor belt carries more eyes on strings (i-devices). Torsos of a man in bathing trunks and a woman in a shift hold their detached heads on strings, signifying the disconnect between characters online and real people. Each of the caricatures is signed in English and Chinese or Tamil by their respective artists.

Tembusu class projects tend toward role play and visual media. A project blue-skies an "aging in place" residence, dubbed O'Town (Old Town) after Tembusu's location in the new University Town (New Town), with its New England–style commons lawn, eating places, coffee shops, and sports facilities. The project is, in part, a response to and a critique of readings on government policy concerns about the aging population. In part it knowledgeably, hence pragmatically, draws on and tweaks already existing policy frameworks and initiatives. And in part it suggests new ways to integrate government concerns to decentralize health care, such as routine physiotherapy, from an overly hospital-centric system and support changing needs and desires as seniors today become better educated and active than previous senior generations. The role-play format stages conflicts of interests and perspectives, allows otherwise shy students to speak up through a mask, and when filmed produces an archivable, sharable, digital product that if done well enough could even be fed into public debate, as, increasingly, student films, such as the powerful *Before We Forget* (on two families taking care of disabled seniors) already are.[70]

Not all of course is digital or filmic. A Tembusu student-organized debate series called "The Elephant in the Room" allows sensitive topics, such as racial harmony, to be debated under Chatham House rules. (Material can be used outside of the meeting but with no attributions to anyone in the meeting.) Students at the nearby University Scholars Program put on a tightly choreographed student-written musical, *White Collar*, satirizing the career pressures of Singapore families, workplace gender relations, maid-madam tensions, hierarchy and arbitrary promotion and demotion decisions, status competition, parent-teacher association politics, tiger moms and no-more-arguments-please dads, the drone work of bureaucrats, and their relations with their less educated working-class parents.

What I want to indicate with these small ethnographic notes, with no space for providing further contextual significance, is something "under foot" in the cultural texture of fast-changing Asian cities. Singapore is neither China nor India nor Southeast Asia, though it has deep roots and live interactions in each of these global arenas of social and cultural change. A new geography of science, of media technologies such as the animation business described by Ian Condry,[71] and of knowledge production in a variety of worlds is already at hand all under the stress of intense global competition.

The largest genomic sequencing center in the world, for instance, is BGI in Shenzhen and Hong Kong, with labs also now in Philadelphia, Copenhagen, and Davis, California. It is not, as popular accounts often claim, just a government-supported, cheap labor factory. Far more interestingly, it grew out of graduate student experience at the Universities of Copenhagen and Washington (Seattle), and those lineages and connections remain strong. Early funding came from starting a small diagnostic startup company and from a municipal loan from the provincial hometown of one of the founders. Sequencing machines were on loan to be paid for over time thanks to a mentoring network connection to the then management of Solexa (now Ilumina), the maker of sequencing machines. Again through the mentoring lineages they secured a role in the Human Genome Project to sequence 1 percent of the human genome. Only then did the Chinese government take notice. For industries such as animation, large "creative industry" parks are being readied in Guangzhou, Shanghai, Beijing, and Chengdu in the hopes that biotech, clean energy, the culture industry (animation, cartoons, games), consulting, software, and education industries can provide new, higher value economic engines than the factories of the recent past. Since 2007 Guangzhou's International Animation Festival has been the largest in the country, with over a thousand enterprises participating in 2009 and 150,000 attendees.[72]

As a new geography of science, culture industries, and global universities takes shape, older geographies, histories, and cultural interpretations are also being rewritten. Some are in a traditional scholarly manner, as in the expanding turn to histories from the perspective of ocean diasporas and sea-traveling peoples, such as Engseng Ho's work on the Hadramut network from Yemen across southeast Asia;[73] Kenneth Dean and Zheng Zhenman's work on irrigation expansion in Putian (Fujian Province), adjudicated by hierarchies of temples resisting and accepting incorporation into state ritual frameworks and the extension of clan houses and temples to southeast Asia;[74] Daphon David Ho's work on sea lords and the maritime frontier in seventeenth-century Fujian (from where many overseas Chinese are descended);[75] and Herman Kulke et al.'s edited volume on the Indian Chola kingdom's trade and naval expeditions across southeast Asia.[76]

Some of these new geographies place local and global stories in compelling regional contexts, hinting at other possible histories, such as Warrick Anderson's account of the competition in 1960s population genetics and virology over whether Papua New Guinea was to be Australian or American scientific turf.[77] This was in the context of the International Biological Program spearheaded in part by the U.S. National Institutes of Health and the search for the causes of the neurodegenerative *kuru* disease (a celebrated case in 1960s medical anthropology).

Other of these new geographies, equally interesting, are new creative arts across borders, of which three from the dramatic arts may stand in for a profusion. Kuo Pao Kun's *Descendants of the Eunuch Admiral* (1995 in both Mandarin and English) is a powerful imagining of Zheng He, the great Ming Dynasty admiral who led seven expeditions across the Indian Ocean, as an emigrant cut off from his roots: as a man (made a eunuch), as a Muslim (taking on a Chinese name and culture), as a family descendant (a Persian ancestor, a Yunan upbringing). These severances function as a powerful allegory for Singaporeans cut off from much of their past in a migrant and globalized world ("To keep my head / I must accept losing my tail / To keep my faith / I must learn to worship others' gods"). Kuo Pao Kun has become a cultural icon himself, having been imprisoned in Singapore for five years and yet the founder of three important theater institutions. Ten years after his death, his work, most recently in 2013, was celebrated with four twenty-minute experimental tributes to his play *Lao Jiu* by four prominent Asian theater practitioners from Beijing (Li Liuyi), Taipei (Li Bao-chun), Hong Kong (Danny Yung), and Macau (Lawrence Lei).[78]

Awakening, the brilliant interpretation of *The Dream of the Red Chamber* with an all-female cast starring the gay Hong Kong–based pop star Denise Ho playing the male lead Baoyu, is done with pop songs, contemporary dress (heels, black skirts and jackets), minimalist geometric sets, and lively choreography in twenty fast-paced scenes. Directed by Edward Lam, along with Danny Yung, a founder of Zuni Icosahedron, the experimental arts group in Hong Kong, and written by Wong Wing Sze, it uses a fairy tale and a hothouse of emotions from the aristocratic red chamber of concubines to explore the impossibilities of correcting past mistakes so they do not repeat. Denise Ho comments, "We cannot possibly overturn the errors from our ignorant youth, so they remain irrevocably etched in the record of our lives. As we see the protagonist head down the same path, helplessly reliving his own ignorance, and experiencing the loss of each one close to him all over again, would this not serve as a mirror for the audience?"[79]

From the India side of Southeast Asian history comes another brilliant reworking, *Glimpses of Angkor*, a classical South Indian dance interpretation of "the churning," the central motif of Angkor Wat, the cosmological churning of the cosmic ocean by the *deva*s and *asura*s pulling on the *naga* (snake) coiled around Mount Meru, and out of the froth is born the elixir of immortality, the *aspara*s, and the goddess of wealth, Lakshmi. In Cambodia the churning is celebrated in the Festival of the Reversing Current (Bonn Om Tuk), when people flock to dragon boat races on the Tônlé Sap to cheer the river flow returning to its downstream direction. During the rainy season water backs up the Sap River from the Mekong, flowing into the Tônlé Sap Lake and causing it to swell five times its dry season size. As the rainy season ends, the river changes direction again, and the lake empties back into the Mekong. The Tônlé Sap is rich in freshwater fish and the surrounding farmlands rich in sediment. The churning is, as well, says the director, Aravinth Kumarasmay, "the churning of our pure conscience in the constant battle between good and evil as we strive toward excellence, the amrita. As artists we battle between spiritual evolution, perfection of our craft and the effects of commercialization in our pursuit of artistic excellence."[80] Aravinth himself is the son of refugees from communal violence in Sri Lanka, and for his family the churning also has a deep reference to this history. The founder of the Aspara Arts Dance Company, Neila Sathyalingam, also born in Sri Lanka, leaving a house burned down behind her, trained in the Kalakshetra Academy in Tamilnadu and brings with her to Singapore a rich socio-aesthetic history of human form moving rhythmically in a series of sculptural poses embodying emotion. *The Churning* (*Manthan*) is the title also of Shyam Benegal's 1976 Hindi film about Amul, the Gujarat milk cooperative, financed by the Gujarat Cooperative Milk Federation.[81] It tells of the churning struggle for just return to labor and increased wealth through cooperation. These several loci tie together Hindu mythic resonances across South and Southeast Asia from India via the Khmer Empire to the Cham of Vietnam, but more important for the contemporary world from labor struggles to dealing with communal violence, making and remaking pluralist worlds under new tourist economies, visual spectacles, and renewing aesthetic approaches to acknowledging both emotion and wisdom.

Beyond mere multisited to also multiscalar and cross-temporally resonating, stuttering, and recommended cultural writing, perhaps the aesthetic form most ethnographic as well as historical are novels, particularly those that, for a post–cold war world, remind and remend the once and now again skeins of the sea and land Silk Roads shuttling from East to West and back again. Among these I would invoke, first of all, the anthropologist Amitav Ghosh's *Calcutta Chromosome* (1996), *Hungry Tide* (2004), and *River of Smoke* (2011), and then Philip Caputo's *Acts of Faith* (2006), Kamila Shamsie's *Burnt Shadows* (2009), David Mitchell's *Cloud Atlas* (2004, and the 2012 film), and *The Thousand Autumns of Jacob de Zoet*.[82] My own sense is that there is more to be learned here about playing the scales of culture than from flat-footed talk of global assemblages, neoliberalisms, hybridities, and the like, which, however corrective and useful in their place, capture only limited dimensions, even of political economy, not to mention cosmopolitics, and listening to the harmonics of cross-cultural and historical interferences and inter-references. As Mitchell nicely says in an interview, "In early drafts I was always trying to devise ingenious ways around the language barrier—and then I realized that this barrier could work for, and not against, the novel. So I stuck my characters into language prison and watched them try to get out."[83] The same might be said of Ghosh's *Sea of Poppies* (2008), where it is we readers who are thrown into a rich polyglot of seafarers.

Playing the scales of ethnographic insight and spatially traveling farther along with the migrants, registering their harmonic repeats, reprises, and multimedia mutations, going on from the *Sea of Poppies*, from eighteenth-century

Bihar into the twenty-first century, Indian documentary and ethnographic filmmaker Surabhi Sharma says, "It is actually my experience of tracking music in the Caribbean, in Trinidad especially, that layered my understanding [of Bhojapuri Bihari music in Mumbai]."[84] She is speaking of the newly politically charged annual *chhath puja* and *Ram Lila* performances on Juhu beach (where Mumbai film stars and industrialists live), the parking lots filled with autorickshaws and taxis of Bihari migrants, many of whom live in the Jari Mari slum next to and directly under the flight paths of Mumbai International Airport. Mirroring the Maharastran *Ganesh puja* a month earlier, this increasingly scripted and megaspectacle *mela* has become a demonstration of visibility against the Shiva Sena and Maharashtra Navnirman Sena's attacks on north Indian migrants. "In the one song, if you noticed, she named every district [in Bihar, from which the migrants come], and the song is basically 'we have come here with our labor and the whole country belongs to us, you cannot throw us out'; and that was soon after that particular year [2008] when the Shiv Sena said we will never allow chhath puja to happen on the beaches of Bombay and Lal Prasad, the famous [Bihari] leader from back home [and minister of railways], had famously said I will perform it at his doorstep if he doesn't allow my brother to do it on the beach."[85]

In Trinidad Sharma was filming how Bihari folk music traditions had crossed over into the popular music industry, infusing chutney, soca, and calypso with the sounds of the *dholak, tabla,* and *dhantal,*[86] and upon her return to Mumbai she was suddenly impressed with how similarly Bihari "folk music comes to the big cities (in Mumbai and Delhi and Patna) and becomes a music industry, pop music, that goes back to the village but which gets further enriched, so [for instance] the mobile phone is a very common theme in the music that goes back to the villages, and is reinvented into a story there that comes right back, a constant" cycle of renewal and transformation. It is a *chutney* of political *visibility*, of rhizomic labor roots across India, from Shilong in the northeast to Mumbai in the west, and across the globe to Trinidad and Surinam, of an organized music industry megaspectacle and of women's-family *puja*s. It contains moments of terrifying massed power, displays of two *lakh*s (200,000) of hands in unison going "Jai, jai, jai!" (victory, victory, victory), and moments of "knowing he is the vulnerable sweatshop worker the next morning, the very vulnerable taxi driver or watchman or whatever, someone in the service sector where there is no security." Sharma says, "I am not so sure I can fix the meaning completely.

Although it is a terrifying moment, but then the small details within the crowd sort of started to make me feel I do not want to complete the story." It is, after all, alive, constantly shape-shifting, taking on new valences, growing, changing as culture does. In Trinidad "musical culture is the space where identity, politics, racial tensions are played out," and similarly in Mumbai: "I realized that this musical culture back home was entirely centered around the notion of leaving home. . . . And suddenly I found this entire music industry that was so completely confident of themselves and self-contained, it was not bothered by the big music industry that is Bollywood music; they were completely banking on their culture, the folk tradition, and in fact very confidently said that it is Bollywood that needs to steal our tunes, because this is where the real music is." Had she not gone to Trinidad, she might not, she says, have seen all these interconnections and transmedia slides from folk music to pop culture industry and from labor migration to scripted megaspectacle and back again, all around her in Mumbai.

The notion of ethnographic insight is crucial: it is both a grounded style of investigation demanded in proliferating places and for multiple checks upon theoretical claims, models built by aggregating analysis, and hegemonic assertion; it is also a kind of yoga, a recognition of the shape-shifting illusions of fixed categories, comparisons, opinions, and perceptions. Ethnographically informed anthropology is the speech, account, reason, or logics of the animal operating semiotically, psychically, emotionally, intro- and projectionally between the bestial and the divine.[87] The anthropo-logics and aesthetics of writing culture include affects and actions that—after giving reasons for actions run out and yet decisions and actions must be taken—leave enduring legibilities, traces, hints, or cues in the rhythms and sounds, the catacoustics of the social text.[88]

A Note to End On

Lévi-Strauss was right: culture is both symphonic and amoebic.[89] Apologies for trying to score it.

Notes

1 A maguffin (or MacGuffin or McGuffin), Hitchcock said, is an apparatus for trapping lions in the Scottish Highlands, where there are no lions.

2 Fischer, "Ethnicity and the Post-Modern Arts of Memory," "Autobiographical Voices (1, 2, 3) and Mosaic Memory," and "Eye(I)ing the Sciences and their Signifiers."

3 Michel Serres's pun on epistemologies or grammars or cultural frames that interfere and inter-reference one another.

4 Biographies of the Gandian social worker and Jain monk Santibalji; the Jewish gnostic Shabbatai Zvi and founding figure of both a modernist circle around Attaturk (the Donmeh) and a kabbalist strand of Judaism; Rabbi Nahman of Bratslav, a founder of Hassidism and perhaps a manic-depressive dealing with his followers' dilemmas of entering a modern world; the Muslim mystic al-Hallaj, executed for his ecstatic utterances and revered by sufi traditions). These biographies are written, respectively, by the former Jain Gujarat minister of education and leading social reformer Navalbhai Shah; Gershom Scholem, who transformed the scholarship of modern Judaism; Arthur Green, who helped introduce a modern orthodox Judaism in America during the cultural turmoil of the 1960s; Louis Massignon, one of the generation of French scholars who found through Islam what they missed in Catholicism.

5 In the three time-stamped periods alluded to here these are (1) the Rice Anthropology Department, the Rice Circle, the Rice Center for Cultural Studies, the Chicago Center for Psychosocial (later Transnational) Studies, the journals *Cultural Anthropology, Public Culture,* and the *Late Editions* project; (2) the MIT Program in Science, Technology and Society, the Program in Anthropology; the Harvard "Friday Morning Seminar" in Mental Health and Medical Anthropology; the Harvard Departments of Global Health and Social Medicine, Anthropology, and the Harvard STS Circle; (3) the Asia Research Institute, the Biopoleis Project, and Tembusu College of the National University of Singapore, the journals *Cultural Politics* and EASTS *(East Asian Science, Technology and Society)*, the Duke University Press book series *Experimental Futures: Technological Lives, Scientific Arts, Anthropological Voices;* the Irvine- and Chicago-based workshops in Knowledge/Value, and Irvine Center for Persian Studies workshops on Ethnographers, Scientists, and Health-Related Air Quality.

6 Foucault, *Discipline and Punish,* and *The Birth of Biopolitics;* Deleuze, "Postscript on the Societies of Control."

7 Negri, *The Political Descartes.*

8 Levon Abrahamian reproduced in Fischer, *Emergent Forms of Life and the Anthropological Voice.*

9 Bourke-White, "Women in Steel"; Friedan, *The Feminine Mystique;* Field, *The Life and Times of Rosie the Riveter;* Coleman, *Rosie the Riveter.*

10 Engels, *The Origin of the Family, Private Property and the State.*

11 Juris, *Networking Futures.*

12 Haraway, *When Species Meet;* Fischer, *Anthropological Futures,* chapter 3.

13 For a different account, and outcomes, of such debates in a distinctively non-U.S. context, see Felt, "Keeping Technologies Out" on Austria; Jasanoff, *De-*

signs on Nature, on Germany and the United Kingdom. The Asilomar conference attempted (and succeeded) to allay public fears about recombinant organisms escaping into the environment by proposing a series of biosafety measures, triggered by Paul Berg's experimental design of inserting fragments of monkey virus SV40 and bacteriophage lambda into an *E. coli* bacterium. Before doing this third step, in response to concerns voiced, procedures were proposed for ensuring that a series of biocontainment measures were in place, under oversight by a National Institutes of Health review process, that could be lifted only as the scientific community gained experience and assurance of safety. The most vigorous public debates were those held in the Cambridge, Massachusetts, City Council meetings in June 1976 and again when the moratorium was extended in September 1976. The debates were videorecorded by the historian Charles Weiner and are available in the MIT archives.

14 "Governments of the Industrial World, you weary giants of flesh and steel, I come from Cyberspace, the new home of Mind. On behalf of the future, I ask you of the past to leave us alone. You are not welcome among us. You have no sovereignty where we gather."

15 Fischer, "Worlding Cyberspace"; Kelty, "Culture in, Culture Out."

16 Havis, "Interview with Chen Zaige."

17 Fischer, "Biopolis."

18 See Appadurai, *Modernity at Large* and *Fear of Small Numbers*; Cohen, *No Aging in India*; Das, *Critical Events* and *Life and Words*; Fortun, *Advocacy after Bhopal*; Hansen, The Saffron Wave; Pradhan, *When the Saints Go Marching In*; Rajagopal, *Politics after Television*; and the journal *Public Culture*, and later the design of covers of the journal *Cultural Anthropology* by an Indian graphic artist.

19 Infosys is not just one of the leading Indian software support companies but an engine of social change, and a social hieroglyph itself, as well as, in the careers of its founders a history of transition in India's technoscientific imaginaries. Founded in 1981 by N. R. Narayana Murthy, who gathered a team of five young visionaries, including Nandan Nilekani, now chair of the Unique Identification Authority of India, to build not just a company but an innovative, and architecturally beautiful, socially and environmentally designed campus in Bangalore with its own back-up water and electricity supplies and satellite connections. Narayana Murthy had worked at the Indian Institute of Management, Ahmedabad, under J. G. Krishnaya, who had spent time at MIT's Project MAC and ran the computer systems at IIM Ahmedabad, attempting to introduce personal computers to a resistant mainframe environment. Krishnaya then started an early geographical information system company in Pune, bringing Narayana Murthy with him. They provided among the first such systems for public planning for the governments of India, Maharastra, and Pune. Narayana Murthy also had experience in Paris developing software for the subway system. (I had the pleasure of interviewing both Krishnaya in Pune and

Narayana Murthy at Infosys in Bangalore in the 1990s.) Nihilani succeeded Narayana Murthy as CEO of Infosys and became involved with advocacy for new forms of governance in Bangalore (and India). His wife, Rohini Nilekani, endowed the Arghyam (Skt. "offering") Foundation, which initially experimented with neoliberal models to extend water systems to the slums outside the Bangalore municipal pipe system when the city could not afford to do so. This controversially involved user payments to contribute to capital costs. It now operates a web-based platform, India Water Portal, that shares water management knowledge among practitioners and the general public across states and jurisdictions.

20 Fischer, "The Rhythmic Beat of the Revolution in Iran."

21 Fischer, "Before Going Digital."

22 Fischer, "Bombay Talkies, the Word and the World"; Fischer, "Iran and the Boomeranging Cartoon Wars."

23 Fortun, *Advocacy after Bhopal*; Callison, "More Information Is Not the Problem"; Wylie, "Corporate Bodies and Chemical Bonds"; MacKenzie, *An Engine, Not a Camera*; Tett, *Fool's Gold*; Lepinay, *Codes of Finance*; Condry, *The Soul of Anime*.

24 Rabinow, *Making PCR*; Dumit, *Drugs for Life*; Petryna, *When Experiments Travel*; Fischer, *Emergent Forms of Life and the Anthropological Voice* and *Anthropological Futures* and "The Rhythmic Beat of the Revolution in Iran"; Franklin and Lock, *Remaking Life and Death*; Kuo, "The Voice on the Bridge"; Soto Laveaga, *Jungle Laboratories*; Sunder Rajan, *Biocapital*; Sunder Rajan, *Lively Capital*.

25 Franklin, *Dolly Mixtures*; Franklin and Lock, eds., *Remaking Life and Death*; Jasanoff, *Designs on Nature*; Biehl and Petryna, "Bodies of Rights and Therapeutic Markets" and *When People Come First*; Fischer, "The BAC [Bioethics Advisory Committee] Consultation on Neuroscience and Ethics."

26 Virno, "Natural-Historical Diagrams."

27 Schroedinger, *What Is Life?*; Fischer, *Anthropological Futures*, chapter 3.

28 Fischer, "If Derrida Is the Gomez-Pena of Philosophy, What Are the Genres of Social Science?"

29 These two paragraphs are adapted from Fischer, "Anthropology of Science and Technology."

30 Mnookin, "Images of Truth."

31 Cole, *Suspect Identities*; Dumit, *Picturing Personhood*; Blanchette, *Burdens of Proof*.

32 Landecker, *Culturing Life*.

33 Kelty, *Two Bits*; Chan, "The Promiscuity of Freedom"; Coleman, *Coding Freedom*; Kumar, "The Yellow Revolution in Malway."

34 Schwarz, "Techno-Territories."

35 Kuo, "The Voice on the Bridge."

36 Cohen, "Where It Hurts" and "Operability, Bioavailability, and Exception"; Petryna, *Life Exposed*; Montoya, *Making the Mexican Diabetic*.

37 Dumit, *Drugs for Life*; Greenslit, "Pharmaceutical Relations"; Prentice, *Bodies in Formation*.

38 Sunder Rajan, *Biocapital*; Jasanoff, *Designs on Nature*.

39 Sanal, *New Organs within Us*; Hamdy, *Our Bodies Belong to God*.

40 Myers, "Modeling Proteins, Making Scientists."

41 Kahn, *Race in a Bottle*; Pollock, *Medicating Race*.

42 Jain, *Injury*.

43 Perin, *Shouldering Risks*; Masco, *Nuclear Borderlands*.

44 Ozkan, "Executive Coaching."

45 Behrouzan, "Prozak Diaries."

46 Garcia, *The Pastoral Clinic*.

47 Helmreich, *Silicon Second Nature* and *Alien Ocean*; Paxson, "Post-Pasteurian Cultures" and *The Life of Cheese*.

48 Callison, "More Information Is Not the Problem"; Lahsen, "Seductive Simulations," *The Role of Unstated Mistrust and Disparities in Scientific Capacity* and "Knowledge, Democracy and Uneven Playing Fields."

49 See Wylie, "Corporate Bodies and Chemical Bonds."

50 Ozden, "Vernacular Economics and Smart Electricity Grids"; Schilling, "The Social Implications of Digital Mapmaking among Insect Ecologists, Geologists, and Aboriginal First Nations Heritage Consultants."

51 Virno, "Natural-Historical Diagrams."

52 Marchetti, "From Mao's 'Continuous Revolution' to Ning Ying's Perpetual Motion."

53 Osanloo, *The Politics of Women's Rights in Iran*.

54 Fischer, *Anthropological Futures*.

55 Adams, "Against Global Health?"; World Bank, "Indonesia's PNPM Generasi Program," 3 para. 3, and finding 2; p. 32 on MIT's Poverty Action Lab, and inexplicable findings, p. 39.

56 Theidon, *Intimate Enemies*; Good et al., *A Psychosocial Needs Assessment of Communities in 14 Selected Districts in Acheh*; Good and Good, "Indonesia Sakit"; Grayman, "Humanitarian Encounters in Post Conflict Acheh."

57 Biehl and Petryna, *When People Come First*; Livingston, *Improvised Medicine*.

58 Murray and Lopez, *The Global Burden of Disease*; Kessler et al., "The Global Burden of Mental Disorders"; Heyman, "Neuroscience and Ethics"; Kleinman, Das, and Lock, *Social Suffering*; Cohen, Kleinman and Saraceno, *World Mental Health Casebook*.

59 For instance, the new billion-euro ten-year Human Brain Project funded by the European Union, the $100 million Canada Brain Research Fund, boosts in funding for the United Kingdom's Brain Bank network, the 2004 U.S. National Institutes of Health Blueprint for Neuroscience Research, the 2013

ten-year $100 million initiative on concussion-related brain damage among professional football players; in Singapore the $25 million Singapore Translation and Clinical Research in Psychosis program, and the new SINAPSE (Singapore Institute for Neurotechnology) at the National University of Singapore funded by the University, A*STAR, and the Ministry of Defense.

60 Fischer, "The Rhythmic Beat of the Revolution in Iran."

61 Behrouzan, "Prozak Diaries."

62 Since 2011 a Telecommunication Industry Dialogue (a group of eight major telecommunications companies, including Nokia-Siemens Networks, Alcatel-Lucent, France Telecom-Orange, Millicom, Telefonica, Telenor, TeliaSonera, and Vodafone) has established a set of guidelines aligned with the United Nations "Guiding Principles on Business and Human Rights." A common platform to exchange best practices, learning, and tools is to be provided by the Global Network Initiative, a coalition of companies, human rights organizations, and freedom of the press groups (Google, Microsoft, Yahoo, Center for Democracy and Technology, Committee to Protect Journalists, Electronic Frontier Foundation, Human Rights First, Human Rights in China, Human Rights Watch, Index on Censorship, Calvert Group, Domini Social Investments, F and C Asset Management, Folksam, the Berkman Center for Internet and Society at Harvard, Center for Freedom of Expression and Access to Information—CELE at Palermo University, Argentina). Aside from the three cases mentioned, there is a case brought by Turkey's Turkcell against MTN, headquartered in South Africa, for using bribery to get a contract to supply Iran with surveillance technology. Not yet a court case, but on free press, human rights, and digital democracy activists' watch list, U.S. companies Net-App and Hewlett-Packard along with Italian AreaSpA have been negotiating to provide Syria with the capability to read all emails and track people's location.

63 Callison, "More Information Is Not the Problem."

64 Ballestero, "Expert Attempts."

65 Fischer, "The Peopling of Technologies"; Biehl and Petryna, "Bodies of Rights and Therapeutic Markets" and *When People Come First.*

66 Wylie, "Corporate Bodies and Chemical Bonds."

67 Faubion and Marcus, *Doing Fieldwork Is Not What It Used to Be.*

68 Cefkin, *Ethnography and the Corporate Encounter;* World Bank, "Indonesia's PNPM Generasi Program."

69 Felt, "Keeping Technologies Out," 16.

70 Singaporean filmmakers Lee Xian Jie and Jeremy Boo were Singapore Polytechnic seniors when they made the film. Both are now studying in Japan.

71 Condry, *The Soul of Anime.*

72 Xuan, "The Global Diffusion and Variations of Creative Industries for Urban Development."

73 Ho, *The Graves of Tarim* and "Empire through Diasporic Eyes."

74 Dean and Zheng, *Ritual Alliances of the Putian Plain.*

75 Ho, "Sealords Live in Vain."

76 Kulke et al., *Nagapattinam to Suvarnadwipa.*

77 Anderson, *The Collectors of Lost Souls.*

78 "Salute to Pao Kun" at the Esplanade Theater in Mandarin and Cantonese with English subtitles, April 5–6, 2013. The Taiwanese producer Vivien Ku set the rules: Each director was allowed one table and two chairs, three lighting effects, and twenty minutes of stage time. The sequence of the plays is shuffled for every performance. Each work is an artistic response to Kuo's play *Lao Jiu* (1990, English version 1993, musical 2005 restaged in 2012). The title character is the ninth and only male child of a Teochew family who has a chance to win a coveted scholarship but can't make himself finish the exams, preferring to pursue puppetry. He wishes not to be a puppet with his path determined for him but to be able to hold his fate in the palm of his hand, like a puppet master. He has grown up around a family friend, Shi Fu, a traditional Chinese puppeteer, and goes to his house when stressed. In the middle of the exams he suffers a crisis of confidence and cannot decide whether to follow his artistic dreams or the more realistic career option strongly advocated by his parents.

79 Denise Ho, program notes.

80 Aravinth, program notes.

81 Screenplay by Vijay Tendulkar, Shyam Benegal, and Samik Banerjee, published by Seagull Books, 1984.

82 There is no space here to do analytic justice to these works, but they are all well known. One of the dilemmas of ethnographic writing continues to be the impatience of many readers (and publishers) with the details of the unfamiliar that are required to understand lived worlds. This is less complaint than writing challenge. The solutions of novelists are not entirely those anthropologists should adopt, but there are lessons to be learned. It is of course not surprising that novelists who deeply research their work should parallel the work of anthropologists. Nonetheless I was deeply mesmerized reading *Calcutta Chromosome* while I was interviewing molecular biologists working on malaria in Delhi and Bombay in 1996, and later went on a pilgrimage to all the sites mentioned in the novel and the histories of Sir Ronald Ross. The history of curing syphilis by malaria fever, and of theosophy, is beautifully done, as is the insistence on local knowledge and assistants who helped the scientists who get the credit in history books. So too is the satire of total computerized water resources control, taking on both at-a-distance management systems and watershed projects such as the Mekong Valley Authority. *Hungry Tide* came out just before the 2004 devastating tsunami broke over the Indian Ocean from Aceh to Bengal and proleptically described the coming destruction. It also provides a compelling account of the settlement frontier in the Sunderbans between colonials and islanders, along with an exploration of cetology and dolphins as sensors of cross-species and ecological interactions. *River of Smoke* is a mesmerizing

account of the European opium merchants in Canton (Qangzhou) and the efforts of the Chinese officials to stop the trade, and a sympathetic account of the mediation instruments and constraints of the Chinese merchants. This novel follows after the account of the manufacturing of opium and export of labor chronicled in *The Sea of Poppies*. Mitchell's *The Thousand Autumns of Jacob de Zoet* does similar work for Nagasaki, while his *Cloud Atlas* explores a series of interlocking vignettes across the generations (much as Neal Stephenson more massively does in *Cryptonomicon*, another of my favorites). Philip Caputo's *Acts of Faith* brings together in interlocking form the humanitarian aid industry, missionaries who free Nuba slaves from seminomadic Arab raiders only to have them be reenslaved later, the South Sudan People's Liberation Army fighters, Khartoum-recruited Arab and Islamicized black Janjaweed fighters, Dinka, Nuer, and Turkana known to the anthropological archive in an earlier era. It is a rich, only lightly fictionalized tableau of the dilemmas of a second (twenty-two-year-long) civil war that puts in context more specialized anthropological, political science, and development studies. Importantly it tells each acting group's story from its own point of view. Shamsie's *Burnt Shadows* begins just before the bombing of Nagasaki (where Margaret Duras's *Hiroshima Mon Amour* also begins, with the burned shadows of vaporized souls imprinted on stone) and weaves extraordinary scenes of cultural sensibilities, moods, and change across time (from Hiroshima to Delhi to New York and Karachi), illuminating through the historical sweep of intense crises the postwar history from the Partition of India to the Taliban's ensnaring of youth. What intrigues me in all these works is the ability to play the scales with explanatory depth and exploration of nonintuitive connections.

83 Mitchell, "The Art of Fiction."

84 The quotes in this paragraph are taken from the question-and-answer period following a presentation of three short films at the Museum of the National University of Singapore, May 16, 2013: *Airplane Descending over Jari Mari* (2008), *The Enactment of Exile in Mumbai* (2011), *Tracing Bylanes* (2011). Sharma's longer films on these topics are *Jari Mari: Of Cloth and Other Stories* (2001), *Above the Din of Sewing Machines* (2004). Sharma has a bachelor's degree in anthropology and psychology and speaks of her documentary methods as ethnographic. Just to complete the circle of references to Singapore in this chapter, one of her shots is of interviewing a man in a Jari Mari garment shop while he is packing pajamas with skull prints on it and affixing labels of $9.99 in Singapore dollars. "He says 'we have to complete this order, otherwise the entire money will not be given to us.' It was being shipped to Singapore and it is being produced in that slum," a residue of closed factories, with labor devolved into putting out systems, the whole slum being illegal, requiring getting water and electricity through extrastate nonlegal connections.

85 See the YouTube videos of the *chhath puja* on Juhu beach from 2009, 2010, 2011, and 2012. In the press the dance between MNS leader Raj Thackeray,

his cousin Uddhav Thackeray, and Bihari politicians, most recently Congress Member of Parliament from North Mumbai Sanjay Nirupam, who in 2011 countered Shiv Sena and MNS provocations with his own, saying that North Indians can bring Mumbai to a standstill and daring Shiv Sena's Uddhav Thackeray, his son Aditya, and MNS's Raj Thackeray to step out without security. In September 2012 Raj Thackeray had threatened to brand Biharis as "infiltrators" and force them out of Maharashtra, and earlier Uddhav Thackeray said a permit system should be implemented for Biharis wanting to live in Mumbai. Both Thackerays claimed that Biharis were the majority contributors to the crime rate in Mumbai. Bihar's chief minister Nitish Kumar strongly objected, and the Janata Dal (United) from Patna issued a statement: "Biharis are not a burden on anyone. They have made Mumbai and we have full rights on the commercial capital of the country. Bihari are there because of their deeds and hard work." In 2012, after Bal Thackeray, father of Uddhav and uncle of Raj and a longtime leader of the Shiv Sena, died, both sides toned down their language, lest real violence be provoked at that year's puja and festival. (For one of many press accounts, see "JD (U) Takes on Thackeray Brothers over Biharis in Mumbai," Z News, September 4, 2012, http://zeenews.india .com/news/maharashtra/jd-u-takes-on-thackeray-brothers-over-biharis-in -mumbai_797643.html.)

86 Chutney music has roots in Surinam, Guyana, and Trinidad at least back to the 1940s and was first recorded in 1958 by the singer Ramdew Chaitoe and became popular with Dropati's album *Let's Sing and Dance* (1968). In the 1970s Sundar Popo (King of Chutney) added guitars and electronics, and Ras Shorty (Garfield Blackman) infused soca (soul-calypso) with Indian instruments. In 1987 Drupatee Ramgoonai (Queen of Chutney) fixed the term *chutney soca* with her album *Chatnee Soca*, with both English and Hindi versions of the songs. The producer Rohit Jagessar in the 1980s took chutney soca worldwide with shows in stadiums and cricket fields, and in 1991, at Weston Outdoor Studios in Mumbai, digitally recorded the all-time highest grossing album *Leggo Me Na Raja*. In the 1995–96 Trinidad Carnival season, the Chutney Soca Monarch Competition became the venue for the world's largest Indo-Caribbean concerts. Various spin-off styles of chutney soca have emerged, including *chutney rap*, *chutney jhumari* (from Baluchistan), *chutney lambada* (from Brazil), and mixes with Bollywood film music. (See Wikipedia's entries on chutney music and chutney soca for more details and references.) Sharma's film is *Jahaji Music: India in the Caribbean* (2007, 112 min.).

87 Fischer, *Anthropological Futures* and "Anthropologia and Philosophia."

88 I take the term *catacoustics* from a brilliant essay by the philosopher Philippe Lacoue-Labarthe, "The Echo of the Subject," and have used it in several essays, especially one several years ago on trauma and depression in Iran (Behrouzan and Fischer, "Behaves Like a Rooster and Cries like a 'Four-Eyed' Canine") and on musicality and rhythm in the aesthetics of politics in Iran in

2009 (Fischer, "The Rhythmic Beat of the Revolution in Iran"). It refers to the "phenomenon of a 'tune in one's head' that 'keeps coming back'" (150). Lacoue-Labarthe finds "the most striking example (and for good reason . . .)" in the opening of Theodore Reik's essay, "Kol Nidre," an uncanny tune that Reik hears (but only later identifies and recognizes from his youth) in Max Bruch's Op. 47 "Kol Nidre," triggering powerful emotions.

89 Lévi-Strauss, *Naked Man*.

CHAPTER 5

Kinky Empiricism

Danilyn Rutherford

It is time for anthropology to reclaim the empirical. But this reclaiming must be accompanied by a rethinking of what empiricism means. What I'd like to affirm in this chapter—and have attempted to practice in my recent research—is a kind of empiricism that builds on the singular power of anthropological ways of knowing the world. A kinky empiricism: kinky like a slinky, twisting back on itself, but also kinky like s and m and other queer elaborations of established scenarios, relationships, and things. An empiricism that admits that one never gets to the bottom of things yet also accepts and even celebrates the disavowals required of us given a world that forces us to act. An empiricism that is ethical because its methods create obligations, obligations that compel those who seek knowledge to put themselves on the line by making truth claims that they know will intervene within the settings and among the people they describe.

There are several reasons why now is a good time for anthropologists to insist on the empirical nature of what they do. The new kinds of interchanges in which anthropologists are engaged create obligations of a particularly pressing sort. There is a price of admission to the politically fraught arenas that anthropologists are increasingly entering. As I have learned in my work in the troubled Indonesian territory of West Papua, paying this price can require us to write and speak authoritatively on issues that matter to the people we have studied. But all too often anthropology has appeared to outsiders to have a tangential relationship to the empirical, producing knowledge that is too partial, too particular, too relativistic or theoretical to bear on real-world questions. However mistaken, such views reflect the long shadow cast by the 1980s, a time when many anthropologists developed new allegiances in the humanities. In reclaiming the empirical for anthropology, we must contend with the legacy of this epoch in the discipline's development. It is in writings demonized as steering anthropology away from "reality" that one finds the clearest expression of the epistemology that is implicitly embraced by the best practitioners of the discipline. These writings make the case for a kinky kind of empiricism, an empiricism that takes seriously the situated nature of what all thinkers do.

Sometimes to find the way forward, one must begin by looking back. In the first part of this chapter, I consider two sources for the ingredients of the kinky empiricism that I would like to affirm as a critical dimension of contemporary anthropology. The first is *Writing Culture*, which, I argue, helped add to the phenomena open to anthropological inquiry by foregrounding the circumstances of ethnography. The second is the work of David Hume, whose epistemology, I argue, proves surprisingly resonant with the empiricism implicitly endorsed in *Writing Culture*. Following the lead of Gilles Deleuze, Brian Massumi, and others who have read Hume in new ways, I consider how this eighteenth-century philosopher, like *Writing Culture*'s contributors, sketched out an empiricism that was both skeptical and ethical because it included among its objects of inquiry the apparatuses through which reality is known.

My aim is not simply descriptive; it is also polemical. Kinky empiricism is a position I would like anthropology to embrace. But it is also a position that brings with it dangers as well as possibilities. In the second part of this chapter I turn to my research in Dutch New Guinea and the pitfalls of ways of knowing that anthropologists and colonial officials have shared. I end by considering a recent ethnography that responds to these dangers and possibilities in a particularly compelling way. Kinky empiricism is always slightly off-kilter, always aware of the slipperiness of its grounds and of the difficulty of adequately responding to the ethical demands spawned by its methods. Being off-kilter is a strength, not a weakness. For anthropology, it is what comes with getting real.

Backward Look 1

In the 1980s, the potted history of our discipline goes, anthropology turned left while its sister disciplines turned right. Significant subgroups within psychology, political science, economics, and sociology began adopting mathematical models and quantitative methods and crafted experiments aimed at producing generalizable findings. Anthropology, for its part, looked inward, producing self-indulgent, jargon-strewn texts that only the initiated could understand. Silliness ruled the day. "I've talked enough about me," the "postmodern" anthropologist in the famous joke says to an informant. "What do you think about me?" "What's the difference between a gangster and a postmodernist?" another joke goes. "A postmodernist gives you an offer you can't understand." For purveyors of this potted history, the move toward dialogue and partial truths represented a retreat from empirical research—above all from the kind of empirical research on colonized and formerly colonized peoples and cultures for which the discipline long was known. And when anthropology did finally come to its senses, the potted history goes on, it turned its attention to colonialism and science: the peoples and cultures that gave birth to anthropology. The fervor of the 1980s left anthropology unauthorized to claim to know others; the best we could do was to know ourselves.

I do not believe in this potted history, even though it was foisted on me at a tender disciplinary age. (The second person to introduce me to anthropology was Steve Sangren, a Marxist anthropologist of the Terry Turner persuasion who wrote a critique of *Writing Culture* and other "postmodern" works that appeared in *Current Anthropology* shortly before I arrived at Cornell.[1] The first person to introduce me to anthropology was Jim Siegel, a student of Clifford Geertz who was so idiosyncratic in his orientation to the discipline that the first course I took, Political Anthropology, had a syllabus that consisted exclusively of serialized novels in colonial Malay.)[2] This potted history makes me squirm whenever I confront it, which is usually in conversations with other social scientists. It's way too easy to get sucked into the narrative. "But we've left those bad old days behind!" I find myself saying. "We're doing all kinds of hard-nosed work!" When we open *Writing Culture* and actually read it, a different view of the bad old days comes into focus. *Writing Culture* provides a warrant for an anthropological empiricism that takes on more reality, not less.

The reality taken on by *Writing Culture* takes two forms. On the one hand, the chapters in the collection extend outward the range of empirical phenomena open to inquiry and criticize those who have limited their studies' scope. Renato Rosaldo discusses the pacification campaigns undertaken in the Sudan shortly before Evans-Pritchard contracted "Nueritis" trying to extract information about local politics from his understandably reticent Nuer informants.[3] Vincent Crapanzano criticizes Geertz's famous essay on the Balinese cockfight for failing to provide enough empirical evidence to substantiate Geertz's claims.[4] "We must go further" is a refrain repeated throughout *Writing Culture*—we must say more about the intellectual settings and professional imperatives that are shaping our discipline, Paul Rabinow tells us; we must say more about the interplay of social phenomena on different levels and scales, George Marcus insists.[5] This dimension of *Writing Culture* reflects what I see as a key strength of the discipline. Because we don't set the parameters of admissible data from the get-go, anthropologists are arguably able to be more empirical than social scientists constrained by survey instruments and the need for large samples. We sacrifice what statisticians call statistical validity, but we gain construct validity: a higher level of confidence that we are doing justice to a messy reality. *Writing Culture* queers this second kind of validity. The chapters reveal a kinky penchant for thoroughly specifying the messy reality with which anthropologists are concerned.

On the other hand, the chapters in *Writing Culture* also, more famously, extend the range of empirical phenomena open to inquiry inward toward the research and writing process itself.[6] Taking the quest for construct validity to an extreme, *Writing Culture*'s empiricism becomes kinky in a second sense: this empiricism loops back on itself. In bringing ethnography's dialogic character clearly into view, the collection raises ethical questions about the enterprise, questions to which some contributors responded by calling for writing practices that more fully represented informants' voices in a work. In the years since *Writing Culture* was published, linguistic anthropologists have provided us with a sophisticated understanding of the issues raised by the book's kinky obsession with reflexivity.[7] As *Writing Culture*'s authors knew well, dialogue never happens between just two sides.[8] Bearing the traces of long histories of interaction, dialogue also never happens in just one setting but rather requires the bringing into relevance of institutions that authorize, valorize, and lend prestige to speakers' words.[9] Dialogue is always fraught with ethical conundrums. To converse is to engage in an exchange of gestures. To exchange is to receive, and to receive is to confront the impossible demand to give others their due. For anthropologists, the conundrums multiply. Fieldwork generates both debts and identities in the back-and-forth through which interlocutors create a sense of what they are up to and who they are. Anthropologists find themselves compelled to do right by a cultural other that fades into a specter as soon as they think hard about what they do.[10] This second dimension of kinky empiricism—its slinky effect, we might call it—eats away at certainty as well as good conscience. When anthropologists look closely at their own research practices, it becomes clear that partial truths are the best they can do.

What I see as the most important contribution of *Writing Culture* is this coupling of the empirical and the ethical. What I have described as two realities are really just aspects of one: the messy reality in which ethnography lives. Unfortunately readers of the collection haven't always recognized that, for *Writing Culture*, looking outward and looking inward are two sides of the same kinky coin.[11] To some degree *Writing Culture*'s editors and contributors were complicit in perpetrating this view, adding references to empirical "standards" almost as an afterthought. In fact there is nothing inconsistent or incoherent about the implicit epistemology articulated in *Writing Culture*. The reflexive turn in anthropology has expanded rather than contracted the discipline's power to represent reality. The ethical challenges that have come out of this recognition are indicative of how much more rather than less anthropology is trying to say about the empirical world. I think we can do a better job of defining and defending this dimension of our discipline. But this may require yet another look backward—to an early champion of empiricism, a thinker whom at least one contributor to *Writing Culture* may have too hastily dismissed.

Backward Look 2

Eighteenth-century philosopher, friend of Adam Smith, "a man of letters and, in a mild manner, a man of affairs," as one biographer puts it, David Hume would seem an odd patron saint for today's anthropologists.[12] Born in 1711, Hume entered Edinburgh University at the age of ten and encountered the writings of John Locke as a teenager before decamping for France. There, in his early twenties, he wrote his magnificent flop, *A Treatise of Human Nature*, and made friends with Jean-Jacques Rousseau, whom he "imported to England" and provided with a house, a dog, a mistress, and a pension from the king. ("But nothing would persuade Rousseau that Hume was not secretly plotting his ridicule and humiliation," D. C. G. MacNabb reports. "The relationship ended in a spectacular quarrel. In self-justification, Hume was forced to publish the correspondence, from which it is abundantly clear that the only man who ever hated Hume was mad.")[13] Hume himself never married, preferring to live with his sister and a cat. Whatever his erotic proclivities—he seems less kinky than quirky by this account—his thinking clearly had twists.[14] Giving with one hand and taking with the other, leading the careful reader on a conceptual loop, Hume proclaimed that all knowledge begins in experience. But he also argued that we have no real reason to trust experience or to believe that what has happened in the past provides a basis for predicting what is to come.

Hume was, among other things, an epistemologist, and hence a proponent of a breed of thinking dismissed in Rabinow's chapter in *Writing Culture* as "an accidental, but eventually sterile, turning in Western culture."[15] But as Deleuze and Massumi have suggested, Hume's work may be more generative than Rabinow would lead us to think.[16] I find it useful to read Hume's work as fodder for an exercise in reverse engineering. If we begin with the view of thought advocated by Rabinow—as "nothing more or less than a historically locatable set of practices"[17]—what kind of mechanism do we need to envision such that thought and the subjectivity of the thinker could both be, in Deleuze's words, "constituted in the given"?[18] Whether or not we call it epistemology, a tacit understanding of how this might work weaves its way through our research in the wake of *Writing Culture*. Hume is perhaps less useful in telling us what we should think than shedding light on what we do think when we are making the most of our methods: the kinky empiricist background assumptions that structure knowledge production in our field.

Two of Hume's terms provide useful tools for grasping these background assumptions. The first is the notion of circumstances, which relates to the first form of reality addressed by *Writing Culture*, the one that comes into focus when one takes in the broader contexts that shape what anthropologists find in the field. Hume is famous for his account of what he calls "moral reasoning," a category that encompasses the lion's share of thought, which, with the sole exception of certain problems in mathematics, proceeds through inference.[19] Inference, for Hume, is an interpretive practice that reads the unfolding of events as signs of what once was and what is to come. Like all sign use, inference cannot occur in a vacuum. Interpretation is an imaginative form of conduct in which what Hume calls the "fancy" moves along grooves established by previous encounters with the world. In describing the aggregated effect of these encounters, Hume draws on the notion of circumstances. Circumstances consist of the patterned distribution of happenings that makes it more or less probable that a certain person will have certain experiences. Circumstances shape the expectations that lead particular people to read a particular cause or effect off of a particular event.

But Hume goes further than the contributors to *Writing Culture* did in exploring how circumstances influence what people think and do. The solid ground of his empiricism grows shaky when he considers the process through which experiences give rise to expectations. Hume asserts that the ability to infer is adaptive: it is the basis not only for science and technology but also for government, civil society, and domestic life. Yet he also does much to show that the practice of inference has no logical rationale. The mind-fuck moment in Hume's writings comes when he argues that the legitimacy of our inferences stands or falls on the assumption that events will have the same kind of causes and consequences in the future as they did in the past.[20] There is no way of adducing evidence in support of this assumption because it is the assumption on which the very notion of evidence rests. (Pause. Think about it!) If we believe in the evidence of our senses, it is because of what Hume calls a "principle of human nature," "custom," which he describes as a quasi-organic variety of the repetition compulsion that drives us to wait for a "tock" following every "tick."[21] Unlike philosophers who draw a distinction between mind and body, Hume finds passion at the heart of reason. Rational thought draws on the same organic forces that drive hunger, lust, and the beating of hearts. Along with fellow feeling, reason is less sublime than lizard-brained.

The same tendency both to trust experience and undermine it runs through *Writing Culture*'s critique of the anthropology of its day. Something like Hume's notion of circumstances makes an appearance throughout the book. The contributors' point is not that anything goes when it comes to interpreting ethnographic data. Their point is that what does go is, to quote Rabinow again, "historically locatable." Interpretations follow grooves laid in the imaginations of individuals and institutions by virtue of their pathways through space and time. Notably interpretations follow grooves left by what Hume calls "artifices":[22] technologies for regulating the imagination, which for him include both police forces and books. What Hume adds to this approach is the proposal that among the circumstances that matter is the form of the organism that thinks. The process of interpretation is anything but dispassionate. Thinking occurs in the body, not some isolated "internal space," and in the company of others linked together through the repetitions that constitute custom. And the process of interpretation is scarcely immune to doubt. Simply "being there" in the field cannot qualify an ethnographer to produce a transparent account of what he or she has witnessed. Every observation is haunted by a multiplicity of places and times. This holds for ethnographers and the ethnographers of the ethnographers, not to mention the people they study. There is no act of reasoning that is not a leap of faith, both embodied and collective. "Contextualize!"

we contemporary anthropologists tell our students. "But take nothing for granted, including context," we always add.

The second term from Hume's repertoire that provides us with a grip on the implicit epistemology we have inherited from *Writing Culture* is sympathy.[23] Sympathy for Hume is not empathy, pity, or any of the other rosy synonyms for the ability to identify with another that we tend to associate with the word. Rather it is the embodied outcome of proximity—occasioned by the placement of human bodies and artifacts in space and time—that leads people to share perspectives and passions. Sympathy is the outcome of inference, but with a twist. One witnesses an event—a gesture, a facial expression, an utterance—and one infers a cause, in this case the passion that led to this effect. Proximity makes the passion vivid, and one comes to feel what one imagines the other feels. The ability to share perspectives and passions, for Hume, is not simply the basis of friendship, kinship, and romance. Like inference, sympathy plays a critical role in public life. Without this passion there would be no state, no economy, and no science. Sympathy is an embodied mode of intersubjectivity; it is the sentiment that provides the grounds of all social pursuits. Sympathy is a source of both power and compassion. It is an instrument of governance. It is also the privileged instrument of ethnography. "Be interested in what people are interested in," we tell our students. We often add a caveat: "Don't presume that simply by seeing things their way you are necessarily doing them any good."

The empirical and the ethical go hand in hand in Hume's work, as they do in *Writing Culture* and the best of contemporary anthropology. Inference and sympathy are key ingredients in every human project. They are ways of getting things done. As kinky empiricists, we would do well to follow Hume in insisting that it is not just anthropologists who engage in "moral reasoning," as singular as our research methods might seem. So do sociologists, psychologists, economists, and political scientists, along with our more distant cousins in the natural and physical sciences. What is distinctive about anthropology among the disciplines—what makes our form of moral reasoning particularly fruitful—is the fact that we refuse to draw a categorical distinction between our practices and those of the people we study. This kind of reflexivity would risk becoming paralyzing if it were not for an insight that Hume also offers. Even though we are aware of the partiality of our truths, we still must act. For Hume, our seemingly most rigorous ways of thinking proceed "merely from an illusion of the imagination."[24] And yet the practical effects of "this capacity to compose fictions to both ourselves and others," as the Canadian philosopher Davide Panagia points out, are what "saves us from the kind of nihilism Hume's radical skepticism might induce."[25] As Jacques Derrida insisted, an ethical question is one that cannot be answered according to a prescription or program.[26] Uncertainty and justice go hand in hand in those moments that force us to choose among contending ways of doing the right thing. The empiricism that characterizes anthropology at its best is both skeptical and committed. The discipline's future lives in the kinks.

Looking Forward

If anthropology is going to remain a going concern, we have to learn to inhabit the ethical quandaries built into our kinky empiricism more creatively by building alliances across some of the barriers we have built around cultural anthropology. I have in mind those that divide us from policy work and the more quantitative social sciences. Counting people is not the only way to control them. When it comes to the consequences of our research, the best lives next door to the worst, as my work on sympathy and colonial state-building makes clear.[27] In my investigation of the establishment of the first government post in the New Guinea highlands, I came upon an episode that stopped me in my tracks. It was in Lloyd Rhys's *Jungle Pimpernel*, which describes the life and times of one of the officers whose expedition reports I pored over as part of the research for a book I am finishing. Jan Victor de Bruijn was the mixed-race son of a planter, an urbane, sophisticated man with a doctorate in Javanese archaeology who responded to the call of New Guinea. De Bruijn made it his mission to bring the "Stone Age" Papuans into the modern world through a carefully crafted program of colonial intervention. He was so devoted to this task that he refused to evacuate when western New Guinea fell to the Japanese at the outset of World War II. Rhys describes the wealth of ethnographic knowledge gathered by de Bruijn during his adventures running from the Japanese. De Bruijn gained an intimate acquaintance with the Papuans' distinct form of justice when a man accused of sleeping with another man's wife took shelter in the house where de Bruijn was staying. The man begged de Bruijn to save him, and de Bruijn almost succeeded, moved as he was by the dread that swept over the unfortunate man. But when the crowd set fire to the building, forcing the culprit to come out, de Bruijn picked up his camera. Rhys recounts what happened next: "When the adulterer had been shot and captured and de Bruijn could do nothing to intervene, he took the opportunity of taking an extraordinary set of photographs of the scene. Like many of his pictures they are unique. No other white man is known to have witnessed such an event, and no other photographs are known to exist."[28]

For de Bruijn, as for other Dutch officials in New Guinea, sympathy was a means of controlling the Papuans. And yet it created obligations—obligations born of the unsettling proximity that de Bruijn had to experience to get state-building done. The fact that sympathy was an instrumental as well as an unavoidable element of governance in New Guinea may have made it easier for him to put sympathy back in his toolbox when its demands proved impossible to fulfill. This is not to say that the obligations born of his proximity to the Papuans were not real. The abruptness with which de Bruijn turned to photography is evidence of the violence it took to turn away when he was faced with the prospect of sympathizing with the dead. However much we might want to distance ourselves from colonial figures like de Bruijn, the scenario Rhys describes should make anthropologists uncomfortable. This is not simply because there is no way fully to satisfy our obligation to others. It is also because an ethnographer and his or her subjects come from and return to different places. He or she and they come from and return to different sets of circumstances that open different opportunities, offer different constraints, and pose different demands.

When Jeff Schonberg picked up his camera in the research that led to *Righteous Dopefiend*, his and Philippe Bourgois's astonishing study of homeless heroin users in San Francisco, it was not in an effort to turn his back on obligations. Like de Bruijn, Schonberg documented suffering: the dusty, trash-strewn roadside where a man crouches to inject himself; the exposed flesh left after the removal of an abscess from another man's neck; the grief on the face of another man near the coffin of a deceased friend. But Schonberg's aim was not to take a distanced view on the distress he witnessed; it was to help create a book that acts as an artifact, in Hume's sense, enlivening the passions—and expanding the imaginations—of anyone who opens its pages. The two authors' prose fulfills much the same function. The book consists of a refreshingly unapologetic combination of divergent kinds of evidence, from statistical data drawn from the public health and policy studies literatures to excerpts from field notes intimately detailing particular people's lives, loves, and torments.

What is remarkable about the book is its ability to track between the empirical and the ethical. The book offers a fascinating analysis of the different ways black and white heroin addicts inhabit their predicament, from their methods of injection to their ways of getting by and the divergent ways they stand, talk, move, and react in a world that is ethnically divided. At the same time, Bourgois and Schonberg get close enough to the complicated lives of individuals to show how ethnic boundaries are crossed. Large-scale circumstances are everywhere revealed in this ethnography as shaping the narrow world the authors describe. These circumstances range from the role of race in fragmenting the labor force that existed before economic change turned this industrialized neighborhood of the city into a wasteland, to the tendency of African American extended families to retain ties to addicted relatives and the streetwise styles of comportment available to black addicts, but not to whites, who appear to the world as pitiful, not fearsome and strong. And yet Bourgois and Schonberg's role in the narrow world created by these circumstances is anything but that of a tourist. They hung out with the heroin addicts. They went with them on "licks"—expeditions to steal enough resalable goods to provide for another fix. They slept in their leaky tents on cold, rainy winter nights. They lent money to the addicts; they gave them rides; they gave them photographs; they documented the stories and images the addicts wanted them to record.

The book stands as a tribute to particular people: Tina, Carter, Frank, Max, Petey, Scotty. And yet it opens and closes as a policy study, a book that yields specific recommendations on how Americans might deal with the problem of heroin addiction more effectively. The research Bourgois and Schonberg undertook was funded to do precisely this: to document the public health implications of different methods of injection. As much as they registered the effects of specifically U.S. modes of sovereignty and governmentality in the lives of those they studied, this lens does not obscure their gaze. The book ends with a bittersweet account of how the authors tried to help the individuals who populate the book escape drug addiction when their twelve years of fieldwork ended. But it also ends with a call to action to transform the circumstances that made the lives described in the book the ones the addicts had to lead. The efficacy of this appeal turns on a methodological eclecticism in which fieldwork is not the only way to illuminate a social world. It is impossible not to identify with the people Bourgois and Schonberg so generously and unflinchingly describe in their joy as well as their pain. But the book's efficacy depends on the authors' ability to step back, to pick up not just a camera but also statistics. There is no question: the bold contentiousness called for in *Writing Culture* is absent in Bourgois and Schonberg's study. *Righteous Dopefiend*'s kinky empiricism is marked by what one might hope is a different kind of bravery: the courage to build alliances with anthropology's disciplinary rivals in the social sciences but to do so on our own terms.

In thinking through what these terms should be, I can't help but miss the voice of Michel-Rolph Trouillot, who would have been a wonderful participant in this conversation. Twenty years ago Trouillot told us that the time was ripe for anthropologists to contest what he called the "savage slot"—the field of inquiry that defined anthropology's place among the disciplines well before anthropology even existed.[29] He had a far less sanguine view of the project undertaken in *Writing Culture* than I have presented here. Anthropological calls for reflexivity were "timid, spontaneous—and in this sense genuinely American—responses to major changes in relations between anthropology and the wider world, provincial expressions of wider concerns, allusions to opportunities yet to be seized" now that the "savages" were gone.[30] Today's anthropologists have in many ways seized these opportunities and undertaken the "fundamental redirection" Trouillot demanded. There has been no shortage of anthropologists seeking "new points of reentry by questioning the symbolic world upon which 'nativeness' is presumed." There is no shortage of anthropologists "claiming new grounds."[31] But even as we engage in research that is creating new contact zones among the social sciences, we have yet to develop compelling ways of describing what anthropologists can—and can't—do better than economists, psychologists, or political scientists. The time is still ripe for what Trouillot called for: "an epistemology and semiology of all anthropology has done and can do."

Kinky empiricism: those who embrace it are attuned to the real-world effects of their own practices and the texts that they put into the world. They are aware of the analytic and ethical twists and turns born of a research method that forces them to get close enough to imagine how it might feel to walk in another's shoes. They are not afraid of dangerous liaisons. *Writing Culture* was not a detour on the way to the projects undertaken by today's anthropologists. In all its kinkiness, it pointed the way.

Notes

1 Sangren, "Rhetoric and the Authority of Ethnography."
2 Siegel developed themes from this course in his brilliant study of Indonesian nationalism, *Fetish, Recognition, Revolution*.

3 Rosaldo, "From the Door of His Tent."

4 Crapanzano, "Hermes' Dilemma."

5 Rabinow, "Representations Are Social Facts"; Marcus, "Afterword" and "Contemporary Problems of Ethnography in the Modern World System."

6 Clifford, "Introduction," "On Ethnographic Allegory"; Fischer, "Ethnicity and the Post-Modern Arts of Memory"; Tyler, "Post-modern Ethnography."

7 Lucy, *Reflexive Language*; Silverstein, "Shifters, Linguistic Categories, and Cultural Description."

8 Bakhtin, *The Dialogic Imagination*. Also see Feldman, *Formations of Violence*; Keane, *Signs of Recognition*. Clifford and others of the time drew on Bakhtin for their notion of dialogue. Read by way of Jakobson, Peirce, Goffman, Derrida, and others, Bakhtin's ideas about dialogue and voicing also run through much of the work cited above.

9 Silverstein, "'Cultural' Concepts and the Language-Culture Nexus"; see also Agha, *Language and Social Relations*.

10 See Siegel, *Fetish, Recognition, Revolution* on this predicament.

11 For example, Sangren, "Rhetoric and the Authority of Ethnography." Clifford, "Introduction" also points to the diversity of the chapters and eschews any effort to reduce them to a single project.

12 MacNabb, introduction, 28.

13 MacNabb, introduction, 28–29.

14 In his introduction to Hume's *Dialogues Concerning Natural Religion*, Richard H. Popkin reports that Hume told Adam Smith that "the only reason he wanted to stay alive was to 'see the elimination of this strange superstition, Christianity, that pervaded the world.' Then, in his usual skeptical manner, Hume added that even if he could carry on his efforts in this direction, he doubted that Christianity would ever be eliminated."

15 Rabinow, "Representations are Social Facts," 234.

16 Deleuze, *Empiricism and Subjectivity*; Massumi, *Parables of the Virtual*.

17 Rabinow, "Representations are Social Facts," 234.

18 Deleuze, *Empiricism and Subjectivity*, 104.

19 Hume, *A Treatise of Human Nature* and *An Enquiry Concerning Human Understanding*. See also Deleuze, *Empiricism and Subjectivity*.

20 Hume, *An Enquiry Concerning Human Understanding*.

21 Hume, *A Treatise of Human Nature*; see also Deleuze, *Empiricism and Subjectivity* and *Difference and Repetition*.

22 Hume, *A Treatise of Human Nature*.

23 Hume, *A Treatise of Human Nature*; Deleuze, *Empiricism and Subjectivity*. See also Panagia, "Inconsistencies of Character."

24 Panagia, "Inconsistencies of Character," 90.

25 Panagia, "Inconsistencies of Character," 90.

26 Derrida, *The Gift of Death* and "Force of Law."

27 Rutherford, "Sympathy, State Building, and the Experience of Empire."

28 Rhys, *Jungle Pimpernel*, 210.

29 Trouillot traced this slot to a *thématique* born during the Renaissance, when the savage became an element in the trilogy, along with order and utopia, that oriented the political and conceptual moves through what we now take as the West ("Anthropology and the Savage Slot," 18). Whether or not representations of the newly discovered "other" had any empirical reality is beside the point, Trouillot tells us, "The savage is only evidence in a debate, the importance of which surpasses not only his understanding but also his very existence" (33).

30 Trouillot, "Anthropology and the Savage Slot," 19.

31 Trouillot, "Anthropology and the Savage Slot," 40, 36. To make a case for the advantages of the kind of knowledge anthropology produces is anything but to invoke what Trouillot refers to as the "ahistorical voice of reason, justice, or civilization" (19). It is to acknowledge anthropology's own situated standing as a science among other sciences—to specify what we can and can't do better than economists, political scientists, or psychologists. We have to learn to think about anthropology within a wider landscape of knowledge production and political action. Patting ourselves on the back for our studies of the state, say, is misguided if we fail to contend with changes in the discipline of political science. The other way of reading our ability to claim new ground is in terms of political science's retreat from the historical specificity associated with comparative politics. The motto would seem to be "Let the girls do it"—that is, leave this kind of empirical work to the relatively feminized discipline of anthropology. The boys, with their elegant rational choice models, remain nestled in the armpits of power. To become something other than specialists in savagery we need to find new ways to authorize our findings as something other than the musings of adventurers seeking the exotic close to home. Trouillot calls on anthropology to intervene more effectively in debates over the Western canon by championing minority voices. This challenge remains, but these days there are also other interdisciplinary fish to fry.

CHAPTER 6

Think about the timing: the 1984 Bhopal disaster, marking the risks of in-dustrial order and the already degraded state of industrial infrastructure. The American plant in central India was underdesigned for safety and had not been maintained. The forty-ton tank that released its contents into the air of a sleeping city on December 3, 1984, is where the many failures of many in-volved systems came together, at a boil.[1] Thousands were killed; hundreds of thousands of others were exposed, their bodies becoming even more laced with toxics than mine, yours, and all others in our late industrial age. Un-derstanding of the chemicals released in Bhopal remains inconclusive; they are among the over 100,000 chemicals registered with governments around the world for routine use; the data haven't been collected, the science hasn't been done, to understand how these chemicals affect human and ecosystem health. Thousands of new chemicals continue to be introduced each year.[2]

The Bhopal plant site today is decrepit and eerie. The old control room is open air and crumbling. The old piping configuration still stands, rusted; T. R. Chouhan, a former Union Carbide worker, can still narrate its workings, pointing out the pathways and junctures leading to the reaction in Tank 610.[3] On the perimeter an old waste-disposal site still oozes chemicals.[4] The smell is truly worse than shit. It is the smell of late industrialism. Children play and cows graze within it.

Zoom out to picture Delhi. New, gated communities house a multina-tional corporate elite. The future they work for, that they have anterior-ized, is that promised and motored by neoliberalism, bolstered by digital infrastructure and wealth but still energized by coal and oil. There are many more cars on the road. And increasing rates of asthma. People can't breathe. Another sign of late industrialism.[5]

Figure 6.1. Tank 610 at the Old Union Carbide plant in Bhopal, India. Forty tons of methyl isocyanate were released from this tank in the early morning hours of December 3, 1984. Photograph by the author.

Figure 6.2. Degraded components of the Union Carbide pesticide plant in Bhopal, India. The site is now abandoned but remains contaminated with pesticides, chlorinated benzenes, and heavy metals. Groundwater serving local communities is also contaminated. Photograph by the author.

And people can't think. According to a survey of "American environmental values" sponsored by the Sierra Club and other environmental organizations, Americans are paralyzed by issue complexity. The survey also reports that "libertarian values are ascendant over communal values."[6] Complexity, but little collectivity. Not a great combination.

This is a world in which Clarence Thomas, a former attorney for Monsanto, becomes a U.S. Supreme Court justice. A world in which Iraqi farmers are told that they are required to plant "protected" crop varieties, defined as new, distinct, uniform, and stable—as Monsanto seeds. Seed saving was made illegal; contracts to purchase herbicides, insecticides, and fertilizers were also required.[7] The complexity of these conditions, the entanglements—of business and government, of law and politics, of war and farming, of natural and technical systems—is stunning, and sobering.

This is late industrialism, where we've come since 1984.

Again, think about the timing: 1986, Clifford and Marcus's *Writing Culture*, a call to rethink thought—about anthropology and ethnography, authority and the purpose and responsibilities of scholarship. It was historically attuned, and a call to remain historically attuned, a call to always ask about the conditions in which ethnography is produced and must work within, a call to recognize how discursive forms, including those of ethnography, stage, direct, and limit what is said and not said, who is heard and benefits, who and what remains subaltern, outside articulation. It embodied and animated what has become known as the "language turn" in the humanities and the human sciences.

The original critique was directed at the conceptual, discursive, and social forms of what could be called high industrialism. The concern was with discursive exclusion and the promise of polyvocalism, with ways around the disjuncture between dominant ways of understanding the world and what ethnographers encountered on the ground.

How, today, do we both stay with and update the call? How, today, at a time when social order and sensibility are worked out on talk shows, a time in which we are *Outfoxed* (2004) by the news, and even the best of coverage insists on "balance," granting equal time to those few who refuse to believe scientific evidence of climate change, working with constructs of fairness and appropriateness that embody simple to the point of simplistic notions of democracy and truth?[8]

It is also a world noisy with new media, streaming through products with planned obsolescence.[9] Cell phones and iPods last a year or two. In

2009, when broadcasters switched to digital TV signal, millions of analog TVs became garbage. Electronic waste piles up and circulates globally, leaching toxins into humans and animals, soil, air, and water.[10]

The pipes that carry water to and waste away from households, hospitals, schools, and businesses are now aging, even in metropoles like Washington, D.C. The D.C. sewer was built in 1889. The average D.C. water pipe is seventy-seven years old.[11] Across the United States water and sewage systems haven't been updated; they leak and overflow.[12] And they have no way to deal with what now passes through them: water laced with runoff from roads and effluents from manufacturing plants, but also with pharmaceutical residues, including synthetic hormones.[13] Amphibians are the new canaries in the coal shaft, exhibiting skewed sexual development and extra limbs.[14] Queer, in a way that cannot be applauded.

And it is a world of even more experts. A world in which cadres of well-trained men and women carry out highly specific functions that maintain the technical and economic conditions of our times. People specialize in very particular domains of production, spending their days immersed in the information flows and practices of biomedical care for asthma, of transportation engineering, of the design of convenience stores or shopping malls. There is incredible particularity and incredible complexity. Incredible skill and pervasive deskilling.[15]

Much of the infrastructure, many of the paradigms that have held it up are exhausted. Things are falling apart, again.

What is the task of ethnography at such a moment?

Questions Concerning Ethnography

How can we leverage the affordances of ethnography to understand and engage a late industrial world? How, particularly, can we leverage understanding of how ethnography works as articulated in *Writing Culture*, in synch with a 1980s flurry of feminist and postcolonial criticism? What would make ethnography "appropriate" to the historical conditions in which we find ourselves today? What designs on/of ethnography should we cultivate?[16] I write here—of leveraging, affordances, how things work, appropriateness, and design—from within science and technology studies, where many of us love, and love to study technology, understood expansively. The word *technology* comes from Greek τεχνολογία (*technología*); from τέχνη (*téchnē*), meaning "art, skill, craft," and -λογία (-*logía*), meaning "study of." Technology, from this vantage point, is something crafted to enable and direct, routing desire, making new things possible and possible to imagine. And it should, etymologically speaking, have an in-built reflexivity, a study of that which is crafted, and of how craft happens and should happen, that occurs alongside the making and use of the technology.[17]

Ethnography can be thought of as a technology in these terms, as a means through which things are enabled. And ethnography, like other technologies, can be designed in different ways—to draw out what is, the state of things, or to show what is at odds with extant theory, ethnography as cultural critique.[18] Ethnography, like other technologies, can also be designed to challenge and change existing order, provoking new orderings of subjectivity, society, and culture, having what Stephen Tyler, in *Writing Culture*, called a "therapeutic effect."[19]

Thus far, it seems to me, we have made good use of ethnography for the first of these, for understanding and critique. And critique, to be sure, is transformative. I don't at all mean to suggest that ethnography has "just" been critique. I do, however, think there are new possibilities to pursue, directed at transformation but without the teleological overtones of activism as usual.

Ethnography, I want to suggest, can be designed to bring forth a future anterior that is not calculable from what we now know, a future that surprises. Ethnography thus becomes creative, producing something that didn't exist before. Something beyond codified expert formulas.

The future is anteriorized when the past is folded into the way reality presents itself, setting up both the structures and the obligations of the future. The future inhabits the present, yet it also has not yet come—rather like the way toxics inhabit the bodies of those exposed, setting up the future but not yet manifest as disease nor even as an origin from which a specific and known disease will come. Toxics, like the future anterior, call on us to think about determinism but without the straightforward directives of teleology.

Derrida, rereading Levinas, remarks that the "future anterior could turn out to be—and this resemblance is irreducible—the time of Hegelian teleology. Indeed, that is how the properly philosophical intelligence is usually administered, in accord with what I called above the dominant interpretation of language—in which the philosophical interpretation precisely consists." Derrida also suggests other possibilities, describing how the concept of the future anterior could have "drawn us toward an eschatology without philosophical teleology, beyond it in any case, otherwise than it."[20]

Derrida writes of the future anterior to think about what both demands and makes possible a future that would not merely be a continuation of the present. The future anterior, he says, puts in place a "lace of obligation" that both binds and unbinds the ethical actor. The possibility of pursuing justice beyond the determinations of law is one important effect.[21]

Hans-Jörg Rheinberger, a biologist and historian of biology and a translator of Derrida, can be read as describing how a future anterior is pursued in science, through the building of experimental systems. These systems are systems carefully designed to work in a way that generates surprises. Experimental systems are not testing devices, designed to confirm what is already known. They are designed to allow for the emergence of questions that could not be asked before.[22]

Ethnography too can be designed in such a way.

Partly because ethnography historically, by definition, perhaps, certainly as articulated in *Writing Culture*, has affordances that call for openness to what is foreign, Other, not yet articulable.[23] It tolerates, indeed cultivates open-endedness.

Ethnography also has a record and a habit of shifting in concert with the times, responsive to both historical conditions and internal critique (of the sort *Writing Culture* offered). And these conditions can be discerned ethnographically. This is a critical step in the design process that I put forward here.

Ethnography, at its best, provides a powerful and efficient way to read historical conditions. It produces both situated and comparative insight, is able to see across scale, and leverage different analytic lenses. It can draw out nested and proximate systems, sensitive to their similarities, differences, and synergisms. Postcolonialism and neoliberalism, for example, can be seen as phenomena that cut across space in similar ways and as phenomena that are exquisitely specific in their instantiations. The ability to recognize both is an ethnographic signature. So too with language games. The discursive dynamics that we observe and parse can be recognized as those of modernity or "the Enlightenment" and Patriarchy, for example, and also as specific to particular problem domains, domains with particular information flows and practices, their own ways of making sense. Many such problem domains today, in our late industrial times, involve complex conditions, conditions involving many nested systems—technical, biophysical, cultural, economic—and thus a multiplicity of interactions, which keep the parameters of "the problem" from ever settling down. Complex conditions resist explanation in available terms, producing what I have come to think of as discursive gaps and discursive risks.

Discursive gaps emerge when there are conditions to deal with for which there is no available idiom, no way of thinking that can grasp what is at hand.

Discursive risks emerge because of a tendency to rely on established idioms and ways of thinking nonetheless.

As when the idioms and thought styles of mechanics are imposed on toxics, for example. The particular dynamics of toxics are then ignored. Ignorance is produced. We are continually told that "there is no evidence of harm to humans" because the evidence deemed necessary is at odds with the condition it is meant to represent. What is Other to the dominant idiom is colonized by it.

Another example is when water and other resource wars are cast as religious or ethnic wars. It may be that religion and ethnicity are part of the puzzle, but habits of reading in these terms produce ignorance about environmental determinations.[24]

Feminist theory has, of course, taught us much about this kind of cycle, and the violences of it. Ethnography can help break the cycle, leveraging its capacity to get at the exacting specificity of a given problem domain. This is critical in these late industrial times in which most problem domains are like the tightly coupled complex systems described by the sociologist Charles Perrow in his seminal book *Normal Accidents*. The industrial systems Perrow describes—nuclear power plants, chemical processing plants, air transport networks—are made of a tangle of technical systems, which are so tightly coupled that it must be considered "normal" to have runaway incidents that exceed what experts can understand, much less control. Ethnography has affordances that enable it to effectively observe and respond to this kind of dynamic, typical of the problem domains of late industrialism.

Designing Ethnography

There are a number of steps in the design process. First, and continuing, is the ethnographic work of discerning discursive gaps and risks. This is ethnography in a somewhat traditional mode, working to understand what is so, discursively, and materially. Again, feminist theory has laid the ground.[25] We need to understand what is said, what can be said, and what is disavowed.

This understanding, ironically, becomes something we can share, make into a collective resource, only by rendering it in terms of established idioms, which we know in advance are inadequate, even violent. This was a key teaching of

Writing Culture. What we can think or say—even within and in the idiom of anthropology—cannot but be within established systems of ideality. Thinking in terms of theory, even poetics, delimits us. So we must proceed with humility, humor, and reflexivity, reaching to move from the overdeterminations of description to provocation, knowing that we will have to design for something otherwise.

We must next loop, leveraging ethnography not only to describe what is at hand but also to respond to the discursive gaps we have come to see and understand.[26]

Our task now becomes creative. We must try, through the design of an experimental ethnographic system, to provoke new idioms, new ways of thinking, which grasp and attend to current realities. Not knowing in advance what theses idioms will look and sound like.

Ethnography must, then, create a space for deliberation, for worrying through, for creativity. It must stage encounters. Operating a bit like performance art.

Readers thus become users of the systems we build; our interlocutors become party to what we say. Ethnography becomes polyvocal, as called for in *Writing Culture,* in a way that literally keeps the conversation going and open.[27]

The goal is not to give everyone a chance to speak, as a matter of fairness. The model is not the town hall meeting or the talk show. But it is about being open to intervention and foreigners, about hospitality and solicitude.[28] The goal is to come together—to literally collaborate, performing the labor of difference, to articulate something that could not be said, could not be brought together before.

Let me provide a few examples of what this might look like.

THE ASTHMA FILES

First, a project that I have undertaken with a number of colleagues, which we call The Asthma Files.[29] I want to highlight the ethnographic looping that I called for earlier—how insight from the research is being fed back into the design of the project, functioning as what we call "substantive logics," which operate alongside what we call "design logics," drawn from what is usually thought of as "theory." These substantive logics lay out the discursive habits, gaps, and risks of the problem domain in which asthma operates, made up of overlapping systems and worlds. The worlds of epidemiology and pollution science, of biomedicine and school nurses, of young athletes and old women, of families in urban housing projects and in rural households around the world in which cooking fuels generate an ever-present, eventually unnoticed but still debilitating smoke.

In studying these worlds and their interactions, we have come to see patterns and habits, incapacity and incapability. A *Lancet* review in 2006, for example, questions whether *asthma* is an overly monolithic term, which glosses amazing variation in asthma occurrence. Operating at more of a micro level, a research group at the University of Texas Medical Branch at Galveston that focuses on severe, life-threatening asthma has recently changed direction, provoked by recognition that established understandings of who is at risk and when are simply wrong or at least out of synch with the data if looked at through the lens of advanced informatics. In recategorizing people according to their "protein profiles" and correlating those to subsets of asthma severity, new research directions have opened up.[30] Hesitations and shifts like these produce important openings for the kind of ethnographic encounter I want to help stage, encounters that would trouble established frameworks, facilitating slippage, so that new questions and idioms can emerge.

Such staging has to consider where the conversation is likely to go. The goal is not to give everyone a chance to voice his or her perspective, rearticulating what he or she thinks and sees. The goal is to create a space of creativity, where something surprising, something new to all emerges.

The ethnographer sets the stage accordingly. In dealing with asthma, many tendencies have to be diverted. First is the tendency to remain disassembled, such that the various parts never come together. Epidemiologists with large asthma cohort studies not knowing about air quality data sets maintained by state and federal government agencies, which they could draw into their analyses, at least attempting a reading for environmental determinations, for example. Another tendency is to hierarchically order the types of data and knowledge in play. Asthma geneticists, for example, reifying the types of data genomics is able to produce, with huge investments of time and expertise, such that the data produced by air chemists and chemical engineers, drawn from monitors along highways and atop schools, are never considered usable, always too noisy, not true enough to what a specific human body is exposed to and incorporates. A third tendency we actively work against is a tendency to locate care and cure in the biomedicalized, inhaler-ready, compliant individual. This is the teleology of most asthma education, carried out by very well meaning nurses, coaches, and parents, a teleology we want to displace.

So we have designed a web platform that supports collaboration among ethnographers working on various components of this puzzle, enabling a collective, multisited ethnography, which we try to keep intensely cross-linked. As the platform evolves, our interlocutors who work on asthma will be drawn in to the site itself so that they too, like the ethnographers involved, are immersed in what we think about as a juxtapositional logic, a logic wherein divergent ways of seeing (often the same thing) are brought together.[31] The structure of Bateson's *Naven* comes to mind here; we want to draw out what one gets when one sees through different analytic lenses, from different vantage points. Not to resolve differences nor to merely celebrate diversity but to provoke encounters across differences that produce new articulations.

This is requiring new kinds of discipline, the discipline to design and then work with ethnographic questions sufficiently standardized to allow juxtapositions to be animated. We query all of our interlocutors about the kinds of data they create, use, and idealize, for example. We also ask about their methodological anxieties, workarounds, and biases. There are about thirty questions we try to return to. These questions must be adhered to for the platform to really work. Forced methods, so to speak, with a critical intent akin to the "forced readings" that Gayatri Spivak showed to be so productive.[32]

Developments in the environmental health sciences have also taught me to be patient with this new discipline. It has only been through hard-won standardization of the metadata on environmental health data sets that environmental health scientists have been able to push into being new ways of understanding and representing toxicity, regional air quality, nested ecosystems, and other objects of concern. Diversity of content and form has had to become interoperable.[33]

Our digital platform thus operates as both a research tool and as a space to share research results. We offer what we think of as staccato readings, short, densely cross-linked articulations that quickly move users elsewhere in the system, where they will see the puzzle from a different vantage point. The system is meant to provide a portal—a designed way in—to the world as it is, in its incredible complexity, while destabilizing usual ways of thinking about the world and its possibilities. So the goals are traditionally ethnographic, in a sense, but with creative intent.

What we want to stage is an encounter with asthma that anticipates discursive habits that pose discursive risks, mindful too of things that need to be articulated, which don't yet have an idiom. Gene-environment interactions in asthma incidence, for example. The connection between air quality and health outcomes. We know in advance that conventional (scientific) constructs of causation won't suffice, so we try to animate other ways of making connections and seeing relationships.

We thus loop, turning ethnographic findings back into the system, an experimental ethnographic system also designed to embody the theories of language that animated the so-called language turn of the 1980s. So it is both a legacy and an emergent system, theoretically inflected and deeply ethnographic.

CONVENIENCE STORES AND THE U.S. (INDUSTRIAL) FOOD SYSTEM

The second project that I want to point to is even more emergent and is focused on a condition at least as complex as asthma: the U.S. food delivery system. The point of entry is the convenience store. Michael Powell, another anthropologist educated at Rice, is undertaking this project in the Los Angeles area, where he works for an architectural design firm that specializes in the planning of urban retail, advertising itself as a firm "with a focus on leveraging consumer perceptions." Much of his firm's work focuses on food retail, including supermarkets, restaurants, bodegas, and convenience stores. Through this Powell has had access to food executives, marketers, cashiers, and customers. He has learned that there are nearly 150,000 convenience stores in the United States, constituting a $500 billion industry, and that this industry knows it needs to rethink itself and the future, partly because tobacco sales, which constitute a huge percentage of convenience store sales, are declining. One type of convenience store also sells gas, which is also likely to move in different ways in coming years. But what will the convenience store of the future look like? Will today's convenience store remain? A small, well-lit box store that sells cigarettes and lotto tickets, coffee, Slushees, and hotdogs off heated rollers on the counter, its shelves stocked with food from who knows where, laced with preservatives, bound up in plastic?

Is something else imaginable?

The food industry planners that Powell has interacted with through his firm want to innovate. And they know how to think about consumer perceptions and how they can be shifted. But Powell has been struck by how little they know about other kinds of thinking about local and global food systems, their interconnections and problems. It is not that his interlocutors are not expert; they are intensively expert, and thus operate in a manner and in a world that is delimited.

In Powell's experience, for example, many food industry experts have never heard of Michael Pollan, a leading voice for people concerned about how healthy today's food is for people, ecosystems, and economies. There has been a surge of work critical of Food, Inc. and its factory farms, incredibly high food miles, and unregulated ingredients.[34] And a surge of interest in obesity and other indexes of food delivery systems gone wrong. But not in the world of the food industry itself.

What would happen if these worlds were brought together? One could predict where the conversation would likely go, based on ethnographic observation of the assumptions, binaries, and expectations of different players. It could well end in uncomfortable silence.

Could the ethnographer stage something different, a carefully designed encounter intended to provoke what neither "side" could say or imagine coming in?

Where should the event take place? What questions should be posed? What solicitation techniques could be used? How could an ethnographic understanding of the ways language and meaning work be put to work?

Powell is now wrestling with all this. I challenge you too to think in these terms—about how the food industry and its critics could be shaken up, but also about ethnography in an array of other problem domains that, in a tightly coupled way, make up late industrialism.

In the Future

What we are after here could be called the *différend,* or *jouissance.* We want to reach beyond established systems of ideality, where Derrida and Levinas locate justice. Philosopher Dawn McCance says it this way:

> This future anteriority of the mirror stage trope distinguishes Lacan's specular subject, characterized by "anticipated belatedness," from the conscious subject of metaphysical philosophy, Hegel's Selbst, for example, whose basis is a perfected present. . . . [It] means that the positioning of oneself as a unified ("phallic") subject within the Law-of-the-Father is an endeavor which inevitably fails. Aware of this failure, yet always attempting to cover it up, the signifying subject is beset by an inexorable anxiety, a disconcerting after-effect, an unrepresentable, contaminating and impossible to integrate, "after the fact [*après coup*], nachträglich"

effect. For Lyotard, this after-effect bears such non-names as "the jews" and *le différend*. Lacan calls it *jouissance*.[35]

Drucilla Cornell, reading Derrida and Levinas, explains how it is about justice:

> As with Derrida, Levinas' conception of time has implications for his understanding of justice. For Levinas, Justice is messianic. The "avenir" is not just the limit created by the aporias Derrida indicates, but instead inheres in the otherness of the Other that cannot be encompassed by any present system of ideality. The Other is other to the system. Incorporation into the system is the denial of the Other. Justice is sanctity for her "otherness." Nonencompassable by the system, the Other is also noncalculable. The right of the Other, then, is infinite, meaning that it can never be reduced to a proportional share of an already-established system of ideality, legal or otherwise. It is the Other as other to the present that echoes in the call to justice.[36]

My point here is not to validate ethnography through philosophy. Instead we can let philosophical teachings orient ethnography so that ethnography produces something beyond philosophy. Theory thus operates as design logics, geared to enable ethnographic articulations that are truly creative, and therein a new kind of truth.

We surely need this. Working with toxics, I know especially well that we, as a society, need to invest in more data, more knowledge. I also know that we need new knowledge forms, that it is not just a matter of quantity.

Ethnography, it seems to me, can be designed to elicit these new forms. Not because the ethnographer is especially brilliant but because she knows how to listen, how to discern discursive gaps and risks, how to tolerate truly not knowing where one is headed. We are trained and positioned, funnily, to tolerate the unknown; we have an affordance for unimaginable futures.

It at times sobers me that I still work with Spivak, Derrida, Homi Bhabha, and kin, not having moved beyond them. But perhaps this is because the kinds of openings they provided have of late been made elsewhere or otherwise.

Perhaps it is ethnography that now does the work of "theory." Perhaps an ethnographic turn has followed the so-called linguistic turn of the 1980s.

The language turn, carried by texts like *Writing Culture*, directed our attention to the ways discursive and textual forms are constitutive of the real, directing what we see and say, and don't, and what counts as true, benefiting some, often at great cost to others. Language also came to be understood as a place of play and supplementarity, out of which quite unimaginable things could emerge. So ideas about systems that permit or even provoke play are not new. We haven't, however, really run with possibilities for building our own systems—experimental ethnographic systems—that leverage the ways we have come to understand language to work.

Such systems could take many forms—that of the book, the digital archive, or an event, among others—but what these systems would be after would be particular subject effects, subjects able and willing, even wanting, desiring, to become party to new ways of thinking about and engaging a particular problem domain, a domain that we have analyzed ethnographically to understand the discursive gaps and risks that characterize it. What we would seek to engineer, then, would be something beyond understanding: a subject with a will to know differently.

Such a subject could be called postmodern or specular. But here, in experimental ethnographic systems, there is ethnographic specificity. The systems are designed to unsettle the subjects and discursive forms with which they deal, in very specific ways. The Asthma Files are designed to respond to the particular discursive gaps and risk of the complex problem space in which asthma is dealt with. Michael Powell's effort to provoke new ways of thinking about the convenience store and the U.S. food system must be designed to attend to the habits and biases, discursive gaps and risks of that particular problem space. Ethnographic knowledge thus provides substantive logics, supplementing design logics drawn from what we traditionally think of as "theory."

This, it seems to me, is what would make ethnography "appropriate" to the historical conditions in which we find ourselves. Conditions characterized by massive violence, marginalization, and injustice, by environmental devastation and industrial recklessness, by stunning hubris and shrill ignorance. Conditions that cultivate a will not to know, not to engage, not to experiment.

It doesn't help, of course, that our politicians are defunding National Public Radio, public education, and the sciences and threatening to "padlock" the U.S. Environmental Protection Agency,[37] an imperfect agency to be sure, but one that today can stand as a signal of what we cannot or will not deal with: problems that we don't know how to fix or even evaluate with currently available tools, problems that won't settle down, shifting as natural, social, economic, and cultural systems continually play off one another.

Really imagine it: a padlocked EPA, a society and culture that refuses to invest in complex problems, deeming all experiments necessary.

Ethnography can respond, reading these historical conditions with great care and solicitude, to stage encounters—in texts, online, in the street, in conference rooms—that are productively creative, creating space for something new to emerge, engineering imaginations and idioms for different futures, mindful of how very hard it is to think outside and beyond what we know presently.

Ethnography thus becomes creative—setting language games in motion, provoking different orderings of things, having patience for what we cannot yet imagine. Writing culture as a future anterior that draws us, with and away from Derrida, "toward an eschatology without philosophical teleology, beyond it in any case, otherwise than it."[38] An ethnographic turn thus supplements the language turn.

Notes

1 See Fortun, *Advocacy after Bhopal.* For a recent review of the Bhopal disaster, see Ansell and Tinsley, "Bhopal's Never Ending Tragedy."
2 See Lyndsey Layton, "U.S. Regulators Lack Data on Health Risks of Most Chemicals," *Washington Post,* August 2, 2010, accessed July 1, 2014. http://www.washingtonpost.com/wp-dyn/content/article/2010/08/01/AR2010080103469.html.
3 I have worked with Chouhan to understand the Bhopal disaster since 1990. During my extended fieldwork in Bhopal in the early 1990s, the plant site was not accessible. It was accessible when I visited in December 2010, with Chouhan as my guide.
4 Centre for Science and the Environment, "Contamination of Soil and Water inside and outside the Union Carbide India Limited, Bhopal."
5 Centre for Science and the Environment, "CSE's Press Release."
6 SRI Consulting, "The American Environmental Values Survey, 2006." The survey was conducted for Sierra Club, Earthjustice, and ecoAmerica.
7 Sourcewatch, "Monsanto's High Level Connections to the Bush Administration."
8 Boykoff and Boykoff, "Journalistic Balance as Global Warming Bias."
9 Slade, *Made to Break.*
10 See details and the plan forward provided by the Electronics Take Back Coalition, http://www.electronicstakeback.com/designed-for-the-dump/quickly-obsolete/. Toxipedia's entry on e-waste is also useful: http://toxipedia.org/display/toxipedia/Electronic+Waste+(E-Waste).
11 Ashley Halsey III, "Billions Needed to Upgrade American's Leaky Water Infrastructure," *Washington Post,* January 2, 2012, accessed May 22, 2012, http://

www.washingtonpost.com/local/billions-needed-to-upgrade-americas-leaky-water-infrastructure/2011/12/22/gIQAdsEoWP_print.html.

12 A plan forward is laid out in "Water Works: Rebuilding Infrastructure, Creating Jobs, Greening the Environment," a report by Green for All, http://www.greenforall.org/resources/water-works/.

13 Zota, "Oral Contraceptives Are Not a Major Estrogen Source in Drinking Water."

14 Lanoo, *Malformed Frogs*; Dashka Slater, "The Frog of War," *Mother Jones*, January–February 2012, accessed March 15, 2012, http://motherjones.com/environment/2011/11/tyrone-hayes-atrazine-syngenta-feud-frog-endangered?page=1.

15 Consider the kind of persona cultivated by and emblematic of the sciences, as described by the feminist historian of science Evelyn Fox Keller in *Reflections on Gender and Science*. They are obsessive-compulsive in their desire for control, not so much of others as of themselves. Attention is subject to the same kind of control as the rest of behavior, leading to a focus so intensely sharp and restricted that it precludes peripheral vision and simply ignores the unusual, staying on narrow, established pathways for thought, going right by anything out of the way. Like tending a garden or forest with manicure scissors. My own research in the environmental sciences suggests that a different figuration of the scientist has emerged in recent decades. Keller's description of the subject effects of intensive expertise nonetheless remains important in thinking about late industrialism.

16 The slash used here refers readers to George Marcus's seminal article, "Ethnography in/of the World System."

17 For a historical reading, see Schatzberg, "Technik Comes to America."

18 Marcus and Fischer, *Anthropology as Cultural Critique*.

19 Tyler, "Post-modern Ethnography."

20 Derrida, "At This Very Moment in This Work Here I Am," 36–37.

21 Derrida, "Force of Law," 329.

22 See Fischer, "Culture and Cultural Analysis as Experimental Systems"; Fortun, "Ethnography in/of/as Open Systems"; Rheinberger, "Experimental Systems, Graphematic Spaces"; Ronell, *The Test Drive*, 45–48.

23 Bhabha, "Articulating the Archaic."

24 See, for example, Vandana Shiva's writing on conflicts around the Kaveri River in South India, *Water Wars*. In "The Science of Catastrophe" the anthropologist David Bond describes another instance of discursive risk: After the *Exxon Valdez* disaster in 1989 the U.S. National Oceanic and Atmospheric Administration (NOAA) committed to being better prepared for ocean oil spills. And they were better prepared in the summer of 2010, when British Petroleum's Deepwater Horizon platform blew up and began gushing oil into the sea. NOAA was prepared for a surface oil slick as in the *Exxon Valdez* case—not for a spill gushing up from a mile under the sea, out of control.

25 Teresa de Lauretis, for example, emphasizes the need to understand both what systems say and what they do not and cannot say. Understanding the gender effects of a social system, she argues, demands "a movement back and forth between the representation of gender (in its male-centered frame of reference) and what that representation leaves out or, more pointedly, makes unrepresentable" (introduction, 25). The analyst must find or invent a way to move "between the (represented) discursive space of the positions made available by hegemonic discourses and the space-off, the elsewhere, of those discourses: those other spaces both discursive and social that exist, since feminist practices have (re-)constructed them, in the margins (or 'between the lines,' or 'against the grain') of hegemonic discourses and the interstices of institutions, in counterpractices, and in new forms of community" (25). Also see Spivak, *Other Worlds*; Haraway, "Situated Knowledge"; Cornell, *The Philosophy of the Limit*.

26 This notion of looping recalls Marcus's effort to vitalize "para-sites," now ongoing at the Center for Ethnography at University of California, Irvine. Marcus's introduction to *Para-Sites: A Casebook against Cynical Reason*, a volume in the experimental Late Editions series, provides a preliminary articulation: "[Para-sites are concerned with] forging spaces, sites, and even objects that facilitate alternative thinking by subjects who are deeply complicit with and implicated in powerful institutional processes in times of heightened consciousness of great social transformations. Our interest in how ambiguously alternative perspectives emerge amid moderately empowered people involved explicitly with major institutional powers has been a motivating component. . . . [The interest is in] functionaries within important institutions . . . who are attempting to come to terms with changing practices, opportunities, and self-definitions. The para-site is thus a space of excess or surplus in a subject's actions but is never fully controllable by him or her. The achievement is to be able to make and operate in such a space at all. This is cultural production as close to the skin of events and engines of change as possible. It is the kind of cultural work that critical scholars or ethnographers, on the lookout for 'found' critical sensibilities, must ally with" (5). Thanks to Kirk Jalbert for bringing this passage back to mind.

27 Derrida points to the aporia and paradox in the way hospitality requires one to be the master of the house or nation, a controlling agent, to lay the table and set the stage for encounters with foreigners and foreignness. To be hospitable, one has to have the power to host; one has to exercise control over the event. One must also, however, give up mastery, ownership, one's possessions, if the foreigner is really to come in, if hospitality is to be realized. So there is an impossibility at the heart of hospitality (Derrida, *Adieu to Emmanuel Lévinas* and *On Cosmopolitanism and Forgiveness*; Derrida with Dufourmantelle, *Of Hospitality*). So too in ethnography. An experimental ethnographic system must be carefully staged, carefully controlled, to make way for something new to arrive. Here too there is an impossibility at the heart of it, but also a promise.

28 *Solicitude* has roots in *solicit* and *soliciting*. Derrida put solicitude at the heart of deconstruction: "Structure is perceived through the incidence of menace, at the moment when imminent danger concentrates our vision on the keystone of an institution, the stone which encapsulates both the possibility and the fragility of its existence. Structure then can be methodically threatened in order to be comprehended more clearly and to reveal not only its supports but also that secret place in which it is neither construction nor ruin but lability. This operation is called (from the Latin) soliciting. In other words, shaking in a way related to the whole (from *sollus*, in archaic Latin 'the whole,' and from *citare*, 'to put in motion')" (*Writing and Difference*, 6).

29 See http://theasthmafiles.org/, last accessed July 1, 2014.

30 The anthropologist Jerome Crowder works alongside this research group and has introduced me. A brief description of their research is at http://www.ut mbhealth.com/wtn/Page.asp?PageID=WTN000571. Examples of the visual analytics used by the group are accessible at http://skbhavnani.com/DIVA/.

31 Our thinking about juxtapositional logic builds on Clifford, "On Ethnographic Surrealism."

32 See Spivak, *Other Worlds* and *Outside in the Teaching Machine*.

33 See Fortun, "Toxics Trouble." Critically the comparisons and juxtaposition in play in The Asthma Files are not generated by simple term matching or even by semantic webs that delineate when things mean the same thing despite being said differently. In The Asthma Files, by digital design, comparison is animated by our ethnographic questions, not by answers, such that answers are not expected in advance to be the same or even patterned in a particular way. The Asthma Files system is thus built to be open-ended rather than calculative. Comparisons are not generated by matching but by questions that make things proximate even if vastly different. It is a different way of ordering things, a way of staging collectivity that does not assume consensus or simple processes of communication. It is meant to embody a poststructural rather than Habermasian understanding of the way language and meaning production work.

34 See the Food, Inc. website, http://www.foodincmovie.com/.

35 McCance, *Posts*, 76–77.

36 Cornell, *The Philosophy of the Limit*, 137.

37 I refer here to intentions articulated in the lead-up to the 2011 Republican presidential primary. For examples, see John Broder, "Bashing EPA Is New Theme in GOP Race," *New York Times*, August 17, 2011, accessed March 15, 2012, http://www.nytimes.com/2011/08/18/us/politics/18epa.html; John Broder and Kate Galbraith, "EPA Is Longtime Favorite Target for Perry," *New York Times*, September 29, 2011, accessed March 15, 2012, http://www.nytimes.com/2011/09/30/us/politics/epa-is-perrys-favorite-target.html.

38 Derrida, "At This Very Moment in This Work Here I Am," 36–37.

CHAPTER 7

Excelente Zona Social

Michael Taussig

In July of this year I spent two days in a camp of displaced peasants in the swamps of northern Colombia where the mighty Magdalena River spills out. I was accompanied by Juan Felipe García, a professor of law in Bogotá, Pablo, his assistant who kept track of our expenses, and Lily Hibberd, an Australian artist who had never been to Latin America. On the first night of our return trip to Bogotá we stayed at a hotel in the heavily militarized town of Agua Chica called Don Pepe's Posada, located, according to its sign, in an excelente zona social.

Jimmy has it worked out. Just as the ancient city of Alexandria was to the poet Constantine Cavafy, so Bogotá is to him. Actually Jimmy lives in self-imposed exile, having grown up in New York City. He attended Columbia University in the 1960s but dropped out searching for a more meaningful life, first in western Ireland, then in Colombia, where he found home. So it seems fair to say he inhabits in his soul two cities. Me too, I want to say, but my other city is not Bogotá but an agribusiness town called Puerto Tejada and beyond that a territory extending over southwest Colombia, from the mangrove swamps of the Pacific over the *cordilleras* to the foothills of the Andes falling into the Amazon. I guess we could continue; Faulkner and Yoknapatawpha County, Hardy and Wessex, García Márquez and Macondo, George Eliot and Middlemarch. But these are fictional names for real places, whereas for Jimmy and me, while the place is real enough, our writing is less so. He aims at what he thinks of as the surreal 1990s into 2010, when Colombia was in his eyes a mix of soap opera, film noir, and horror film, now on "pause," while I myself zigzag between ultrarealism and irony, seeking a way out though fable and allegory. In either case the life rendered is largely unlivable and the violence unspeakable. Yet the monstrous slips away into the banal everyday of low-grade paranoia punctuated by language as exaggerated as that which such language tries in vain to tell you about.

Cavafy has a poem he wrote in 1896.

Confusion

My soul, in the middle of the night,
is confused and paralyzed. Outside:
its life comes into being outside itself

And it awaits the improbable dawn.
And I await, am worn down, and am bored,
even I who am in it or with it.

On a balcony on a brand-new high-rise facing the inky blackness of the mountains rising sheer in our face, an elegant young law professor, whiskey in hand, expounds on the history of the new Constitution of 1991. But each story requires another to explain it. We get locked into a labyrinth of interconnecting but incomplete stories in a sort of hysteria of history with the native being egged on by the outsider (me) for the sake of the newcomer (Lily). It is cold under these stars with all this glass and shiny steel around us of the New City built on top of poky redbrick two-story bourgeois homes with Tudor façades considered elegant in their day before becoming abortion clinics and brothels and then Xerox shops, universities, and rapid-delivery mail stores. Twenty-two stories below thread the lights of traffic like a string of pearls. The new Constitution came about largely because of the student movement, he says, a bunch of eighteen-year-olds, many from the Jesuit university, La Javeriana. The M-19 guerrillas came aboard later, as did the FARC guerrillas, who were ready to sign on but the government couldn't tolerate that so bombed them from the air, he explains. The government needs the guerrilla, the enemy within, the anti-Christ, their best ally, better even than the USA. The students had a stimulating conversation with the leader of the M-19 when he signed on. What was meant to be a five-minute formality extended to three hours of animated conversation. Next day he was assassinated. The stars are fiercely alive at this height although technically dead. It's just that it takes so long for their light to reach us through this cold air. A burly ex-M-19 *guerrillero* looks on but does not say much. He seems strangely absent, now a nonbeing on the wrong side of history, out of place in these shimmering towers. He belongs to the impenetrable blackness of the past, where history becomes someone else's story.

Faulkner not only told stories but told the language, something that in his case at least might have been easier because he worked in a circumscribed area that was his territory if not his home. His novels were auto-ethnographic, and the exotic lay more with his readers and his use of language moving back and forth across that thin membrane where inner and outer worlds meet and dissolve. He saw words glued to what they meant, and then he unglued them so they soared. He wrote with the limitless power of what I came to call in Colombia "multiple realities," whereby each person sees the same thing differently, like *As I Lay Dying*, in which he had separate chapters for the thoughts of each member of the dead woman's family. Susan Willis told me that Faulkner wanted the book printed such that each person's chapter would have a separate color. In my town in Colombia this multiplicity of reality became apparent to me under three conditions: stories of origins of local saints, stories of how corpses on roads into town got to be there, and stories I wrote when I started to write about these things.

Sometimes when you write field notes time stands still and an image takes its place. On occasions the image is tactile. Just about the softest thing I ever touched was powdered coca leaf prepared by the Huitoto Indians of the Igaraparaná and Caraparaná affluents of the Putumayo River, which itself runs into the Amazon. Jimmy had some coca powder in the fridge but said it was a little old to *mambear*, meaning put into your mouth with lime and hold it there a while like a wad of tobacco. It's good for writing, he says, but makes you want to chain-smoke cigarettes. But hey! Anything for writing. His kid Rafael made a phony Nobel Prize for Literature certificate and hung it on the wall above his desk. Feeling the coca powder with my finger and thumb was beautiful, like the softest velvet, resonating with the subtlety of its color between light green and gray, like stardust, if you know what I mean. Dust, that's for sure, the dust so fine it's where substance gives way to immateriality. It takes the Indians ages to make, I believe, toasting it, then mixing it with ash, then sorting it with deft hands using green leaves as funnels. These are the hands of alchemists, pharmacists of the rain forest.

Juan Alvaro, who teaches anthropology in a university deep in the Amazon, has a plastic bag of much fresher stuff than Jimmy's and uses it quite a bit. He hangs out with Huitotos and speaks their language. I have memories of him in his glassed-in penthouse in downtown Bogotá, surrounded by all manner of exotic plants such as a giant San Pedro cactus from northern Peru.

His house is like a watchtower, tilting to one side with a spiral staircase inside and a loopy old dog whose claws make scratchy noises as she clambers up and down. Modernized apartments stare at us from across the way as the trendy new-style Colombians dream of hedge funds and banking. He is sucking his finger dipped in concentrated tobacco juice at the same time as he chews on the coca powder, like Huitoto men do when they gather in a circle to talk and tell stories. He keeps the tobacco juice in a small bottle shaped like a penis. It is extremely strong. His voice is soft, like the coca powder. The ink-black tobacco juice drips down either side of his mouth as he speaks, giving him black fangs. His mouth—organ of speech—has become transformed, as has therefore his face. It is no longer a mouth but more like a cave dripping with fungi or decaying organic materials, dark green and black. No wonder he often seems a little high and drifting, but that could be because of what I take to be his mission. He wants us to gather close, *mambear*, suck tobacco juice, and have each person in turn tell their story. Years back I was told about the importance Huitotos attach to stories, the stories that abetted white conquest, and the stories of the rubber boom atrocities which, so it was said, only sorcerers listen to so as to gain power to kill people. I think Juan Alvaro is continuing this chain of storytelling as that which has the power to change the world. He wants us to change. At least a little. He wants us to live a little like Huitotos and nudge the world and especially its sense of words and language and what it is to tell a story and inhabit multiple realities. He is trying to live both like a forest Indian and as your not so regular middle-class professor intellectual. His decades of experience and his modesty make this a reality. In his quiet way he inhabits a space every bit as fictive, every bit as real, as do Faulkner and Cavafy, only he is in two places at once and has the language and drugs to make it work.

Having a place resonates with having a territory, but what if you live emotionally in two places? What sort of territory is that? And what about not having a territory or, rather, feeling you have one but you have been displaced from it so it's more a phantom territory like a phantom limb? This has happened throughout history, as with the Jews who, after two thousand years' absence, nevertheless claim they have an indisputable claim to a territory so they feel fine pushing Palestinians off, Palestinians who were actually working the land and have had a continuous, working relationship with it presumably since before the Jews fled Egypt. The Jewish sense of territory is fraught and mythic, now sustained at gunpoint, which is different from the mythic properties of what Jimmy is claiming for Cavafy in relation to Alexandria, or as regards Jimmy himself in connection with Bogotá.

It is said that in Colombia some 4 million poor country people have been forced in the past twenty years to flee from the land they cultivated and regarded as theirs. This forced displacement has been especially severe in northern Colombia, where first cattle—the armed tank of the large landowners—and now biofuels lay waste the land and the people who once farmed it. But just as the new type of large landowner moves to monocropping biofuels, cultivating African palm or sugar cane, depleting local resources and creating plantations, so there is an opposite and opposed development in which displaced or resistant peasants have come up with the idea of "territory," meaning their territory based not on commodity values but on use value bound to histories of possession based on use, on closeness to the land and now something new or newly articulated, namely conscious care for the sustainability of the environment. This is the direction or tendency of struggle now with echoes worldwide. It is similar to what Marx predicted for the proletariat, that in their coming together in ever larger factories, workers would create socialism. But it didn't happen. Yet something like this is occurring in agriculture, at least in the Third World, wherein the means of production, thought of as territory and history, are to be treasured as an end in themselves.

Powered by a small outboard engine, our canoe, known as a Johnson, pushes through brilliantly colored flowers—white, purple, and a bloody red—that spread like a floating carpet over the surface of the water. Great white herons stand solitary on one leg in haughty disdain, flying off slowly at the last minute as we approach, stretching open their enormous white wings like fans against the bright green. They are extremely clumsy and extremely graceful, catching themselves as they seem to fall. Black ducks skid across the clear brown waters. After flooding there are plenty of fish in the swamps. *Mojarra.* I got to know the taste well. This enormous area of wilderness, of swamps that go on forever, is one of the world's great and least known paradises. What a fate to plant it in African palm row after row for diesel fuel.

My law professor friend Juan Felipe García has been here in these swamps of northern Colombia fifteen times, usually accompanied by his law professor colleague Roberto Vidal. It takes two days of travel from Bogotá by plane, bus, taxi, launch, motorbike, and Johnson. They work pro bono. On either side of Juan Felipe's office in the Jesuit university in Bogotá are law professors who work as paid consultants for large landowners. "It was always the

Jesuit way," he explains. "To help the poor while at the same time sustain the system." His mission is to get the land restored to the 120 families displaced first by a drug lord, Jesus Emilio Escobar, a relative of the infamous Pablo Escobar, laundering money and growing coca. In the early 1990s in its efforts to curtail drugs the state claimed the land which thereafter lay abandoned and the peasants occupied it, claiming it should revert to them. Paramilitaries from the Bloque Central forced them off in 2003. But the peasants returned. Then Jesus Emilio returned in 2006 with an army and forced them off again. One of the wealthiest men in Santa Marta—site of Joseph Conrad's novel *Nostromo*, located far away on the Caribbean coast—bought the property or the rights to plant African palm from Jesus Emilio in 2006, and since then African palm cultivation has proceeded apace, alongside the plantations of the sons of former president Uribe, who had the Medal of Freedom bestowed on his scrawny chest by George W. Bush for his fight against terrorists.

One of the curious aspects here is that the peasants rarely held title to the land they farmed, and if bought out by the rich it was not the land but the so-called *mejoras* or improvements that were sold. You have to, first, ask yourself why the peasants did not acquire title and, second, see in this not merely neglect, ignorance, or lack of means to deal with bureaucracy or pay a lawyer but also a clash of civilizations, one based on writing and the state, the other based on knowing the land and claiming it through working it.

Juan Felipe and Roberto have won the first legal battle. The case went to the top court in the land, the Constitutional Court, which held that the use of riot police to force the peasants off the land, for the third time in the past thirty years, was illegal. Now the decision as to who can claim ownership rests with a government-appointed institute until recently stacked with the paramilitary friends of ex-president Uribe.

Photographs shown me by the peasants of their confrontation with the riot police are mythic in their reach. The police are encased head to toe in dark blue riot gear, like the exoskeleton of some primeval reptile. They stand shoulder to shoulder, faces impassive, clubs at the ready, looking out at nothing, holding large shields to the side, their faces smoothly shaven, plump, and pink, while the unarmed peasants, half their size, skin burnt by a life in the sun, stand and squat at all angles, awaiting the first move. It took at least an hour for the ring of police to slowly advance, step by step, towards the hacienda building to make the peasants leave. It is strange to see such police in the swamps, far from the city that is their customary habitat, just as it is now strange to have the peasants hand me these photographs and be propelled back in time to this decisive moment. Both the riot police in their caiman-like gear and the photographs compress time, abutting the prehistoric life of the swamp with the leviathan of the modern state.

In the village of Buenos Aires on the river before I got to this camp I had seen a video of a similar confrontation showing the dark-skinned lawyer of the *palmeros*—as the African palm plantation owners are known—with his bodyguards berating the peasants with all manner of high-flown legalese to make them leave. I was with Misael's family. Every now and then someone watching the video with me would make a comment. The past is not what it used to be, not with video cameras on hand.

A neurologically disturbed mute girl, perhaps like this since birth, age about eighteen, would walk back and forth and occasionally come in and glance at the video, wringing her twisted hands, her arms knotted with tension. She would sit and lie in a sand pit made especially for her so she could carve ephemeral shapes back and forth. Outside on the one street constituting the village, two small girls age ten or so were making castles or mansions in the sand, decorated with flowers. A small boy whose mother took off unannounced one day and abandoned her family so as to go to the USA was nursing a broken arm. He had been taken by Johnson all the way downstream to El Banco and from there by ambulance all the way to Santa Marta to have it set and put in plaster. An epic journey.

The peasants first came to this region with their burros in the 1920s, exploring the tributaries and winding rivulets of the Magdalena. Living in these vast swamps of mud and floating plants, the peasants became amphibious, adapted to the rise and fall of the waters as had the Indians long before them. I have even seen suggestion of an "amphibious mode of production" in Orlando Fals-Borda's 1978 three-volume study, *Historia doble de la costa*, an experimental historical ethnography that, amphibious in its own right, puts travelers' tales, anecdotal observations, and phenomenological impressions on the left-hand page and social sciencey stuff on the right—hence *historia doble*. It is incredible how dated the right-hand side has become, testimony to our need for theory and how boring it can become, while the left-hand side seems to increase its power over time, like a good wine.

Something else stands out with this amphibiousness that is every bit as exciting, every bit as enchanting, as the romantic idea of *nomadism*, and that is the role in history of people who live in or close to swamps and changing water levels at the mouths of great rivers. Much of world history includes such folk, and much of world history and now its impending disasters can be summed up not only as the clearing of the world's forests but also as the drainage of and building walls against rivers.

To live in the swamp bespeaks enormous adaptability and working with the environment, not against it as we find in such graphic detail with the dikes along the Mississippi and the wreckage caused not by Katrina per se but as a result of building up the mouth of that mighty river with oil refineries and cities based on assumptions as to the advantage if not necessity of stable and fixed homes and property in land and buildings.

What appears now as a devastating blow to amphibiousness and what it implies for living with, and not against, nature, is African palm, which, unlike other crops, can withstand flooding and does well in swampland while destroying it. Huge swaths of Colombia and the tropics fall victim to this hunger for biofuel. Clearing the swampland for these plantations is said to release enormous amounts of carbon dioxide such that the net effect is to enhance global warming.

What is also lost is the everyday peasant and indigenous knowledge of living in harmony with water and floods, something that will prove increasingly necessary as sea levels rise along with the increased use of biofuels to power motor vehicles.

Juan Felipe brings official maps. He wants the peasants to check and annotate them with historical referents and discuss a map of utopia showing how the territory would be used if they were able to get it back, complete with new artificial waterways for transport, a swamp reserve of forest, replanting trees along with land set aside for private plots of rice, yucca, and cattle. The peasants call him "Profe" as in *professor*, a term of endearment and respect.

Everyone but the children gathers. Don Efraín starts a prayer. It is early morning and still cool. "We have to create a new language," says Juan Felipe. "The *palmeros* have theirs, and we need to show the world an alternate model." Then he asks, "Who recalls the founding of the village of Buenos Aires?" A man steps forth, puts his elbows on the table while standing, and starts a lengthy genealogy. Don Efraín writes it all down. The witness has his back to the audience and is speaking very softly. Then another elderly man lists all the houses, one by one. It seems tedious to me, but there are guffaws and rippling mirth. Misael asks four elderly men to name the houses in the *calle atras*. We are off on a journey through time, threading names and events onto a new map of swampland territory.

Don Efraín, around sixty, finds it hard to walk due to a misplaced injection in his buttocks when he was a kid. In a physically taxing world this is a problem, but he somehow compensates by being the scribe of this little community living in jeopardy, squatting on the land they consider theirs but now being planted in African palm. He keeps a daily journal and has drawn his own map, which he shows me. What did he do before the troubles started, I wonder, when perhaps a chronicler was not necessary, and why does he do this? I see one entry in the journal which begins with "Today was a day full of promise." It is, I suppose, no surprise that he has tremendous knowledge of the region, as expressed in his map and ensuing discussions about it.

His map accentuates the cemetery, the crops, and the "beaches," which I guess are the fertile levees along the rivers that, if memory serves me right, are like common lands and cannot be alienated. Efraín's map is as much a text as a visual diagram, more a mimesis than an abstract diagram in that it strives to bring out the use, meaning, history, and utopic future of the land and settlements. His map is messy and differs a great deal from the official maps on account of its abundance of information and something like love or at least intimacy.

The maps are placed on a crude table chest high, and the men cluster around, then drift away after an hour, leaving the discussion to a handful of elders and the scribe. There are no women, other than those young and middle-aged women tending great tubs of fish and yucca. As the sun gathers force, excitement around the maps wanes. Heat rises under the black plastic ceiling.

Two kids four years old are playing in the dirt to one side of us, making their own sort of map, an imaginary road system for their cars, two old cans of tuna. Why tuna? Aren't there loads of fish here? The label on their underpants is visible. It says "American Rangers." Kids, pigs, and dogs roll around together in spiraling confusion. The pond in front of us is covered with thick green slime and at night there are so many frogs croaking you can barely think.

Much of the week the peasants live in a village on the edge of a river called the Brazuelo de Papayal, which runs into the Magdalena. But to keep alive their moral if not legal right to territory, they built this tent city two hours' walk away (at their speed of walking), right next to the hacienda building built by the *palmeros*, or African palm cultivators who dispute their claims. They have divided into three such that every two to three days a new group stays in the tent city and the others remain in the village by the river. I see a young man and woman walking back through the swamp carrying their belongings in a large plastic trash bag. No LL Bean or North Face wilderness gear for these folk, the real denizens of the wilderness, physical and political.

At sunset the peasants form a guard along the fence dividing this black plastic encampment from the hacienda building in which three or four employees of the African palm growers reside. I look for a place to take a shit and find there is none, or rather everywhere is possible, and am pointed vaguely to a field full of young African palms, like fat pineapples, in neat rows. It is hard to walk anywhere because of the mud. Once I had to get hauled out when my calf-high rubber boots stuck in the mud. It is satisfying—indeed a sublimely revolutionary act, is it not?—to shit in their palm field as the sun sets over the ridge. I am told that a guard made of Indians all the way from Cauca in the south of the country have been here, armed with nothing but their staves to provide support, and there is a group of Swiss who do the same thing frequently, "bearing witness," as they say. In my cynical way I ask why not have three German sanitary engineers here for a week to make some toilets? I'll take that over people bearing witness any time.

Looking out over the squat African palms I sit with six of the younger men sprawled on a piece of farm equipment quietly watching the colors in the sky. The mood has shifted from the practical to the poetic, like shitting in the palm field. Alexander is here, age twenty-nine. I call him "the poet." He has no job, he says, and has never worked. His father allowed him to finish high school, and that he did at twenty-three. How can I understand his not working? The valleys in the far-off ridges of what I take to be the *serranía* of San Lucas fill with a golden haze, while along the hilltops the gold forms a thin ribbon running along the bluish green of the hills. Not a word passes between us. Triggered by the hysterically ascending price for gold, the serranía is now subject to a gold craze, with miners using mercury that gets into the waterways here, a man told me. But not much, he adds. The serranía is also the home for the guerrillas, first the ELN and then the FARC. All that is there, on the horizon. And now the whole sky is flecked, purple and red. Meanwhile the employees of the hacienda switch on an electric generator, which makes a terrible racket. Their lights will glare the whole night long, making our sleep difficult. It is all so strange: our camp and their camp, cheek by jowl, our camp of black plastic sheeting, theirs a solid-looking hacienda building with a powerful backhoe as its guardian. It gets stranger still, as two of the men hired by the hacienda are accomplished accordion players who join us on our return canoe trip, complete with *tambor* and *aguardiente*. Best of pals.

As the darkness gathers I decide to copy Lily, who has been accompanied by a group of women to a bathing place by the side of the African palms. I walk through the mud with a flashlight accompanied by a one-armed young man named José who appears out of nowhere. We reach a small pond the size of a bathtub four feet down a muddy slope that has crude, slippery steps set into it. He holds my hand in his good hand. I slip as I descend. His grip is firm and comforting. It is pitch black. He wears swimming trunks and nothing else. With infinite care I take off one sandal, then another. Then he hands me a container for scooping up the muddy water so as to douse myself. Out of fear of offending him I do not strip completely naked. Then like a crab I make my way up again. This one-armed gentle man who appeared out of nowhere has become my guardian angel.

Only 30 percent of the people are behind this movement to claim territory, Juan Felipe tells me, and they are mainly middle-aged and elderly. What's up with the rest? I wonder. Coming to this place in the Johnson took about five hours as the motor refused to start. The current was with us. We drifted as the *motorista*, sweating profusely, tried again and again to yank the motor into action. Up front sang the balladeer. He answers my questions with songs of violence and violation, of betrayal by the "black Judas" who swore a deposition in the state capital, Cartagena, that the peasants had not been forcibly displaced, this same Judas who now has a salaried job with the African palm owners. Sung in a high falsetto, like Woody Guthrie, these *vallenatos* sung to a Hohner accordion (always a Hohner; always from the same town in Germany), are famous throughout the north of Colombia as songs of protest as much as of love and betrayal. The hours pass. The sun beats down. The great white herons spread their wings like the swan enrapturing Leda as we float downstream through the floating verdure. He sings of the paramilitaries and the terror they create, chopping up bodies and heaving them into the river we are floating on with its vivid flowers. He stops singing for a moment and tells me how, when swimming in this river, he felt an arm and then a hand clutching at his throat. I don't believe a word of it. Why exaggerate like this? Did I hear right? Then he starts singing again. We stop to fix the motor at a bunch of houses made of packed mud. A stout schoolteacher joins us. Her blood pressure fell suddenly, and she was taken here for medical attention. The conversation turns once again to the violent and bizarre, stage 2, you might say, of an ongoing dialogue as the canoe, now moving briskly, raises a fine spray in a glistening arc overhead. What would the Huitotos say about this? Are we like the sorcerers, gathering tales of atrocity with which to empower ourselves? What is our humanism, really? Why do we gorge ourselves on these stories? What of Walter Benjamin and his claim—at once dubious and convincing—that storytelling is a dead art, especially in times of war? Why do they put the bodies in the river? I ask. Because they won't let them be buried, she replies. This takes time to sink in. Life is important, but I get the feeling burial is more so. Don't Vico and Bataille see in burial the first sign of culture, the first sign of being human? Therefore not to bury and, even more, to refuse burial strikes at the heart of life, human life, that is, what separates whatever it is we designate "human" from non-human, meaning not only animal but also the inhuman. Yet the inhuman is every bit as religious, every bit as sacred as the pious rites that help move the corpse from its frightening negative state to that of hallowed ground. Is it not this arc of sanctification of the corpse that lies at the center of its disposal not in the graveyard but in the river? A body is the ultimate territory, and a chopped-up corpse adrift in the river is the absolute denial of such territory, the deepest possible exile of the soul. Thus does deterritorialization achieve its most definitive state of non-being. Could this be why the counterforce claiming territory as mythical power is now every day ascendant in Colombia, after two decades of paramilitary violence aimed at dismembering both land and body?

The territory of the body, that is the corpse, is not lost on Vladimir either. He is an ex-paramilitary who deserted through fear and, of all things, because he hated oatmeal for breakfast. I can't stand *avena*, he explains. He was recruited in Caicedonia in the Valle and was taken to a training school lasting forty-five days near Libano in Tolima. He spares no detail. They cut open the body of a guerrilla fighter, stuffed it with cocaine, and drove it to Medellin in a hearse. Another time he was working on a dairy farm in Antioquia and had to walk somewhere at three in the morning. He saw headlights of three pickup trucks in a stream and then he saw two bodies, one being cut to pieces with a belt around the man's mouth to stop him screaming. The other man was dead, and his body was being packed with what most likely was cocaine. Vladimir crept past. Walking up the hill he heard the sound of a motorbike of *alto cylindrage* coming down the hill, *muy suave*. The driver stopped and asked him if he'd seen anything down at the stream. Oh no! He replied. Are you sure? Of course I'm sure.

The tent city, like the hacienda building next to it, is built on a platform about three hundred feet square and thirty inches high so as to resist floodwaters, and I am told it was used for dwellings and cultivation in pre-Colombian times. It is marvelous to be on this platform continuing a tradition one thousand or more years old, yet so modest, a mere raising of levels. Misael brings out two stone cutting tools he has discovered there, about five inches long. They are surprisingly heavy. It is strange to live in this gridwork of black plastic homes erected on pre-Colombian earthworks with heavy stone tools scattered around. I recommend it to anyone in search of a territory in this modern age—the permanence of the earth below, itself an artifact, sustaining the impermanence of the black glistening plastic shelters above.

It must seem frivolous if I pause to consider my fieldwork notebook as territory in this sense too, but then is not the notebook as much our means of production as is the watery land the peasants work as use value? Might this be even more so as regards the phantom land that, now displaced, is filled with turbulence and hope of redemption every bit as glowing as those ridges of the serranía de San Lucas, with the sky now flecking purple and red? And just as land as territory is a lot more than means to an end, can we not say the same about the fieldwork notebook, which quickly becomes an end in itself, a veritable fetish cherished as a work not only of documentation but of secret signs and even art as well?

I had been thinking along these lines for several years, ever since I published in 2003 a diary of two weeks in a Colombian town in 2001 taken over by hired killers identified by many as paramilitaries. In reorganizing my diary of those two weeks so as to create a book, I realized that an ethnographic notebook or diary can mean very different things and be written in a great variety of ways, such that in the final analysis the very notions of the Self to whom one purportedly writes dissolves no less than the meaning of writing and representation along with—and this is crucial—the events and thoughts depicted. A diary thereby matches the fragmented and multiple nature of social reality, analogous to the terror I experienced in Colombia. I came across a note in my notebook of this trip into the swamp that read, "These trips become as much a trip into one's past and into one's being as they are journeys into the unknown. What effort must be expended by travelers and anthropologists to ignore this."

Aspects of this came to light for me when a student at CalArts directed me many years back toward Brion Gysin and William Burroughs's 1961 scrapbooks based on what Gysin called the cut-up principle. With that I got to thinking about fieldwork notebooks as having the potential—at least the potential—to be considered modernist art objects, fetishes, talismans, and, like any true collection, according to Benjamin, magic encyclopedias with some divinatory power.

Here Benjamin's radio stories for children and his concepts of *colportage* and the *Denkbilden* are relevant. The colportage strategy or disposition was to mix walking the city, taking drugs, and cinematic montage into a mode of perception and representation. The Denkbilden, or "thought figures"—as hit upon in his two summers in Ibiza in 1932 and 1933—combined surrealist juxtapositions of experience with philosophical observations or aphorisms coupled to combinations and permutations of ethnography, recording of stories, drug experiences, recording of dreams, and making up one's own stories. He had already tried something like this in his small book of 1928 entitled *One Way Street*, but the trips to what he thought of as an "outpost" of Europe, namely Ibiza, brought this to a head.

All this suggests—like Clifford and Marcus's *Writing Culture* and, before that, Marcus and Fischer's *Anthropology as Cultural Critique*—that field-work is inseparable from writing work and that the notebook has its own riches of form and content that cannot and should not be seen as mere stepping stones to the polished end product of a book or article.

If there is something absurd if not insulting about ethnographic writing based on two days and two nights, with some additional material based on notes from the days prior, is it not also the case that first impressions are generally more vivid than subsequent ones? What are we to make of this? And what of the responsibility to oneself as much as one's hosts to put something of those impressions out into the world, together with the responsibility to get it right? Most of all, what is that urge that compels one to put order into experience, as Graham Greene once described his novels? I understand that *The Power and the Glory* is based on a mere six weeks' travel in southern Mexico, yet it reads as if he had spent years. But if he had, maybe his senses would have dulled.

To this it should be noted that what happens when notes are "written up" is that what I call "afterthoughts" kick in. By afterthoughts I mean secondary elaborations that arise on top of the original notes, photographs, and drawings. Through stops, starts, and sudden swerves the original is pulled into a wider landscape. To reread and to rewrite is to tug at the memories buried therein as well as engage with the gaps, questions, connections, conundrums, and big ideas that lie latent and in turn generate more of the same. In essence this chapter is exactly that, a fifteen-page afterthought that, with the passage of three weeks, has slipped away from its moorings while preserving the imprimatur if not the character of the original.

I feel impelled to ask, therefore, if anthropology has sold itself short in conforming to the idea that its main vehicle of expression is an academic book or a journal article? This is not a plea for exact reproduction of the fieldwork notebook but rather a plea for following its forms and its mix of private and public in what can only be called, as in cinema, a "dissolve" or "fade-out" that captures ephemeral realities, the check and bluff of life.

At the end of the day one is left with an image of a cocaine-rich man with a checkbook and a lawyer turning up one day in the swamp saying it's all his now, recorded in the deed book of properties in far-off Cartagena, capital of the state, a walled port built over two centuries by slaves from Africa baptized by the Jesuits in the cathedral of San Pedro Claver. Other rich men follow in order to plant African palm in neat rows for diesel fuel to power the endless stream of trucks running north and south night and day along the highway connecting Barranquilla, the port at the mouth of the Magdalena, with the interior. The trucks are beautifully illuminated with row after row of twinkling lights and full of mystery. The landlords build roads through the swamp that interrupt the flow of waters. A songster sings of feeling a chopped-off arm and hand clutching at his throat while he swims in the river. The more swamp the men with the checkbooks take, however, the more they provoke an idea of territory in place of alienable land, territory meaning a place with a history that, depending on your outlook, is evidenced by Indian earthworks going way back in time, or black plastic villages where now the map is being rewritten as memory opens like the fan of the great white wings of the heron against the green of the swamp.

CHAPTER 8

Ethnography Is,

Ethnography Ain't

John L. Jackson Jr.

The Death of Marlon Riggs

I remember watching Marlon Riggs dying. It was 1994, and I was in graduate school, quite literally so, scrutinizing his ghostly image in a classroom on the fourth floor of Schermerhorn Extension, the building that houses Columbia University's Department of Anthropology.

The dying, the death, was no less real for its unviewed finale or for the fact that I witnessed it by way of a rolled-out video console's totemic stacking of a TV monitor atop multiple VHS players, audio-video wires and power cords dangling carelessly off the sides.

In a form of filmic reflexivity far more rigorous than anything I'd seen before, Riggs, a controversial documentarian who'd already been denounced on the floor of the U.S. Congress as a pervert undeserving of government funding for his previous film, *Tongues Untied* (1989), a meditation on black gay manhood, had decided to use his final documentary, *Black Is, Black Ain't* (1994), a film on the *openness*, although not the *emptiness*, of blackness as a signifier, to chronicle his own end, his own death, his body more and more emaciated from the HIV virus with every passing scene.

Black Is, Black Ain't, anthropological in its luscious holism, flags and chronicles all the overdetermined markers (even clichés) of purported blacknesses: hair textures, facial features, skin tones, striding gaits, musical genres, political histories, vernacular legends, existential anxieties, stereotyped burdens, sexist acculturations—everything, including shots of kitchen sinks, the preparation of gumbo, a southern Louisianan stew, being its central metaphor of African American eclecticism and heterogeneity.

By the end of the film, however, a couple of images haunt most: out-of-focus shots of a bony Riggs, naked and alone, jogging, as best his sickly body could, through sunlit woods; and a bedridden and hospitalized Riggs, effort-fully explaining how he wants his film to end, an ending that he himself would most certainly not witness. Riggs's narration, by the final few sequences of the film, is punctuated by precise calculations of plunging T-cell counts and lost body weight, a heating pad on his bloated and nondigesting stomach, nods to the slow-moving finalities and mutating materialities of human life, what Emerson once called "the irresistible democracy" of physical decomposition itself, of all earth going back to earth—ashes to ashes, dust to dust.

I have always considered *Black Is, Black Ain't* an illicit and uncanny auto-ethnography of courageous strangeness, especially with its mesmeric ability to cast its viewers as unrepentant and willing voyeurs. And I eased into my own willingness on that score, locking eyes on death and refusing to turn away, unable to do so. It is the kind of hyperreflexive film that pricks and prods at the soul, offering (at least to me) an early trip to one mass-mediated field site from which a portion of my own anthropological subconscious has never completely returned.

Several years later I would get my first chance to see Barbara Myerhoff's filmic depiction of her own demise, the 1985 offering *In Her Own Time*, a meditation on her relationship to Judaism, released about a year before the publication of *Writing Culture*, the volume that helped to foreground reflex-ivity as one of anthropology's central interventions, concomitantly energizing the field's main flank for cross-disciplinary ridicule: its supposed solipsism, a disciplinary reflexivity purportedly taken to unhealthy extremes. Myerhoff's film is not cited and invoked nearly as much as it could be, for reasons that might have to do with how it carries its investment in reflexivity—a reflexiv-ity that is as much *art* as science.

Devouring *Writing Culture* had me chomping at the bit to conduct my own ethnographic fieldwork. Admittedly less because of the intrinsic lure, the interactive rough-and-tumble of "the field" (with its sometimes threat-ening and unwieldy exchanges, the kinds of exchanges for which I conjured up Anthroman, my ethnographic alter ego) and more because of the license the book provided for thinking unabashedly about writing itself, nailing shut the centrality of anthropological assumptions about ethnographic mono-graphs as unproblematically transparent windows onto some cultural tundra out there beyond the text. It meant a valuable black-boxification or surre-alization of ethnographic representation (as opposed to what I considered qualitative sociology's more positivist longings), even as it meticulously set about delineating the writerly techniques used for manufacturing scientific authority in the first place. This seemed like a powerful paradox: explication and mystification at one and the same time. Although the accompanying critiques of its racial and gendered exclusions (from scholars such as Faye Harrison and others) seemed legitimate,[1] I was still determined to write myself into the writing culture project, to embrace its flights of representational fancy, unabashedly recognizing the inescapable aesthetics of all anthropological writing, a social science (like any other social science) coproduced through rhetorical flourishes and even literary artistry.

Anna Grimshaw describes the difference between an oft-disparaged *aesthetics* and the aspirational objectivity of a truly social *science* as one of the foundational fault lines disqualifying filmic offerings from their rightful place in the academy.[2] For some readers, the discussion might hearken back to the time Clifford Geertz famously chastised researchers for trafficking in "intuitionism and alchemy" or mere "sociological aestheticism."[3] Such concerns and critiques would help explain, Grimshaw argues, why even though anthropologists have used film and then video technology in ethnographic endeavors since the early twentieth century, the American Anthropological Association would still need to put out a statement almost a hundred years later imploring academic institutions to take films into account when assessing scholars for tenure and promotion. It is one of the reasons ethnographic films aren't given nearly the same weighty significance as books or articles in most academic contexts. The filmic's problem, she might say, is that it always bends toward the aesthetic, the emotive, the artistic, the affective, and maybe even, as Thomas Csordas would put it, the "preobjective."[4] This aestheticization of anthropological inquiry has always been, for a contingent of anthropologists, precisely what beckoned, seductively, and *Writing Culture* represented a critical point of entry into substantive engagements with such scholarly desires.

John Durham Peters argues that new media technologies, from telegraphy to the telephone, radio to television, photography to film, have always been predicated on an attempt to beat back death, to transcend our own mortality (indeed, he'd add, even our own humanity) in search of ways to finally communicate like (and to) angels or gods—unmediated, without the tawdry materiality of signifiers, smashing our way through the walled-in interiorities that ostensibly separate and alienate us from one another.[5] All media communication is, in a sense, communication with the dead, he says, which is one interpretation of what Roland Barthes claims about the indexicality of photographs: that they are all really spirit photographs, glimpses of our own pending death and a way to see across that great veil. It is an attempt to watch ourselves dying.[6]

Riggs muses about his film providing for a certain transcendence of death, even as he invokes the loving caresses of family members as what will ultimately allow him to die in peace. Increasingly "the filmic" serves as a central instantiation of culture, the ubiquitous metacultural fact of contemporary existence, as my Penn colleague Greg Urban might frame things.[7] This is a notion of the filmic that is increasingly tied to the nonlinear, temporally textured, and even potentially death-defying logics of new digital technologies—the "digital" boasting almost fetishistic powers in some contemporary scholarly evocations. What does this "digital" imply for the writing of culture today? To what extent is watching Riggs's film (via VHS tape, admittedly, not DVD) a necessary component of what it might mean to study "culture" in the twenty-first century? And how does one write up such viewings, even before one begins to play with the possibility of filming them? What kind of writing does the potential digitizalization of culture demand and afford?

The Time Machine

Early in this new millennium a group of bearded men from a seemingly eccentric spiritual community based in southern Israel approached a successful African American entrepreneur with a business proposition. The Philadelphia-based businessman knew very little about these men's lives or about the transnational group that they represented, but he was intrigued by the ambitiousness of their pitch. The relational terms of their proposal would change radically over time (from a request for hands-off venture capital to more collaborative configurations of cross-Atlantic partnership to a final scenario that found the American businessman and his family playing a decidedly leading role in the entire endeavor), but the idea itself, the intended enterprise, was clear and fixed.

The men from Israel wanted help procuring rights to sell and lease an invention that imperceptibly and automatically shortens television programs, allowing networks and cable outlets to add even more minutes of advertising time to their daily broadcasts. This relatively new apparatus did not delete entire scenes or large contiguous sequences from shows, one traditional (and fairly conspicuous) technique that networks deploy to "reformat" theatrical motion pictures so that they fit television's conventional scheduling mandates. The technology was also far more sophisticated than earlier inventions that attempted to squeeze films into advertisement-punctuated time slots by speeding up certain sections, another simple (although sometimes distractingly noticeable) way to decrease a show's overall running time.

These men were pushing for the proprietary acquisition of a newfangled mechanical device based on advanced digital technology, and they walked their potential business partner through the specifics, providing details about the machine they coveted, which works at the unit of the frame, prescanning and digitizing material and intermittently eliminating single "redundant" frames that function as duplicates to the human eye, making the deletions nearly imperceptible. There are enough "redundant" frames in the rebroadcast of an average feature-length motion picture or football game to open up space for several additional thirty-second ads—and without any substantive impact on narrative content or temporal flow. The machine offers a way to profit on media outlets' predictable interest in subtler ways of squeezing more advertising revenue out of every standard hour of commercial television, selling a way to game the media system itself (by hyperexploiting its dependence on advertisers). In some ways the men's social lives back in Israel's Negev region help to explain some of the reasons why they might be interested in this bit of technology—and motivated to capitalize on a media industry's cultural logic that productively interfaces with their own.

I invoke this short rendition of a tale about one business arrangement organized around a piece of media equipment that precisely manipulates temporality (by appearing not to do so) as a way to begin discussing how such new technologies reframe and reformat traditional (predigital?) formulations of diasporic community—and of ethnographic representation. In a manner akin to the difference in scale between, say, a *scene* and its constitutive *frames*, a difference most easily (even automatically) exploitable by digital technologies like the gizmo designed to intricately trim programs without noticeably impacting story lines or frustrating the visual and auditory aspects of our sensorium, I intend this brief chapter to evoke some of the ways we might construct a productive conversation about reconfigurations of ethnographic time and space through digitality and its varied deployments.[8] Indeed all I want to highlight here is a simple (although somewhat controversial) claim that "the diasporic" and "the ethnographic" have, in a sense, gone "digital" as advanced modalities of mass mediatization create and re-create forms of sociality and even intimacy that demand and reward critical attention. Of course, this digitalization is disproportionately distributed. Even as arguments are proffered about "digital diasporas" not being simplistic extensions of, say, race-based "digital divides," the digital can still have ethnocentric inflections when uncritically presumed to be the sort of universalist rubric that it is not.[9]

The men who approached that would-be financier in 2002 have a particularly interesting diasporic tale themselves. They were emissaries from a group of African American expatriates who emigrated from the United States to Liberia in 1967 before finally moving to Israel in 1969, where they have resided ever since. This group, the African Hebrew Israelites of Jerusalem (AHIJ), provides one example of what a notion of "digital diaspora" helps to capture. Digital and "new media" technologies provide the glue that keeps their deterritorialized spiritual community together, a community that spans four continents and continues to successfully compel new people to join its ranks.

It is not just happenstance that such a group would gravitate to new technological innovations predicated on reframed temporalities. Their own time travel (including "exodus" from a Babylonian America, sojourn in the "wilderness" of Liberia, and eventual resettlement in "the promised land," a modern state of Israel regeographized as "northeast Africa") is based on a robustly refashioned sense of temporal possibility, on a contemporization of the Old Testament story of ancient Israelites, considered genealogical forebears by the AHIJ community. I will leave a closer interrogation of the community's subtle rereading of the Old Testament to another time. In this short piece I simply wish to juxtapose various frames and scenes of mass mediatization that constitute the community's present diasporic regime with a claim about how the ethnographic gambit itself is implicated in such a discussion. AHIJ community members travel transnationally, and it is their implementation of the newest media technology (online radio shows, community-maintained websites, YouTube uploads, the circulation of community-produced digital-film content) that provides some of the most powerful mechanisms for cultivating forms of commonality and mutual investment that have allowed this emigrationist community to survive for over forty years.

I would like readers to interpret the series of short sections that follow as constitutive *frames* for thinking through various forms of digital mediatization that overdetermine ethnographic practice in the contemporary moment. This is an invocation of *frame* both in the sense of a gesture toward contextualization (a conceptual framing of the relevant issues) and a singular impression captured in time (as in the presentation of a framed painting or the relative irreducibility of a film or video still). But this capturing is not meant to invoke a kind of taxidermy, an unchanging and lifeless simulation of inert and frozen lived realities. As Bhabha, Clifford, and others have reminded us, diasporic and minoritarian temporalities are always (to use a Taussigian term) "nervous" with movement and agitation, recursive and fractal organizing principles that offer nonlinear logics of diachronic possibility—nonlinearity being one version of the digital's fundamental difference. Kara Keeling argues that such nonlinearity (assumptions about differential access to nonchronological temporal logics) has long determined Africana exclusions from modern Western subjecthood, the latter getting mapped onto a purportedly linear trajectory called "progress." Keeling's point is that the Africana exception is increasingly becoming the global rule, providing angst and existential nervousness for those newly nonlinearized through the rise of digitality.[10] What might be called "ethnographic temporalities" have a similar nervousness, and Keeling's claims have implications for both ethnographic and diasporic discussions. My mobilization of the *frame* intends to channel Keeling's point while also providing a productive metaphor for marking what Brian Axel calls (in his conceptualization of diaspora) "disparate temporalities (anteriorities, presents, futurities), displacements, and subjects."[11] I offer these frames, then, as building blocks for an analytical montage that provides a quick look at some of the concatenations and imbrications that constitute diasporic and ethnographic possibility today.

The Audio-Visual Truth Center

The African Hebrew Israelites of Jerusalem are based in Dimona, but "saints," as adherents are called, can be found throughout Israel and all around the world. Community members spent the 1970s and 1980s as "temporary residents" in Israel, which meant that they received little governmental assistance and were banned from legal employment. They worked anyway, often doing construction jobs off the books, secretly building homes for nomadic African Bedouin forced into sedentary living by a census-taking and tax-collecting Israeli state. They would sometimes get rounded up and deported to the United States while out on such jobs, which necessitated concocting elaborate (and sometimes illegal) schemes for their successful return to Israel's Negev region.

The AHIJ extends beyond contemporary Israel, consisting of satellite communities all around the world. If 2,500 to 3,500 saints currently reside in Israel (some claim as many as 5,000), many more make their homes abroad in the West Indies, Africa, Europe, and the United States. The group has official "extensions" all across the United States (Chicago, Atlanta, and Washington, D.C., being three of the largest communities) and semiofficial (or rising) communities in other parts of the world, including Ghana, South Africa, and Benin.

The AHIJ's Ministry of Information rests on the edge of their compound in Dimona, one of the many corrugated steel and cement edifices that encircle a small concrete lot at the center of their *kfar* (village). The Ministry is linked to the School of the Prophets Institute (the community's own self-accredited tertiary educational, or "dedicational," institution) and encompasses the Audio-Visual Truth Center (AVTC), their media-production arm. The latter is where I would spend much of my ethnographic time during stints in Israel, talking with the saints who run the media facilities and looking at their vast video collection.

The AHIJ are incredibly purposeful self-archivists, which means that they videotape many of the community's annual holidays, including the New World Passover ceremony, a festive two-day event commemorating the original group's departure from the United States in 1967. The AVTC captures special events with Ben Ammi, the group's Messiah, all around the kfar and the country, and they record relevant programming from various U.S. and European satellite television channels. Consequently their video facility contains thousands of hours of video footage in DVD and VHS formats, the majority of that material videotaped by the saints themselves. Several young members of the community are filmmakers (taking classes at nearby schools and developing their craft on community-based productions), and they are the ones responsible for many of the film and video shoots organized out of the AVTC (in consultation with the minister of information, the *sar*, who oversees the entire operation). When Bobby Brown and Whitney Houston visited the group in 2002, an event that received international media attention, the entire visit was chronicled by AVTC producers in digital video with hours and hours of footage. When a new kfar-like complex was completed in Benin, a grand elaboration on the Dimona version and fully designed by saints from the community, AVTC made sure to videotape the entire site, even before it was fully functional, profiling its many institutional features (banquet halls, manufacturing facilities, farming areas, classrooms, etc.), capturing its vast size (which dwarfs the Dimona kfar), and describing its potential impact on Benin, culturally and economically.

For a community sensitive about its public image and prone to being dismissed as a cult, the Ministry of Information and AVTC (in conjunction with the community's Public Relations Office) are ground zero for discursive counterattacks against accusations of pathology and criminality. Just a few months after my first visit to the community, the *Jerusalem Post* ran an article, "Distrust in Dimona," reporting that Israel's National Insurance Institute (NII) had placed an undercover agent inside the AHIJ community to investigate rumors that saints were filing fraudulent benefit claims allegedly worth millions of dollars.[12] The FBI and the U.S. State Department were said to be collaborating with the NII on the investigation.

Early in the twenty-first century the AHIJ were finally given permanent residency status (an attempt to "normalize" their links to Israel and explicitly formalize their path to full citizenship), which meant that they were newly eligible to file for NII benefits. According to the *Jerusalem Post* article, "Israeli authorities" expressed concern about the fact "that they couldn't gauge the community's exact population, as estimates range from 2,000 to 4,000. (Again, some claim as many as 5,000 in 2012.) Even now, while the adults who have received permanent resident status have identity numbers, the community's size is impossible to determine. The children are born within the community, without the use of hospitals or conventional medicine—and, of more concern to the NII, with no official listing. Authorities have no accurate way of registering newborn babies or deaths." The community's relative impenetrability to the state's prying eyes is consistently deemed one of its more threatening features in such recurring news stories and investigative reports. Indeed calls to make them full citizens are at least partially predicated on the idea that such a move might finally create a kind of social transparency more amenable to bureaucratic inspection.

There have even been ongoing allegations that the community's leaders were explicitly encouraging different AHIJ women to register the same children with NII officials under distinctive names so that the community could receive multiple benefits. The article lists many of these claims but provides no hard proof, only speculation based on the group's relative secrecy and opacity. Still, the community is on guard against such negative press, and the Ministry of Information (through the AVTC) is charged with helping to disseminate counternarratives of AHIJ's successes and positive strides, which is why some detractors might dismiss their media productions as little more than propaganda. These productions are usually pitched to two sets of viewers: saints in the kingdom (in the Dimona kfar and all around the world) and outsiders who might be prone to dismissing them as a crazy cult (for relocating from the South Side of Chicago to southern Israel and for their claim that African

Americans are genealogical descendants of ancient Israelites, the latter serving as justification for the former). The way their media productions negotiate the differences between those two audiences pivots on a fine-grained appreciation of temporal and discursive elasticities that both bind and banish.

The Birthday DVD

When Nasi Asiel Ben Israel, the AHIJ's international ambassador plenipoten-tiary extraordinaire, turned sixty-five, the community's Audio-Visual Truth Center produced a forty-minute documentary about his life.[13] This video narrates his birth (as Warren Brown) on the South Side of Chicago in the early 1940s and his early childhood in the infamous Ida B. Wells housing project. His individual story is told in the context of a larger African American narrative highlighting the Great Migration of black southerners to the urban North, the brutal murder of Emmett Till, the creation of Motown Records, the Sixteenth Street church bombing, Rosa Parks's refusal to re-linquish her seat at the front of a public bus, and the founding of the Black Panther Party for Self-Defense, all canonized aspects of most retellings of African American life in the twentieth century.

The documentary also covers Brown's graduation from Dunbar High School (at the top of his class), public recognition of his status as one of the best high school graduates in all of Chicago, and his subsequent enrollment at DePaul University. While getting his undergraduate degree, he became a member of the Alpha Phi Alpha fraternity, an African American organiza-tion, met his future wife, Harriet, and began to sell jukeboxes to black busi-nesses as part of his father-in-law's successful Chicago business. When he was twenty-six, Warren and Harriet were able to purchase a home in a middle-class Chicago neighborhood, and the people who knew him best thought that his combination of intelligence and leadership might eventually make him a good bet for citywide public office, maybe even as Chicago's first black mayor. He was successful by most community standards, but according to his wife, "he was still not satisfied."[14]

Warren met Nasi Shaleak Ben Yehuda (then L. A. Bryant) in 1966 and learned about the AHIJ's message. By 1971 he was in Israel with the rest of that "vanguard group" of emigrationists and had been anointed one of Ben Ammi's twelve princes, Nasi Asiel (Prince of Blessings). Asiel was tasked with bringing more people into the kingdom, and he proved an incredibly effec-tive ambassador. The documentary, an homage to a group elder, is a visual "thank you" for his lifelong work on behalf of the community. But it is also an interesting instantiation of the AHIJ's complicated relationship to African American culture.

One of the first striking things about this short film is its attempt to integrate the AHIJ community into a larger narrative of African American cultural authenticity. For a group often categorically disqualified from valid racial-social belonging as a function of its distance from conventional (and stereotypical) notions of African American spirituality (linked to normative claims about African Americans' more understandable connections to Christianity and the Nation of Islam), this is a very calculated move. Their literal (as opposed to just metaphorical) identification with the ancient Israelites marks them as radically different, even strange. Moreover their own discourse about African American cultural specificity usually finds them defining themselves as quite decidedly outside of that normative cultural formation.

According to the AHIJ, African American culture is pathological as a function of its corruption by a dysfunctional U.S. culture. Their project is a classic example of what Anthony Wallace described as a "revitalization movement," which attempts to challenge just about every aspect of its pregiven cultural moorings; for the AHIJ, this means distancing themselves from African American cultural practices: dress, diet, music, worship, and education.[15] Every aspect of African American cultural particularity is suspect and in need of rehabilitation, which makes the documentary's move to link Warren Brown's narrative to canonical moments in twentieth-century African American popular and political culture—Parks, Till, Motown—so fascinating. This gesture appears as an attempt to fold the community back into a classical story of African American life and culture, a story that they are usually attempting to cut themselves out of. Indeed this video of Brown's transformation might even be said to produce a kind of traceless temporal suturing analogous to the inconspicuous deletions of that frame-snatching televisual device. In fact the birthday video reads like a PBS documentary about African American history in the mid-twentieth century, in ways that are purposeful, self-conscious, and pretty effective.

Even more interesting than a narrative logic that would otherwise be fairly unexceptional (were it not for the community's adamant refusal of traditional African American cultural practices) is the documentary's use of images and sounds to reinforce its story. The film begins with canonical footage (stills and videos) from famous documentaries about African American life, some of the same PBS documentaries it simulates. The redeployed scenes from that earlier fare are noticeable for their own canonical status: oft-replayed black-and-white video of Emmett Till's photo above his open casket, classic footage of segregation's public pronouncements of "Whites Only" water fountains, images of peaceful black protesters, mere children, met by dogs and police batons. For African American viewers, most of these images have been seen many times before, and they are clearly still under copyright protection, but they are simply recycled from DVDs and VHS tapes of documentaries like *Eyes on the Prize* and integrated into this celebratory video without explicit citation. The closing credits list none of the original films included in the reproduction. The offerings are lifted without permission or conventional citation.

The video's use of music is similar. Its narration is delivered above recognizable jazz compositions (including "Kind of Blue" from Miles Davis) and classic Motown hits, which reinforce the video images of (and narrative references to) early Motown and its artists. Again none of the songs is listed in the credits. Instead they are sampled without permission or compensation—in a manner similar to early hip-hop redeployments of musical productions. Such infringements of copyright bespeak a certain calculated indifference to the organizing principles and cultural logics of contract-driven capitalist relations.

The DVD itself seems to further instantiate a kind of anticapitalist form of mass-mediated circulation. Like other videos made by and through the AHIJ's media production offices, some of which quite clearly carry ISBN numbers or noticeable price tags taped to the corners of DVD jewel cases, a substantial portion of the community's video work seems to mobilize the trappings and accoutrements of commodification as a kind of ruse for gifting, both within the community and to nonmembers. In a sense the commodity form (and its contextual mandates) almost seem simulated as a kind of protective cover for a different form of exchange, a mode that potentially puts community building in productive tension with the mereness of commercialization. Such a dynamic is hardly new, especially as more and more cultural groups become increasingly invested in forms of self-commodification predicated on the capitalization of ethnic and racial difference itself.[16] Just as the DVD's content mobilizes audio and video commodities to produce a text without genuflection to standard legal expectations about such intertextuality, its would-be commoditized form appears to play with the architecture of commercialized transactionalism without making such mandates absolutely mandatory. Of course such gifts demand other obligations, but they short-circuit some of what ostensibly constitutes the commodities' distinctiveness.

Tellingly Ben Ammi's books, AHIJ sacred texts, don't seem to be exchanged in the same extracommercial manner, at least not nearly to the same extent. He's published at least ten of them, and they are almost exclusively *purchased* by saints, not given away. Even the interested anthropologist otherwise plied with free DVDs or CDs of many different AHIJ events and productions pays for his copies of Ammi's sacred offerings, which circulate almost exclusively as commodities for sale as opposed to gifts shared without payment. Something about the interesting irony of sacred books for purchase and secular media representations given away for free seems to demonstrate and reflect one version of the productive paradox animating the nexus in which the spiritual and the economic meet in a time of "millennial capitalism." The AHIJ's effort to harness the capitalist needs of media outlets (by way of a machine that allows them to shoehorn more advertisements into daily broadcasts) bespeaks a kind of tension between the sacred (their project of spiritual redemption for all mankind) and the seemingly profane (the global media system) that makes a virtue out of erstwhile vice while attempting to negotiate a mediatized moment still ripe, it seems, for the celestial picking.

It should also be pointed out, even if just in passing, that the endgame for the AHIJ is eternal life, physical immortality. They don't believe that anyone has to die. So they don't want to document the inevitability of life's end. They intend instead to dramatize the exact opposite, providing a very different way of thinking about how human beings might defy death. Not metaphorically, via video documentaries that allow us to see the dead in reanimated life, but literally, by allowing human bodies qua bodies to live longer, much longer. Forever. They use veganism (what they call an Edenic diet) as the central plank of their argument about the body's capacity to regenerate (at the cellular level) into perpetuity, which is just one more reason why they should be included in any discussion about revamped conceptualizations of temporal possibility in the contemporary age.[17] And this immortality might be persuasively theorized as yet another form of nonchronological temporality or even a different way to think about the digital—as something that lasts forever, a "sexist" blog post, a "racist" YouTube video, an "inappropriate" tweet, all of which continue to circulate in something close to their original forms even after their authors have taken them down.

Ethnographic Insincerity

Let me close with a point about the extent to which ethnographic research-ers are increasingly accessible (even surveillable) in unprecedented ways as a function of digital technology, which includes, but is not limited to, those purposeful constructions of public selves found on websites such as Twitter and Facebook.

Not too long ago I was asked to give a lecture on the West Coast based on my research with the AHIJ, and it was advertised months ahead of time on the school's website. A few weeks before my trip from Philadelphia to California, I received a call from one of my research subjects wishing me luck on my forthcoming lecture and asking for more information about what I was planning to say about them. I hadn't mentioned my pending talk, but the saint had little difficulty finding it. Even a fairly uninspired Google search of my name and the community would have pulled it up. And as we all know, after such campus talks are completed, they are often posted online, such that presentations of even works in progress continue to be accessible via the web long afterward. So even if community members did not catch wind of the talk ahead of time, they can watch the video many months and years later.

Given the way we increasingly render our professional lives on the In-ternet, it is becoming easier for research subjects to study and follow the eth-nographer's movements in the "backstage" region (outside of the specifically ethnographic context). Indeed it might just be an example of how the ethno-graphic is expanding to include spaces that would have once been described as beyond its purview. With respect to that lecture out West and its poten-tial afterlife online, we have one small example of the easy access to ethno-graphic back regions that the contemporary moment affords. Although not all populations have access to the Internet, let alone equal access, we might imagine a world where such access (no matter how lopsidedly and unevenly distributed) becomes increasingly prevalent even if never close to universal. And with this emerges new questions shot across the ethnographic bow. For instance, does this ethnographer talk about his project the same way in the academy as he does when he's in southern Israel representing himself and his work to his subjects?

Traditionally the ethnographic project has been predicated on an ethnog-rapher's being expected to thoroughly access the "primitive" others' back-stage without necessarily divulging too much of his or her own—at least not in the same way or to the same extent. Clearly the ethnographer is always managing a complicated cross-cultural dance in the field, and he may perform missteps that portray him in ways that he would prefer to mask. Still he could always hide some of his backstage material inside his proverbial tent. But even more than that, he would eventually leave for home with a kind of finality that kept such distant locales decidedly off limits, even for the most interested of informants.

With new media technologies like the web and academia's concerted commitment to redeploying those technological possibilities toward pedagogical ends, it has become increasingly easy for ethnographers' formerly backstage presentations of self (back home in the Ivy Tower) to be accessed and assessed by subjects in the field, even if said subjects could not, say, find a way to physically attend an ethnographer's scheduled presentation. Of course there are many things gained (at least potentially) from such emergent backstage access, and research subjects mining this new portal is just one aspect of the changing state of ethnographic relations. It makes sense to think seriously about how ethnographers are redisciplined in a world where their backstage (at home) continues to shrink into ethnographic view. It might be another leveling of the ethnographic playing field, maybe even a welcome one, but it does demand that we reconfigure the ethnographic context to include the kind of feedback loops and postfieldwork exchanges that the Internet and other new (increasingly inexpensive) technological outlets beget.

Johannes Fabian has written about the possibility of a "virtual archive" that allows ethnographers to disseminate material quickly, providing the opportunity for almost immediate response and critique from research subjects themselves.[18] This real-time exchange is not just another way to think about ethnographic writing (another excuse for "dialogic" narratives). It might also mark the beginning of a radically different set of relations between ethnographers and their would-be subjects. No matter where they are (and increasingly no matter how much formal education they have completed), the Internet is becoming more useful as a mechanism for humbling the ethnographer's aspirations for a kind of one-sided voyeurism. The researcher is ever more researchable. And if a fundamental portion of the bygone backstage is no longer out of view, at least not the way it once was, we might very well be witnessing a fundamental shift in the nature of ethnographic research and in the kinds of ways ethnographers can be held accountable for their representations of others. Such a shift, even if subtler than I claim, should have serious implications for how we go about writing culture today.

Although I would use the term *ethnographic sincerity* to mark some of this relatively newfangled tension between ethnographic and scholarly regions, between center stage and its rafters, I do not mean to simplistically imply that such sincerity is unproblematically transportable, a universal category applicable always and everywhere. Anthropologists have provided compelling examples of social groups around the world who do not share basic Western ways of understanding subjectivity and selfhood. The linguist Bambi Schieffelin, for instance, has worked with a community in Papua New Guinea that had little notion of subjective interiority or potential individual (in)sincerity, no language for imagining a flip side to taking what people say at anything other than face value—that is, before relatively recent and sustained contact with outsiders.[19] For the AHIJ, my own intentions and motivations for engaging their community are almost, at one level, beside the point, prophetic mandate and divine intervention acting as more powerful explanatory frameworks than any tale I might proffer about how I ended up attempting to conduct research with or on them. The difference between *with* and *on* clearly has major implications for this discussion, but my sincerity is partially what's at stake in either reckoning of things.

Many scholars studying identity issues in the United States argue that self- or misrepresentation is not the only way to understand Western selves and notions of subjecthood. All that is true, but my goal is simply to maintain that ethnographic sincerity points toward a slightly different kind of real-unreal in a mediatized global landscape—and toward an ethnographic field site that is concomitantly getting reconfigured as a function of newfangled media technology and its digitalizing of ethnographic research.

Reflecting on my California lecture on my return to Philadelphia, I cringed at some of my overly flippant answers to audience questions, an occasional tone or terminological choice that ventured some distance away from my presentation of self in the kfar. I might not be duplicitous, at least I hope not, but that is an empirical question, one the AHIJ saints will decide. And they increasingly have access to more of the data they would need to do so.

The digital rewires anthropological possibility, creating new frames and stills of, from, or for our most romantic of disciplinary dreamscapes. Digitality's bending of time and space recalibrates the dyadic relationship that serves as centerpiece and pivot point for the entire ethnographic encounter. The traditional ethnographic project, arguably monological in its Malinowski-bequeathed form, has gone digital, and we should continue to think quite pointedly about what that implies for the future of anthropological research and the versions of writing culture it might require, even as we take seriously the claim that an uncritical invocation of the digital easily traffics in a too comfy ethnocentrism. The digital might still be good to think with. If nothing else, it requires recognition of the fact that ethnographic subjects are already (quite authoritatively!) writing, filming, and observing themselves (and us)—and that that might just be (ironically enough) what saves the discipline from what others prophesy as its pending irrelevance.[20] Stealing a page from Marlon Riggs and Barbara Myerhoff, actively capturing our own demise (in images, sounds, and words) might be one way to negotiate such disciplinary death and dying, just one more way to make a case for what the future of ethnography is and ain't.

Notes

1 Harrison, *Decolonizing Anthropology.*
2 Grimshaw, "The Bellwether Ewe."
3 Geertz, *The Interpretation of Cultures.*
4 Csordas, *Body/Meaning/Healing.*
5 Peters, *Speaking into the Air.*
6 Barthes, *Camera Lucida.*
7 Urban, *Metaculture.*
8 Ginsburg, "Rethinking the Digital Age."
9 Everett, *Digital Diasporas*; Ginsburg, "Rethinking the Digital Age."
10 Keeling, "Passing for Human."
11 Brian Keith Axel, "The Context of Diaspora," *Cultural Anthropology* (2004) 19:1, 27.
12 Yaakov Katz, "Distrust in Dimona," *Jerusalem Post*, December 8, 2005. http://www.jpost.com/Magazine/Features/Distrust-in-Dimona.
13 In 2011 Prince Nasi Asiel made a very public split with Ben Ammi and the African Hebrew Israelite of Jerusalem after more than forty years of service to the community. Although I won't discuss it here, I believe that this recent split is an important thing to analyze if one wants to understand the fluidities of Africana spiritualities in the twenty-first century. I save that discussion for a later time.
14 This quote comes directly from the documentary "Prince Asiel Ben Israel, International Ambassador Plenipotentiary Extraordinaire."
15 Wallace, "Revitalization Movements."
16 Comaroff and Comaroff, *Ethnicity, Inc.*
17 The community is also unabashedly against homosexuality, which, along with Riggs's omnivorous diet (as flagged by his film's literalization of a gumbo metaphor), would be part of what they would use to explain his physical mor-

tality. These are manifestations, they would argue, of a disregard for our ancestors' covenant with Yah, a disregard that directly translates into the inevitabilities of death. Eternal life, they argue, is possible only by repairing the links to Yah (i.e., obeying his commandments).

18 Fabian, *Ethnography as Commentary.*

19 Schieffelin relayed this point to me in a conversation we had after a presentation of my earlier work on race and sincerity. Some of her research on language ideologies among communities in the Pacific (e.g., Makihara and Schieffelin, *Consequences of Contact*) helps to explain such culturally specific assumptions. Similarly, according to Webb Keane ("Sincerity, 'Modernity,' and the Protestants"), overinvestments in such sincerity are often a kind of Christian (specifically Protestant) predilection or borrowing. For my own take on sincerity, authenticity, and racial reasoning, see Jackson, *Real Black.*

20 See Greenhouse, *The Paradox of Relevance.* Greenhouse does a lot to problematize this notion of sociopolitical relevance in terms of ethnographic practice and writing.

CHAPTER 9

From Village to

Precarious Anthropology

Anne Allison

In 1986, the year *Writing Culture* was published, I earned my doctorate in anthropology from the University of Chicago. While hardly canonical, my dissertation adhered to the kind of ethnographic truth-seeking tied to a grounded site so critiqued by that volume. Mine was a variant of a village study that sought to examine its subject from an "Archimedean point," a "place of overview (mountaintop) from which to map human ways of life."[1] And the predominant metaphors I adopted in research were precisely those James Clifford held up to scrutiny: "participant-observation, data collection, and cultural description," with their presumption of a standpoint of outside looking in, "or, somewhat closer, 'reading,' a given reality."[2]

In truth I chose a rather nonconventional village to study: a hostess club in the heart of Tokyo where salarymen staged outings on company expense. This was not an easy sell in my department, where Japan itself was considered an odd object choice in the late 1970s. One prominent faculty member queried why, if I was intent on Japan, I didn't go to a (*real*) village in the countryside. I answered that the edge of corporate capitalism bred by the hostess club—like, but not quite, capitalist enterprise in the West—bore a unique vantage point for studying what was emerging to be not only "Japan" at this moment of globalized, postindustrialized, fantasized existence but the world more generally. With this I was allowed to go to Japan but only after being told that I had to do sufficiently rigorous "anthropological" work (not to be subsumed by the place or culture of Japan, making it mere "Japanology").

In my attempt to uphold rigor, I went to the city, and its nightlife, but wound up treating it like a village. A unit of space, organized by persons and relations, that operates according to rituals and codes that I could learn to "read" by positioning myself as the hostess or anthropologist on the ground;

this was what I looked for, and found. Trusting there was a there there—a reality, even culture of sorts—this is how I wrote it up, in my dissertation and then book (*Nightwork: Sexuality, Pleasure, and Corporate Masculinity in a Tokyo Hostess Club*). An ethnography of the "water business" (*mizu shōbai*) where hostesses ply customers with ego massages that make men "feel like men" and build trust between business partners and coworkers in what was then said to be the cornerstone of Japanese capitalism: long-term ties to workplace and durable social bonds (*ningen kankei*, human relationships).

As I look at it now, my village study of a Tokyo hostess club does a decent job of capturing a slice of Japanese corporate capitalism that was operating at the peak of its bubble economy when I did fieldwork in 1982. But what I was able to do then, both in terms of the ethnographic toolkit I took with me and in terms of Japan itself as an economy and place, running according to a map of (relatively) durable attachments and relations, is no longer possible even if it were desirable (which it's not). Japan has radically changed in the thirty-year interim. In 1982, having rebounded from its defeat in World War II, the country had established itself as a global postindustrial power with high-paced economic growth, off-the-charts productivity, and security of everyday life for its citizens (90 percent of whom by this time identified as middle class). What Lee Edelman calls "reproductive futurism"—working hard in the moment with the expectation that the future will be better for oneself, one's kids, the nation-state—was not only a dream but considered a reality for most Japanese.[3] But after the bursting of the bubble economy in 1991, the slide into a nagging recession as well as flexibilization and precaritization of labor (one-third of the labor force but one-half of young workers between the ages of fifteen and twenty-four are now irregularly employed in contract, dispatch, temporary, or part-time jobs), and two decades of "lost" futures and spectacular crises—most recently the Great East Japan earthquake and tsunami on March 11, 2011, that triggered the nuclear meltdowns in Fukushima—this promise of a good life measured by security and stability has come undone. Or at least for an increasing segment of the population, the so-called losers: those who lack steady employment, marriage, or kids, the consumerist lifestyle of the middle class.

This is the subject of my most recent research, conducted almost thirty years after my study of hostess clubs. I call it "precarity"—my gloss of a host of Japanese words used to index insecurity, unease, socioeconomic disparity, a slide downward, un(der)employment, the working poor, social withdrawal, loneliness. I also adopt precarity from its usage by the autonomia (post-*operaismo*) movement in Italy and France in the 1970s to reference the economic and social insecurity of the un(der)employed, mainly youth, and also the political potential of the "precariat" (the precarious proletariat, a word that has been picked up by Japanese activists) to reorganize the capitalist rubric of labor, life, and wealth. The term includes, but is not limited to, the economic sphere of labor and work. For even if it gets triggered by material or job insecurity, precarity spreads outward to a much wider sense of social dislocation, existential angst, cascading anxieties over just about everything. As Kathleen Stewart and Lauren Berlant note, precarity clutches one in the senses when longing for the good life doesn't stop just because it's out of reach.[4] This means it's also, or often, beyond words as well as (not) any one definable thing. Precarity is not only the state of not being grounded; it defies groundedness itself.

How, then, to study it? Quite a different state of affairs from what I found in and as Japan in the early 1980s and what I took with me as my village-like model for doing anthropology. What I share in the rest of this chapter comes out of my book *Precarious Japan*. My ethnography, there and here, is scattered rather than schematic and driven more by a sensing—the senses I came to associate with precarity and how I came to sense it myself—than by anything definitive or concrete in the way of a research plan. And in my essay here I look at efforts being made to confront, survive, and try to move beyond precarity: what I take to be, as do those involved themselves, a modicum of hope arising from a biopolitics waged by, for, and beyond the social precariat themselves.

Banking Care

I am riding on the *shinkansen*, the network of high-speed railway lines (bullet trains) that, first built in the period of reconstruction following the war, became a sign of Japan's miraculous recovery and, with its rapid economic growth, emergence as a global industrial power. By 2010 the moment feels radically different. As has been much reported in the news, Japan is struggling with a long-lasting recession, political instability, an aging and declining population, and, among the people, rising levels of homelessness, poverty, suicide, and despair. This is what I have come here to study: the contemporary moment and how people are dealing with the insecurity of the times in navigating, quite literally, the ecology of life and death. Based mainly in Tokyo, I am pursuing tangents wherever I find them on the social sensibilities and fractures of survival: how relations with others—of care, belonging, recognition—are showing strain but also, in a few instances, getting reimagined and restitched in innovative new ways. Social precarity is what I'm calling this.

This is why today I am on the shinkansen, returning from Osaka, where I have gone to check out a social welfare program devised to serve people needing basic help in life. It is through a newspaper article that I've learned about what the reporter dubbed a "welfare bank" (*fukushi ginkō*): a system that stores and lends "welfare" in a country where citizens are increasingly living and dying alone but also are expected to maintain an ethos of individual responsibility (*jiko sekinin*) in getting by.[5] As I've heard often from Japanese—and will hear again in the wake of the 3/11 disaster—self-reliance is valued and dependence on others abhorred. Not wanting to burden their children is the number one reason elderly give for choosing to live alone, often at great risk to themselves, the investigators of a study on Japan's *muen shakai* (relationless society) discovered.[6] The welfare bank caters to just such a contingency: it provides a resource for daily living that doesn't depend on money, the family, or the state.

Officially called Nippon (Japan) Active Life Club (NALC), the program operates through a currency of caregiving calculated in time. Started in 1993 by Takahata Keiichi in Osaka,[7] NALC now has 135 branch offices with over thirty thousand members nationwide and is run entirely on its own resources (raised mainly from the annual fee of 3,000 yen [$37] that members pay). The foundational principle is its chief operation: the "time savings system" (*jikan yotaku seido*) whereby one hour of labor earns one point that is recorded in a bankbook (*techō*). All labor is equal, whether it is raking leaves or teaching a computer class. Members are divided into two categories, users (*riyōsha*) and donors (*teikyōsha*), though the assumption is that a donor is a future user (true so far for only about 10 percent of current users). In principle, then, caregivers are proxies for their future selves; one gives care while still able and cashes in when needing care oneself. But recipients can also be family members (defined as spouses, parents, and disabled children), and, if a donor dies with unused points, family members can apply to activate them. More pertinent for the way the system has utility for families is its convertibility across not just time but space. If someone donates time in Osaka, for example, she can convert this into care for her aging mother in Tokyo. In fact, though, while open to families, the currency of care operates more on the assumption of the family's absence or erosion as primary caregiving unit in Japan. And, organized like a bank, NALC donors and users are transacting the labor of care primarily as individuals.

As in capitalism, value is produced through labor measured in discrete units of time. And by treating it as a currency like money, NALC converts care into an impersonal medium that can be brokered between strangers rather than relying on one's personal ties of family (and thus abstracts and homogenizes into exchange the use-value of care). As Takahata elaborates, what drives the need for care in a program like NALC is scarcity. There is a "care deficit" in Japan today that starts, though hardly ends, with the elderly.[8]

The example Takahata gives is of elderly dying alone. Given that this is Japan, there is a word for the phenomenon, *kodokushi*, which literally translates as lonely (*kodoku*) death (*shi*). Loneliness (*kodoku*) is a pain all its own these days, what one hears from people young and old about existence spent too much alone, isolated from others, and disconnected from the social fixtures that (once) anchored identity and human relationships such as the workplace. The national broadcasting network NHK televised a special in 2009 on *muen shakai* (relationless society) that, among all the other stories, highlighted the escalating rate of elderly who die alone (the figure given was thirty-two thousand deaths in 2009, a figure that kept appearing on the screen in large numbers). As Takahata described the phenomenon to me, "lonely death" is increasing nationwide, with more and more discoveries of putrefied bodies of elderly who have died deaths days, even weeks before. One just happened next door in New Town.

As Takahata showed me, this is the lead story in the monthly newspaper NALC puts out: "How to Make the Streets in Our Town Safe(r) for Preventing Lonely Death" (July 10, 2010). Life is risky, and not just for the elderly, Takahata points out. Many people have needs in managing everyday life and insufficient resources (human or financial) to tend to them, such as being an invalid who needs to get to the doctor or a single mom whose kids need to be picked up at day care because she's working. Sitting next to Takahata is Nishimura, the person who coordinates all the work transactions for NALC in Osaka. This is a job she works at everyday from 10 to 4, five days a week, on an entirely volunteer basis (which, she admits, is "quite a job"). It is Nishimura who enumerates the diversity of care needs and services NALC trades in: everything from teaching children to swim to tending to the elderly by helping them bathe or drying their hair. As she cheerfully observes, what gets exchanged is driven by not only need for a specific service but also the desire for something pleasant (*tanoshī*): the pleasantry of having human companionship. The two merge here. For, as described in the pamphlet I'm given, NALC runs on the logic of love and mutual contact (*aijō to fureai no ronri*), drawing on and filling the gap in human relationships. As NALC implicitly acknowledges, there is a care deficit in Japan today. And a deficit in sociality.

Time is at the heart of this time-savings system. One donates time in the form of care as an investment in one's future. Indeed in its promotional literature NALC is called a "storehouse for the future" (*mirai no kura*), appropriating the word for storehouse (*kura*) that merchants and farmers have traditionally used to store goods (rice, silk) that will be later sold on the market and converted into money. But in NALC value is measured differently—as human care rather than material wealth—and temporality is not merely storing for the future. Speaking for himself, Takahata recounts how, in a society where people retire in their sixties and are living twenty years longer, volunteering fills up one's time with an activity at once meaningful and productive.[9] Now eighty, Takahata relates how busy he is. Rather than sitting home alone, cut off from the social world that, for four decades, he'd been tied to through work, he feels both useful and alive—a far cry from the loneliness and isolation suffered by so many elderly (and other precariat) in Japan today. Staying active in the present is another form of life insurance in what is labeled, after all, an "active life club." This is what Takahata himself seems more invested in. Having donated care at NALC for seventeen years, he's accrued a sizable "savings" but imagines he could well die before spending any of it. The thought pleases him immensely.

Something to do, a place to be, utility in life (when one has outlasted productivity on the job market)—this is what NALC gives Takahata as a volunteer. The rhythms of an everyday life, of being "nearly normal" himself.[10] As such NALC's currency of care serves as an alternative economy in a society where, because productivity is the medium of social value, those beyond (or outside) regular employment get left out or dumped. This is how the activist Amamiya Karin describes the exclusion she felt working as a *furītā* (nonregular worker). In serial jobs where she could be fired anytime, wages were minimal, and anyone could do the tasks she was assigned, Amamiya became a disposable laborer.[11] Yet even more pressing, alongside job insecurity and an unlivable wage was the sense of disbelonging—of lacking recognition (*shōnin*) from others—that she found the hardest to bear. The experience of being cut off from society and existentially irrelevant filled Amamiya with a despair that drove her to cut her wrists, overdose, and attempt suicide (multiple times). In her mind lack of shōnin is the biggest hurdle facing those in her generation (the "lost generation" or precariat). For, as scholars from Durkheim to Marx and Arendt have long understood, belonging to some unit beyond the singular self whose endeavor lasts beyond the here and now is critical to the social condition. Estrangement from this unit not only deadens the soul but evacuates everyday life.

Stretching Home

There are *obāsan* [old women] who go to the convenience store because they're lonely. Hearing the cashier thank them when they are handed their change is the only human contact they have in the day. There are children who have no place to play with other humans in days spent commuting between school, cram school, and home. There are mothers who have no one to help them shoulder the responsibilities of child-raising. In Japan there are a lot of people who are somehow lonely. We've slipped into a big darkness [*kurayami*] of loneliness. And, in just an instant, this darkness has transformed Japan.
—*Chiiki no chanoma*, "Niigata-shi"
(www.sawayakazaidan.or.jp/ibasho/case/04koushinetsu/uchinojikka.html; accessed June 15, 2012)

Japan is in trouble today, Chiiki no cha no ma (Regional Living Room) announces on its website. But the reason is not economic decline or a sinking birthrate; rather it is loneliness, the infrequency with which humans bump up against one another or help one another out. Whether for the old woman living alone, the child overregimented by school, or the mother struggling with child raising, loneliness has become generic, a "darkness" in the social fiber: a crimp and crisis in the home (in the Bachelardian sense of sheltering the spirit and nourishing the imagination). "Darkness has transformed Japan" in that something basically human seems amiss. As in missing from basic living in what Butler identifies as the precariousness of social life:

> Precariousness implies living socially, that is, the fact that one's life is always in some sense in the hands of the other. . . . It is not that we are born and then later become precarious, but rather that precariousness is coextensive with birth itself (birth is, by definition, precarious), which means that it matters whether or not this infant survives, and that its survival is dependent on what we might call a social network of hands.[12]

Where does one turn to for a "social network of hands" in an era of increasing self-responsibility (*jiko sekinin*) and the retreat of those institutions and networks—workplace, family, neighborhood—that once were re-lied upon for anchoring relationality, positionality, and care? Recognition of the problem alone is insufficient. What Chiiki no cha no ma offers instead is something more active: a way to sense (out of) precariousness by staging human contact. This is an ethics of the social premised on the logic and need for mutual touch, a social premised on the shared condition of precarious-ness where people come together on the basis not of identity but responsi-bility. And less responsibility to and for oneself ("self-sustainability," as this gets called by the government) than an ethics of life geared to one another, even strangers, thus creating a new "we."

> Who then is included in the "we" that I seem to be, or to be a part of? And for which "we" am I finally responsible? This is not the same as the question: to which "we" do I belong? If I identify a community of belonging on the basis of nation, territory, language, or culture, and if I then base my sense of responsibility on that community, I implicitly hold to the view that I am responsible only for those who are recognizably like me in some way. But what are the implicit frames of recognizability in play when I "recognize" someone as "like" me? . . . What is our respon-sibility toward those we do not know . . . ? Perhaps we belong to them in a different way, and our responsibility to them does not in fact rely on the apprehension of ready-made similitudes.[13]

Chiiki no cha no ma defines itself as a space for mutual human contact: a *fureai ibasho* (*ibasho* is a place where one feels comfortable and at home; *fureai* means mutual contact or touch): "Children, the elderly, middle-aged people, we can get energized [*genki o moratte*] by exchanging smiles. In an ibasho with no divisions, this is power. Starting with ourselves, let's build such an ibasho. From a long time ago [*mukashikara*], this is what we've done: we've built ibasho and come to inhabit them."

A nationwide movement that currently has about two hundred establish-ments all over the country, Chiiki no chanoma refers to the room in a tradi-tional home (often in the countryside, *chiiki*) where Japanese tea is made and served (*cha no ma*) to guests. The aim is to refurbish but remake the referent, as *chiiki no cha no ma* are intended to be homey without being family homes. The two I visited in fact had been empty homes that got reclaimed as a new kind of drop-in or hang-out center where membership is fluid and open rather than bounded or pinned down (by family or private ownership). What NALC does in terms of time—offering a way of providing and calculating care work outside that of wage labor and capitalist productivity—Chiiki no cha no ma does in terms of space, offering a homelike space for contact and companionship outside of family or kin. Quite pointedly, in fact, there are rules (or antirules) designed to remap the kind of sociality fostered here. For example, in the "regional living room" I visited in Niigata City (on the Japan Sea, two and a half hours from Tokyo on the bullet train) the rules were both posted on a wall and written on the handout I was given immediately upon entering.

> In the *genkan* [entrance] enter your name in the registry and pay your
>   fee by yourself.
> When people enter, don't stare or ask "Hey, who's that?!"
> No one is to wear an apron outside the kitchen.
> There's no clear distinction between those caring and those being
>   cared for.
> Don't talk about people in their absence.
> There's no set program; spend time here as you like.
> Come and leave whenever you want.
> Ask for help in those things you can't do, but let's help each other in
>   what we are able to.

Uchi no jikka—"my home," using the term for natal home—is the name of the regional living room in Niigata. It was started in 2003 by Kawada Keiko, a vibrant powerhouse who earlier founded a volunteer care service in Niigata (called Magokoro herupa, Heartfelt Helper) when faced with what was the overwhelming chore of tending to her husband's parents all alone. "When nothing exists, start it yourself," she cheerfully recalls about that venture. Realizing how lonely she found so many of those using Heartfelt Helper, Kawada then launched her local chiiki no cha no ma out of an abandoned house. Essentially a drop-in center, Uchi no jikka is open from 10 to 3 every day and welcomes any and everyone to, basically, hang out: drinking tea, playing cards, talking to one another, eating lunch. The entrance fee is 300 yen ($3.20), as is lunch; staying overnight (which requires a reservation) costs 2,000 yen ($21). The day I visited in June 2010 the air was muggy and still—much like what I found inside this older house down a side road, in a quiet neighborhood. Stepping into the genkan and removing my shoes, I entered the main eighteen-mat room. Doors opened to the outside, with a row of low tables and cushions and tatami mats on the floor, it effused both energy and calm. A flurry of notices filled an entire wall.

That day eighteen people visited: a mix of men and women, mostly middle-aged and elderly but including a young woman with Down syndrome (who was being tended by those at her table) and another woman in her twenties who introduced herself as a Chinese migrant who had just settled in the area. Everyone seemed comfortable and engaged; one man rushed over to give me a paper cup (returning later to make sure I hadn't lost it), and another invited me to play cards. At lunchtime we sat wherever we wanted to and fussed over the food prepared by two preassigned participants who rotate by the day. Some lingered; some jumped up immediately. But everyone seemed to be comfortable and "lightly passing the time." One retired man in his sixties told me he came here about three days a week, traveling on a bus from his home thirty minutes away. A woman in her late fifties confided that, though she shared a nice home with her husband close by, she preferred the atmosphere here (because her husband didn't accompany her?) and came almost every day.

Another man, possibly seventy years old, recounted the accident that, years ago, had stopped him from working and had rendered him basically useless, a condition that confounded his doctors, lawyers, and family alike. Distressed and feeling abandoned, he was told about Uchi no jikka and Kawada, who, in his words, brought him back to life again. Calling her his "*kokoro no sensei*" (heart teacher), the man started crying. So did Kawada, standing next to him, who took over the story: "Well, he lives in a neighborhood with a tofu vendor who makes the most amazing tofu in all of Niigata. So he brings this to us every day. Every day he feeds us delicious tofu and we appreciate what he does for us. Everyone has something they're special in, you know. Everyone. And here we recognize that."

Recognition and acceptance (shōnin)—the very hole in human (un)relatedness that agonized Amamiya more than anything as a furītā. And what she, in her work as an activist, tries—along with activating for furītā unions, reforming the law for *haken* (dispatch) work, and organizing precariat May Days (on the theme "freedom and survival")[14]—to humanly foster in those suffering hardship in life (*ikizurasa*). It was she who, at a Stop Suicide event I attended, answered the question raised by a woman during the Q&A about how she could keep going. Identifying herself as a *hikikomori*—social isolates who stay confined to a room or apartment they do not leave for work, school, or anything else—the woman said she hadn't left her room for a year, and confessed to thinking about suicide all the time. Hearing this, Amamiya commended her for coming out, praising the courage this took and acknowledging both her pain and her strength. "You were bold to come out tonight. And you're not alone. We all have experienced pain. But we're here; and we're here for you. Email me anytime." Recognition is at once personal and generic here; the woman becomes both a singularity that stands alone and a part that stands alongside the multitude of those suffering "hardship of life" (in the live-house where the event was being staged that night as well as the country as a whole these days).

The same is true at Uchi no jikka, where anyone can enter and everyone belongs. Membership is open rather than contingent, depending on neither workplace, family, nor even geographical proximity (as in residence in a certain neighborhood). This also makes for a sociality that is unbounded by commitment or time. Rather than a community per se, it is more like a watering hole, a space where people come and go and are expected only to behave humanly once there. This is a far cry from the principles of hierarchy and differentiation that Nakane Chie, in her canonical text on Japanese society, *Vertical Society* (*Tate Shakai*, 1967), written at the height of postwar fordism, outlined as at the core of social relationality in the Japanese company, family, and nation. In this ontology of the social, hierarchical difference structures all relationships (older brother and younger brother, teacher and student, senior and junior colleague); indeed without it people don't know how to behave toward one another, Nakane wrote. At Uchi no jikka, by contrast, the operative term is not *relationship* but *connectedness* (*tsunagari*), which is postidentitarian and premised on mutuality and care. This is a zone of "mutual contact" (*fureai*) where everyone is to give and receive ("everyone should help to the degree that they can"), no one should be identified by even an apron (no apron wearers outside the kitchen), and all are to be infused by "a human energy" that is rejuvenating (*hito no chikara ni yotte hito wa genki ni narerumono*).[15]

On the evening of the day I visited Uchi no jikka I witnessed how electric this connective charge could get. The small house throbbed with energy— filled to the rafters with lively chatter and convivial sociality—on what was its monthly festive night: two hours for eating, drinking, talk. Over seventy people gathered, many apparently to learn more about the operation of Uchi no jikka: social workers, local officials, persons involved in care work, students (some taking classes that Kawada teaches at the local community college). As three of these visitors told me, Uchi no jikka has become legendary, so there is much interest in learning how to duplicate or link up with Kawada's efforts. One, a prefectural office worker, was in the midst of establishing a chiiki no chanoma in her own ward that summer. Another woman, working with local homeless, hoped to build alliances and share information about the worsening conditions she was finding among the jobless and working poor in Niigata. But this was not an occasion for only those here to observe. Regulars visited as well, and a number I had seen earlier in the day were back this evening, intermingling with the others. The man who had lost his job and found life rekindled here sat at a table, drinking beer and eating sushi. When his turn came to introduce himself, the ritual seemed important to him. Standing up and speaking to the room, he chose his words carefully. "I am Yonezawa Hiroshi. I come here every day. And tonight I am wearing the *happi* coat I once wore as a sake vendor." Standing proud in his blue happi coat, dressed as the worker he'd stopped being long ago, Yonezawa embraced the applause from the room, accepted here at Uchi no jikka, just as was I when, upon introducing myself as here to learn how this "mutual contact zone" works in practice, people urged me on with nods of the head and hearty claps at the end.

A potential—as in a reserve, a reservoir, a cushion—is what I understand the activist Yuasa Makoto to mean by the word *tame*.[16] Whether money in the bank, academic credentials, family, or homeownership, tame are (material, social, personal) reserves that can be drawn on in hard times and stockpiled for the future. But with the downturn in the economy and the rise in job and life insecuritization, such reserves are drying up for more Japanese every day. This constitutes precarity to Yuasa: scarcity of tame. For not only does this make life hard in the here and now, but it crimps one's ability to imagine any outside or possibility beyond, what José Esteban Muñoz (borrowing from Ernst Bloch) calls a there and then and also—and I, following them—hope. As Yuasa explained to me, tame has value more in being saved than in getting spent in the expediency of the moment. It generates "energy," this excess beyond the present need that exists, as a potentiality, *within* the present ("a certain mode of nonbeing that is eminent, a thing that is present but not actually existing in the present tense").[17] A human reserve whose potential for something there and then energizes and adheres to the here and now. This would seem the formula for Uchi no jikka. Like, but even more than, NALC—where, alongside a "storehouse for the future," donating care time gives volunteers something meaningful to do right now—Uchi no jikka operates less as a service provider than as a zone of possibility. One can come here, for help and companionship, anytime. This is the tame it creates: a reserve for human connection. Serving those who feel lonely or uninvolved, Uchi no jikka constructs a space for belonging, a space that draws energy ("light") from the potential within the human need for others and the loneliness of lacking that ("darkness") in contemporary Japan.

Being Nowhere, Expanding Somewhere

As Japan has modernized, places to gather like those that once existed have disappeared across the country. Chiiki no chanoma is one strategy for resolving this.
—Uchi no jikka website

One of the names given newly constructed, openly flexible "meeting places" is *ibasho*, which basically means a space where one feels comfortable and at home. This word has become something of a catchword of the times, as in lacking ibasho (*ibasho ga nai*), which I heard constantly in the circuit of media and public discourse about the state of de-sociality plaguing Japan and Japanese today. People feel disconnected (ibasho ga nai), I was told time and time again when doing fieldwork on this project in the summers of 2008–10. But when I asked people where or what their own ibasho was—a standard question I included in interviews and conversations—most answered positively with replies that ranged from family and work to "wherever I am" or "in the morning when watering the plants." The question struck her as odd though, a friend finally pointed out. For ibasho is more commonly used in the negative: a referent less to the presence than the absence of human connection and security in an unrelational society. (Almost) everyone, she continued, has *some* place or space where living feels right. Or they have the memory, the fragment, the occasional sake with friends or a character toy that goes everywhere on a cell phone or purse strap. But the problem is how troubled and scarce the zone(s) of comfort have become, and how panicky and insecure so many feel more and more, or all the time. Ibasho (ga nai) indexes this. A state of not-ness: not feeling quite right, sufficiently secure, noticeably human. A slippage from a time when things were (remembered or fantasized to be) better, when home meant social security—the stable job, middle-class lifestyle, a place in society and a future—through one's kids. Which makes "home" today seem, well, not (ibasho ga nai).

Certainly this existential, social dis-ease (of panic, depression, and deadness, in Bifo Berardi's terms) is not experienced by everyone in Japan today.[18] But signs are that it is common enough. And it is this wound in the soul that practices like NALC, Uchi no jikka, neighborhood night patrols to ward against lonely deaths, and Stop Suicide events have sprung up in response to. A response to and from a precariousness that, increasingly shared, also becomes a source for a new commonwealth of people and life.[19] Such endeavors draw upon a potential in the present conditions of twenty-first-century Japan: what is at once a pain in and a protest (of sorts) against the insufficiency of the social state to sustain life for its citizens. And out of this human discomfiture—and the response to not simply endure it but to change the conditions of everyday living—we can see the germs of an emergent sociality, one based not on exclusive belonging or normative rules but on mutual caregiving and open acceptance. This is a biopolitics from below, spurred by a shared sense and conditions of precariousness. Advocating for a modicum of basic human life for anyone regardless of his or her place or identity within relations of (re)productivity, property, and wealth.

I return here again to Muñoz and the radically utopic potential he sees in the very condition of exclusion from normative belonging.[20] Distinguishing between what he calls "queer time" and "straight time," Muñoz aligns these two temporalities—and social spatialities—as a materialist critique of the present. Rather than exiting the social or acceding to marginality or death, those who are queered by heteronormativity are uniquely positioned to advocate for change, forcing the lines and lives of who and what gets included to be remapped. Resisting "no future"—or future altogether—for those insufficiently (re)productive or refusing the construct of reproductive futurism altogether.[21] A reterritorialization of the social. The soul on strike. Using Muñoz's example of queer versus straight time, I propose a similar distinction between what could be called care or human time and productive or capitalist time (and family-corporate time within it). When those who are excluded by the rubric of (re)productivity—the elderly, precariat, unemployed, hikikomori, NEET—refuse to simply withdraw. When, instead of not participating in the social (the de-sociality much noted about Japanese youth today), the social gets redefined and redeployed. When those who have found hardship in life "throw up" (*hakidasu*) their pain or reconstrue the "pus" of their disabilities as "broken people" (*Kowaremono saiten*, a performance group located in Niigata City in which each member has a disability). And then go on to make spaces and times within the present and the everyday where not only they but diverse others can find connection and belonging.

Turning the notness of ibasho into a positive: a place to touch and sense others (*fureai ibasho*). This is the descriptor of Uchi no jikka. Making "watering holes" (*tamariba*) to "lightly pass time" (in patchwork, learning local history, sharing a meal to which everyone takes turns bringing the pickles)—as is the format and name of another chiiki no cha no ma I visited on the outskirts of Tokyo in July 2010.[22] Building on and out of the edges of the precarious everyday, a form of social recorporeality, human survival.

Soul on Strike

I end with two final stories. One starts with a boy so panicked by the pressure and his failure to academically perform that he had bald spots in his hair from pulling it out at age five. This is Suzuki, a man in his mid-thirties who videotapes the Kowaremono (Broken People). Growing up lonely, bullied, and chastised by his parents for being a poor student, Suzuki was essentially a hikikomori, someone who withdrew into himself, though, in his case, managed to move away from home after high school and finish his university degree. After graduating, Suzuki spent a long period basically isolated and unemployed but immersed in reading. Just as video games had given him a fantasy world to escape into as a child, now it became books—on psychology, social work, child abuse, object-relations theory—that opened his soul as a young adult. No longer convinced that he was to blame for the rejection by others that traumatized him growing up, Suzuki started reimagining his horizons of possibility. Reimagining a world where belonging and worthiness did not depend unilaterally on performance in school, money in the bank, or a wife and kids of his own. Though unable by these tokens to be counted "a winner," Suzuki started building a life where he refused to discount himself and others like him as "losers." When I first met him, in summer 2008, Suzuki had just made a documentary film of the Kowaremono and was working as a social worker for the *Niigata chiiki wakamono sapōto sutēshon* (Niigata Regional Young People's Support Station), directing support groups for hikikomori and their parents.[23] Two years later, when I was back in Niigata, Suzuki took me to his most recent venture: another new zone straddling the precarious everyday where socially withdrawn youth and economically depressed elderly meet up for mutual assistance.

Nuttari yori dokoro (Nuttari Place) sits in a renovated shop in what is the depressed "old town" (*shitamachi*) section of town. Youth have fled because there are no jobs, and the scattered old people who live there have few resources or stores for shopping. Next to the port, the neighborhood of Nuttari is filled with abandoned storefronts: rows of wooden structures that were once filled with markets, brothels, workshops, and bars. Funded for three years by a nonprofit organization run by Suzuki called a *bansōsha* (literally, someone who runs alongside a bicyclist to give support; Suzuki's is named *Wake e shu ra*), Nuttari yori dokoro consists of two rooms. In the front, a shop sells fresh vegetables at a cheap price to the (elderly) residents of Nuttari; a plaque calls this the "vegetable village" (*yasai mura*). In the back, the open space is subdivided into four areas: a workspace, an area with a table and chairs to sit down, a café (that operates as a lunch restaurant, with plans to open at night as a bar), and a corner for hanging out. The sign here reads "*ibasho supēsu*" (space for ibasho). Here is where those hikikomori involved in the venture gather to learn skills, do some work, get socialized, and start reintegrating into a world outside the rooms many of them have been living in (alone) for up to years.

The day I visit eight are present, all males between eighteen and thirty-five who are sorting through clothing donated from neighbors for a recycling bazaar that will be held on the premises the next month. As the staff member who oversees their training tells me, activities vary by day and the schedule is pretty loose. But for those who show up and for the duration of time they are there, the objective is to get them doing something they stick to and to communicate with other humans: running the café, selling the vegetables in the shop, learning about computers, doing minor labor (for 500 yen/hour, $5.31) for local merchants or house-bound elderly.

The day I visit things are pretty slow. The guys seem to be tired, and only three elderly from the neighborhood pop in for their veggies. But the very idea is extraordinary: a meeting place for two different contingencies who—due to quite different circumstances—rarely meet other humans at all. By putting them in contact with one another, the hope is that the two groups will help one another out: the elderly, deficient in resources and company, and the hikikomori, impoverished in human wherewithal. A potentiality in a precarious present deployed toward a not yet future that draws upon, by reworking, the past: the village (*mura*), the local region (*chiiki*), the family tea room (*cha no ma*), the hang-out (*tamariba*), the natal home (*uchi no jikka*), the homey space (*ibasho*). A conference on volunteerism I attended in summer 2010 in Tokyo labeled the activities represented there *harappa*. Literally this means "grassy fields," but here it meant something metaphoric: the fields left untilled to keep the potential for future crops (or something else) alive. Grassy fields in the idiom of sociality. Cultivating fields on and out of the edges of society:[24] the handicapped, the elderly, the homeless, the poor, the un(der)employed, the socially withdrawn, the suicidal, the broken people. *Harappa* captures Nutarri yori dokoro, the attempt to make a field—for life and human connection—out of the very precariousness of the socially displaced. Such fields, grassy if marginal, need to be cultivated. When they are, they "spin hope."

The second story comes from one of many interviews I did with college students in the summer of 2010. In all the interviews the final question I asked was how they saw the future of Japan. One woman answered that the future seemed dark. What with an economic recession and low birth rate, the vitality of the nation is at risk. She proposed a governmental response: additional support to families so they can raise children "naturally." A reinscription of the principle of reproductive futurism with futurity and national brightness (still) linked to the heteronormative family working hard—now with increased state support—to (re)produce.

But another young woman gave a different answer. Reflecting on something she couldn't quite name, she started to speak. Then paused. "It's something just ordinary, banal, no big deal." But actually, for her, it stood out. So she continued. One night recently she was walking home from the train station and it started to rain. She lives in a Tokyo suburb with her parents, a "bedtown community" that sprang up in the prosperity of postwar times, where men, and increasingly women, commute long hours to and from the city for work. There's little sense of community here, she pointed out; no one knows his or her neighbors or greets another on the street. Everyone moves about in anonymity, including herself. But walking home she encountered someone coming the other way. No one she knew, a woman a bit older than she, getting drenched in the rain because she'd forgotten (or didn't have) an umbrella. And to this stranger she spontaneously gave the extra umbrella she was carrying. A gift with no expectation it would be returned. A gesture with no agenda—and the refusal not to act because of this.

The act deeply affected her because it was so atypical, for her or anyone in Japan (or at least Tokyo) these days. Sharing humanness alongside precariousness in the zone of the ordinary everyday. "This," she said—not giving it a name or definition—"is what Japan needs more of in the future."

Not more babies, more families, more national growth, more competitive achievements. But more attention paid—by the state, social expenditures, people themselves—to sustaining one another in life rather than allocating responsibility to the self ("self-sustainability"). Not dismissing or discounting those who can't make it: the disposable laborers, disappearing elderly, human waste. Not sacrificing more and more of life to the encroachment of capital that produces wealth for the "winners" but insecurity for "losers"—an increasing majority. Instead of "social reproduction of affluence that rests on a foundation of starvation,"[25] there needs to be a revaluing of life as wealth of a different kind (based on the humanness of a shared precariousness—and shared efforts to do something about it).

This would lead to a new "we," a radical reconfiguring of home, a rekindling of hope, and a reterritorialization of the social—the soul on strike in precarious Japan.

Notes

1 Clifford, "Introduction," 22.
2 Clifford, "Introduction," 22.
3 Edelman, *No Future.*
4 Stewart, "Precarity's Forms," this volume; Berlant, *Cruel Optimism.*
5 One-third of all Japanese live alone today.
6 NHK Muen shakai purojekuto, *Muen shakai.*
7 Takahata adopted this from Edgar Cahn, whose "Time Dollar" initiative he learned about when visiting the United States in the early 1990s.
8 Ehrenreich and Hochschild, introduction.
9 See Muehlebach, *The Moral Neoliberal Italy,* for a discussion of how the Italian state actively incorporates and promotes volunteerism from its non- and postwage citizens like the retired.
10 Berlant, *Cruel Optimism.*
11 Amamiya and Kayano, *"Ikizurasa" nitsuite.*
12 Butler, *Frames of War,* 14.
13 Butler, *Frames of War,* 35–36.
14 For an account of all the multifarious activities, events, and activism Amamiya either participated in or sponsored herself in the year 2008, see *Amamiya Karin Tōsō Daiarī* (Amamiya Karin's battle diary).
15 Quotes are taken from handouts I received at Uchi no jikka; this information is also repeated on its website.
16 Yuasa, *Hanhinkon.*
17 Muñoz, *Cruising Utopia,* 9.
18 Berardi, *The Soul at Work.*
19 Hardt and Negri, *Commonwealth.*
20 For a postwork society engineered, in part, by a policy of basic income, Kathi Weeks in *The Problem with Work* advocates for what she calls a "utopic demand."
21 Furuichi, *Zetsubō no kuni no kōfukuna wakmonotachi.*
22 In Saitama-ken, Sayama-shi, on the outskirts of Tokyo, its full name is Tamariba sekireitei.

23 Niigata chiiki wakamono sapōto sutēshon: a subsidiary of the government-sponsored "Hello Work" that offers classes, counseling, and training to young people struggling to find work.

24 This was the Japanese Volunteer Academic Conference held on June 26 and 27, 2010, at Meiji Gakuin University, Shirogane Campus. Codenamed "The Shirogane Mass Harappa Meeting" (Shirogane harappa taikai), its descriptor was "cultivating fields, spinning hope on the edges of Tokyo" (*harappa ho umidasu: tōkyō no ejide kibō o tsumugu*).

25 Bakker et al., "Introduction to Part IV."

CHAPTER 10

Kinship by Other Means

Charles Piot

This chapter examines Togolese applying for and attempting to game the U.S. State Department's Diversity Visa (DV) lottery, a visa scheme that annually awards up to fifty thousand residency visas to those from countries with low rates of immigration to the United States.[1] Applicants apply online, and those who are selected in the raffle submit to a lengthy process of medical exams and embassy interviews. If they successfully jump through these hoops, they receive a green card and become eligible for U.S. citizenship. Because of the hefty embassy interview fee ($813 in 2011) and the cost of a plane ticket to the United States, many winners exploit a loophole in the system: because applicants may add spouses and children after being selected, they may add the children and spouses of others instead in return for help in paying the interview fee and plane ticket. The embassy knows all too well that this gaming is going on and spends much time before and during interviews trying to ferret out "real" from "fake" marriages. For their part, winners know what's coming, and they (and their visa spouses) spend weeks, sometimes months preparing for the interview—for the trick questions the embassy will throw their way. My research has focused on this cat-and-mouse game between street and embassy, as seen through the eyes of a visa broker, Kodjo, who enrolls hundreds, sometimes thousands of Togolese in the DV each year, then arranges the financing for winners and coaches them as they prepare for their interviews.

When I visited Kodjo on a steamy day in July 2010, he was vexed by the case of a young couple going for their second embassy interview. The wife had been pregnant when they went for the first interview (to present their documents)—pregnant by her real, not her fictive, spouse—and a sympathetic consul told them she hoped the verification process went quickly so that they might arrive in the States before their baby was born, thus avoiding having to pay an additional $775 for the baby's visa. But months went by before they were called for the second interview, and the woman gave birth in the interim. Kodjo's worry now was that the embassy might demand a DNA test before giving a visa to the baby, thus threatening to uncover their ruse.

Given the risks, the couple and their financier in the States (the husband's sister) thought it best to leave the baby at home for the second interview, hoping the consul wouldn't remember their earlier meeting. But Kodjo worried that an alert consul with a good memory might wonder why they hadn't brought the infant to the interview, given the large upside of getting a visa for the infant right away. Waiting to apply would not only mean that mother and child would be separated for several years but also certainly set the couple up for a DNA test, whose results would reveal that the child and its mother's visa spouse were unrelated, also potentially reopening the entire case. In the end Kodjo convinced the couple that the risk of taking the baby was less than leaving it behind—that, as he put it, once having "opened the door [of pregnancy] they couldn't turn back now."

In prepping the couple for the interview, Kodjo insisted on one thing: that they enter the interview room with the "father" holding the baby and that they pass it back and forth during the interview (but, he also instructed, not *too* often). The strategy worked like a charm. The consul was friendly from the start and appeared positively taken with the infant, even leaving her perch behind the window to hold it in her arms. After a few minutes of light conversation—and no hint of a DNA test—she granted visas to all three.

Kodjo drew an important lesson from this case and stumbled into a new strategy. While he was initially upset at the couple for getting pregnant without telling him because of the complications and risks the pregnancy introduced, he now realized that a woman's bulging stomach or a baby in hand might have a powerful legitimating effect. There seemed something incontrovertible and real about a mother with a child (or about her husband showing it affection). Here the baby seemed to stand in for the spoken part of the interview itself. Instead of earnest and believable responses to the consul's questions or proof-of-marriage photos constituting a couple's authenticity, the pregnancy alone appeared to do that work, with words no longer necessary.

_____

An additional dilemma presented itself during the run-up to this couple's second interview: since the mother had already given birth, which father's name should be put on the baby's birth certificate—the birth father's or the fictive father's? Kodjo insisted that for the interview, it had to be the latter (but he also suggested that the parents obtain a second birth certificate with the birth father's name, so that it would be easy for the child to later reclaim his natal identity). Still the fictive father (the lottery winner) worried about giving his name to another's son—as did Kodjo, after a case he had been involved in two years earlier in Minnesota (in which the child's biological father tried to claim child support from the lottery father). With no guarantees in sight, however, Kodjo and his client had to rely on the couple's word that they were "devout Christians" and would not take advantage of the winner.

"Here's another interesting detail," Kodjo added in further parsing the case. He loves working his way through these details. Had destiny treated him differently, he would have been a gifted courtroom litigator. "After arriving in the U.S., the woman will divorce her visa spouse, before returning to Lomé to remarry her husband and apply for a visa for him and an older daughter of theirs. However, since the consulate's registry has her married to another man without daughter, she won't be able to claim their daughter as hers. Instead, her husband will say she's a daughter from a previous marriage and will have to generate the appropriate papers—a birth certificate with another 'wife's' name on it and a letter from that imaginary wife allowing him to take 'their' daughter to the U.S. It's also likely," Kodjo concluded, "that the consul will ask for a DNA test [to ensure that the daughter is indeed the second husband's child], but the man will be up to the challenge."

Notice how culture and the law—U.S. immigration and jurisprudential categories, American notions of biological kinship—reconfigure categories of relatedness and belonging at every step, and how this couple must calibrate their future together and their identity according to its logic and through the gaze of its purveyors. Not only must the wife marry a stranger, but she and her husband will divorce and then remarry, give another man's name to their infant (before changing it back), claim their daughter as his but not hers, and create a fictitious former wife for the husband—all the while spending years apart before reuniting as a family.

Here I follow the cases of several visa lottery selectees, exploring the ways situational kinship creates new desires and family forms. Located in the interstices between known practice and imagined category, visa lottery kinship is at once reiterative and innovative, drawing on everyday patterns while also refiguring them—kinship-with-a-difference, as it were.[2] Moreover DV kinship is "performative" in the fullest Butlerian sense,[3] often bringing into being and making real that which it enacts.

———————

I grew up on the cusp between pre–and post–*Writing Culture* moments, entering graduate school and going to the field in the early 1980s, then getting my first job at the end of that decade. While change and paradigm critique were already in the air in the early 1980s—Marx, Wallerstein, feminism, and Derrida were everyday fare in my grad classes—certain verities of the discipline remained unchallenged, especially the call to study in a village *elsewhere*. It was critique of the Orientalist divide and of the anthropological scale of analysis (the bounded village)—pillars of the *Writing Culture* moment—that had their most profound impact on me. After defending my dissertation—about a village in West Africa—I rewrote it from beginning to end to think the village beyond its borders and to see its connections to the modern and the global, a shift in scale that has carried through all my work since. It is ironic, then, that in this project on Togolese participation in the U.S. visa lottery—a project set in transnational space, driven by global fantasies, organized by post-9/11 biometrics and big data, implicating the anthropologist in blurred-boundary complicities—I also find myself returning to the oldest of village-study topics, that of kinship and the intimacies of everyday social relations. Of course it's kinship-with-a-difference, and with a different set of theoretical touchstones, but kinship all the same and in some of its classic guises. Plus ça change . . .

Faux Real?

Note that visa lottery couples (*faux* couples) go through a (real) marriage ceremony at the courthouse, before witnesses and a judge. After exchanging vows and rings, they take pictures with family and friends on the courthouse steps, often following this up with "honeymoon" photos on the beach or at the swimming pool of the five-star Hotel Sarakawa. In prepping for the embassy interview, they imagine themselves sweethearts—falling for each other the first time they met, honeymooning together—and become versed in the affective and bodily intimacies of the other (favorite foods and colors, every-day habits, body scars), as if lovers of long standing. As well they often live together for at least a month before the embassy interview—in case the con-sulate's fraud unit calls for an impromptu house visit—and again for several months after arriving in the United States (while awaiting their green cards).

Given the intensity of this performed conjugality, it should not be surpris-ing that some visa couples fall in love, or better put—since that term betrays cultural bias—end up staying together and having children. While Kodjo warns his clients to avoid any romantic involvement until after they get the visa—it's a "business" relationship, he insists, that will be vastly complicated by a failed romance—some can't resist and throw caution to the wind before the interview itself. Others wait until they have the visa before indulging their desires. More commonly desirous couples hold off until they're in the United States—with enough distance between themselves and spouses or lovers at home—before deepening the relationship.

I've met couples who have fallen for each other at each of these stages: before the interview, after the interview, after arriving in the United States. The last is the most common, not only because distance conceals but also because of the shared intimacy of being together in a faraway place. Regard-less of prior commitments, if attracted to one another, if their social indica-tors (age, class, ethnicity) line up, if the man has paid the interview fee and plane ticket (but usually not the other way around), the couple could well decide to stay together and have children.

But DV romance isn't always so neat. One married winner who began an affair with his lottery wife (before the interview) never told his (real) wife he'd been selected, let alone that he was sleeping with the other woman. The plot thickened when his wife found the money for the embassy interview (sent from the States by the man's sister) in her husband's belongings and—not knowing what it was for, though clearly having no qualms about stealing from him—replaced several $100 bills with counterfeits. The fake bills were discovered when the man tried to exchange them on the black market—luckily not at the embassy itself—before the interview. He suspected his wife but couldn't accuse her since he'd never announced his planned departure for the United States or that another woman was paying his way.

Another Kodjo winner, who also began an affair with his lottery spouse, carelessly left his papers on the table at home, with the other woman listed as wife. When his (real) wife found the papers, she imagined the other woman was trying to steal her husband and went to the embassy to rat them out. Needless to say, his loss was doubled: the man was denied his visa *and* lost his wife.

In a case that is ongoing, two friends—one married with three children, the other engaged to be married—won as a married couple. (Two friends sometimes apply together as a lark, never imagining they'll be selected.) Since they filed together, their "marriage" won't get flagged as a "pop-up" by the embassy computer,[4] and since the primary applicant has a baccalaureate, their case should sail through the vetting and interview process. All they need are appropriately backdated marriage papers, which are easily obtained from a judge friend of Kodjo's at the prefecture. But entanglements at home intervened. The man's wife (who doesn't know her husband has been selected, nor that he applied with another woman) has already accused him, apparently wrongly, of having an interest in this female friend. Moreover the man is a pastor, who will now have to set Christian principles aside to engage in a second, polygamous union. For her part, the woman is hesitant to go through a marriage ceremony with a man who is not her fiancé.

Because of these complications, the couple decided not to proceed. But a friend sent them to Kodjo, who recognized a sure thing and urged them to stay the course, insisting that this was the chance of a lifetime, that their visas were virtually guaranteed, that all would be forgiven at home when the man's wife and children (and the woman's fiancé) were on the other side of the Atlantic. Not surprisingly Kodjo won out, but he insisted that the couple tell no one of their good fortune, especially the man's wife, until after they received their visas. He worried that if the wife found out, she would go to the embassy and spoil the case. Kodjo also eased the woman's disquiet about "marrying" her friend by getting the judge to let them sign the marriage papers without appearing in court.

Kodjo himself is not untouched by such dynamics. He has married three of his clients but failed at the embassy interview each time, so now he is trying to send his (real) wife to the States as the spouse of one of his winners (where, once on the other side, she'll divorce the winner, remarry Kodjo, and bring him to the United States). But given all these infidelities—real marriages that dissolve, fake marriages that become real—shouldn't he be worried about marrying his wife to another? "You ought to be," a friend cajoled in his office one afternoon this July. "Your wife is a beautiful woman. If given the chance, I'd sleep with her in a minute. When she and her lottery husband are far away in the U.S., you don't think that man, and perhaps your wife as well, will be tempted?" "I've thought of that already," Kodjo countered, "and will send my wife to live with one of my friends, perhaps even *l'Americain* here, not with her visa spouse. But the lottery is risky business, and that's a risk I'm willing to take."

Bridewealth, as It Were

If performing conjugality can produce conjugality, it is also the case that conventional conjugal entitlements may seep into lottery practice. Thus some financing "husbands" see the visa payment as a type of bridewealth, which entitles them to marital rights. In one instance a States-side Kodjo client expected his visa spouse—the one he'd financed—to cook for him and share his bed. Another case, of a man who paid the woman's fees and plane ticket, then felt entitled after their arrival in the States, had an unusual twist. The woman refused the man's advances while keeping the door open, insisting that if he wanted to sleep with her, he would have to return to Lomé to ask her parents for her hand and pay the marriage gifts. Only then would she consider capitulating to his desire.

Precisely because arranged DV marriages can so easily blur into the real thing, some women, especially charismatic Christians (who have a strict view of the sanctity of marriage), refuse to participate in them. "Marriage is a once-only event, performed before God, and I won't marry someone just for a visa," an undocumented woman in the United States said to me (and this was someone who's applied unsuccessfully for the past fifteen years). "If I win the lottery myself, God will help me find a way to find the money." But she worried not only that an unholy marriage might put her in a tight spot with God but also—drawing on rumors that circulate among West Africans in the United States—that a visa spouse short on cash might try to blackmail her before agreeing to divorce.

"Certainly, why wouldn't it?" Kodjo responded to my query about the bridewealth analogy. "The boy is investing in the woman's future. This is what a woman looks for in a husband, someone who will take care of her." He then added, "As confirmation that it is a type of *dote* [bridewealth], think about this: all the arranged marriages that become real are when the boy is financing. If the girl is paying for the boy, it's unlikely they'll continue as a couple. Girls don't pay *la dote*."

But consider the upshot: among other things, the diversity lottery is a marriage-generating institution, enabling Togolese to meet one another and fashion futures together. When I put it to Kodjo in this way, he laughed and said, "Yes, of course the lottery can be the occasion for marriage. But what's the difference between meeting your future wife at the beach, at the shopping mall, or through the lottery?"

Identity Exchange

An extravagant case of improvisational kinship—what the consul who described it to me referred to as "identity theft"—came to the embassy's attention in 2011. A lottery winner had put his wife's name on the application but couldn't afford the interview fee or plane ticket and found a financier in the United States who needed papers and was willing to assume his wife's identity. The gambit worked: the woman returned to Lomé, obtained a birth certificate and passport in the wife's name, passed the embassy interview, and, after returning to the States, finally had her green card. Of necessity she kept using the name of the other because all of her papers were in that other's name, and at one point she returned to Lomé to renew her passport, again in the other woman's name. A few weeks later that woman—the man's (real) wife—applied for a passport and was turned down because, she was told, she already had a passport that had been "recently renewed." Confused and angry—she had no idea her husband had sold her name to this woman—she filed a complaint with the Ministry of Justice, which traced the passport and contacted the embassy. After confirming what had transpired and speaking to all parties involved, the State Department began deportation proceedings against the woman (though, surprisingly, not against the man).

An even more byzantine case of DV identity substitution—a man taking on the identity of his deceased cousin and his wife marrying the dead man, what anthropologists are fond of calling a "ghost marriage"—came to a sad denouement in 2008. A man who had been selected in the lottery died before he was able to go for the interview. Not wanting to let a golden opportunity slip by, his cousin decided to step into the shoes of the deceased and go for the interview in his name. He thus applied for a passport in the cousin's name (while using his own picture) and married his wife to the dead man. There was a delay at the passport office, however, with rumors circulating that authorities were tightening up on fraud, and he decided not to retrieve his passport, thus forgoing the embassy interview.

As luck would have it, the man's wife was selected in the lottery the following year—this time as herself. Since she had a baccalaureate and had listed her spouse and children on the application, theirs should have been an open-and-shut case. But at the interview the consul asked if she'd ever applied before—she had chosen to leave blank the section of the application where they ask you to declare any previous spouses—and she replied no (preferring, she said later, to risk that the consul hadn't noticed she'd applied the year before as the spouse of another rather than having to account for why she'd married two men in the same year). But the consul had run a photo-recognition test, which checks an applicant's picture against all others in the system, and held up the one she'd used on her application the previous year, asking if it was her picture. She admitted it was and, caught in a lie, was denied the visa. Sad, not only because she and her husband were fully legitimate and had an application that met all the requirements but also because, sensing a sure thing, they had mortgaged home and property to come up with the interview money for themselves and each of their three children—over $3,000.

How Different Is This?

While stretching relatedness into novel terrain, visa lottery kinship is nevertheless cut from the same cloth as Togolese everyday kinship. Improvisational pragmatics, the privileging of interest over love (or biology), assuming fictive identities, document manipulation—all these are the stuff of kinship as known and practiced, and all have the same goal: satisfying concrete needs, both material and social, by whatever means possible. This is why few Togolese I have spoken to find what Kodjo does odd or suspect, and why even high-ranking state officials are his clients.

In July 2012, for instance, an acquaintance from northern Togo told me he'd just married his fiancée but registered it as a "false marriage" at the prefecture—where, he said, they have "two marriage registers, one real, the other false"—because he didn't want her father to find out that they were married. The father, a local politician, was against the marriage because my friend was Christian, not Muslim, and because he couldn't stomach the idea of his daughter marrying "the son of his enemy." (The father had been a lifelong political opponent of Togo's dictator Gnassingbé Eyadéma, who hailed from the same ethnic group as my friend.) By registering the marriage in the shadow register, my friend was attempting to ensure that the girl's well-connected father wouldn't be able to discover their clandestine union and spoil their plans for a future together.

But all Togolese I know have stories like this—of document manipulation, of assuming the identity of another, of turning relatedness upside down to meet needs, of counterfeits and shadow deals all around. In the northern community where I work, villagers recently gamed a Danish nongovernmental organization that was sponsoring girls to attend school—though only one per family—by sending second and third daughters to live with relatives or friends (where those friends claimed their daughters as theirs). In the same village a man I know has three birth certificates for each of his children—one from when they were born, another from when a schoolteacher urged him to take four years off their ages (so they wouldn't be disadvantaged when looking for jobs), and a third from when this man discovered that the teacher had taken his money and run (never registering them and leaving the family with fake certificates).

These are everyday realities in this postcolony, and it is in this sense that I mean that visa lottery practice is of a piece with rather than a departure from quotidian kinship. Togolese inhabit a world one might call "allegorical," in which there are hidden meanings to every text, to every encounter, to every relationship, and in which little is as it appears. Nothing is self-evident, and "transparency"—that keyword of the international community and of the consulate—finds little place in people's everyday lives or lexicons.

But is it only Togolese or West Africans who traffic in nontransparent or compromised identities these days? Are we not living in a global age when moving between real and fake (assuming for the moment those categories have stable meaning) defines social personhood broadly, and in which the boundary between the two is forever blurred? Product piracy is virtually synonymous with global capitalism today—how to verify, for instance, whether or not your Nokia is real, whether your North Face jacket is a knockoff, whether you were taken for a ride when you bought a piece of designer clothing? Then too Americans cheat on their taxes and their spouses with such regularity that noncheaters are today the exception, and American university students plagiarize essays (by purchasing them on the Internet) and cheat on exams at alarmingly high rates. Wall Street investors—well, we all know what they did in 2008, nearly bringing the global financial system to its knees, with their shadow accounts, their swindling of clients, and their complicity in allowing the biggest Ponzi scheme of all time to flourish in the belly of the beast. Nor is it any accident, and indeed I see it as symptomatic, that American pop culture is positively obsessed with conspiracy theory. Many of the most watched television shows of the past five years are dripping with conspiracy thinking, driven by the message that things are not as they appear and that there are dark forces lurking behind every event. Americans too, I would insist, inhabit allegorical worlds.

DNA Surprises

DNA testing became the new embassy fix in the mid-2000s, promising a surefire (transparent) way of catching those trying to add the children of others to their dossiers. Despite the apparent certainties DNA testing provided, however, surprises and unintended consequences remained in store for both sides—providing yet another example of the difficulty of closing loopholes to eliminate fraud and of using the latest science to do so.

The embassy was especially likely to ask for a DNA test if children were not declared on the original application but then "popped up" after selection. If they were declared on the original application, the consul assumed that they were the couple's own (biological) children. But of course such is not always the case. In Togo, and throughout much of the subregion, child fostering is common and children circulate between households all the time (both within village and city and between the two). Moreover a child's father is defined by marriage, not genealogy—by social rather than biological criteria. Thus a woman's child by anyone other than her husband—a lover, even a rapist—belongs to her husband, not to the biological father. Therefore it is unlikely that all Togolese children claimed as such will conform to American definitions—definitions that lie behind the DNA test—or that those enlisting the names of siblings' children are doing so dishonestly.

While the embassy's romance with DNA made it harder than before to add nonbiological children after selection, Kodjo, always parsing fine differences, found a small window that he felt would give him room to maneuver. He wondered whether adding small children to a dossier, infants who had been born since the time of application, namely children under two—it can take two years from time of application to interview—might get through without being called for a DNA test. He guessed right, and in the two cases he tried in 2010–11 he was successful. Both were children of others who, in possession of a fictive birth certificate, passed as the children of a winner.

Moreover he toyed with the idea that some wealthy nonapplicant who wanted U.S. citizenship for his or her child might try such a strategy and bankroll a couple in need. While unlikely—who would care for the child in the States?—it's not entirely far-fetched. A recent fad among well-off Togolese women—wives of ministers, members of the political elite—has been to get pregnant, then apply for a tourist visa to the United States, then give birth on American soil so that their child will have U.S. citizenship.

But in jumping on the DNA bandwagon, the surprise in store for the embassy was that a DNA mismatch might reveal not so much a fake marriage as a marital infidelity. In December 2011 the consulate was pulled into just such a case. When a Togolese couple in the United States applied to bring over their three children and was asked to get DNA tests, positive matches with both parents were found for only two of the children. The third was positive for the mother alone. When informed of the results, the couple, presumably distraught and quarrelling, pleaded with the consul in a barrage of emails from the States to not tell their families back home, where the children were staying. The irony in this case was that, since the wife already had U.S. citizenship, she could have applied on her own to bring over all three. But of course had she attempted to do so, her husband would have discovered her secret. This case had a happy (or semihappy) ending, however, as the consulate, in a generous gesture, allowed the woman to apply again to bring over the three children—but now on her own.

But consider the upshot: the consulate won't permit polygamous unions (or give visas to the children of such unions)—indeed if you're a polygamist, you can't go for the embassy interview—but they will allow adulterous ones, or at least they were willing to in this case.

Consular Kinship

Cultural specificities attend the definition of the kinship unit, the "family," that lies at the heart of the visa lottery system. Those who apply for the lottery and go for the interview must conform to consular, Euro-American definitions of family: that of a husband-wife pair and their biological children. But, as suggested earlier, Togolese family definition is far more capacious, consisting not only of a man and his wife or wives but also all those children, whether biological or not, that a conjugal unit is taking care of and feeding.

Since they are calling the shots and offering citizenship as a gift, it is of course within the State Department's rights to set definitions as they wish. But in so doing, in insisting on American kinship norms, they create all sorts of problems and suspicions for themselves. Namely they suspect Togolese of trying to scam them (that is, of deliberately lying or engaging in fraud) when they add the names of siblings' children or girlfriends' children to their dossier, when in fact they may just be playing by local rules—caught up in different cultural understandings of family.

The cultural bias that interests me even more, however—as it lies at the very heart of consular anxiety about the so-called fraud that surrounds the entire system—is the one that tries to differentiate a real from an arranged or "fake" marriage. In the normative American view, romance, not interest, defines the conjugal unit. But how—in any marriage, anywhere—to discover whether interest or love is operating? And how is a consul going to pass such judgment after a ten-minute interview?

One index the consulate relies on is whether the couple declared themselves as such on the original application. In such a case the consuls assume it was a legitimate ("real") marriage, rarely doubting its authenticity and subjecting the couple to cross-examination. But recall the case of the two friends (one already married, the other engaged) playing together as a lark, with both names on the original application. They will get their visas without the consul batting an eye. Or what if a married couple appears on the original application whose marriage *was* arranged, influenced by the heavy imprint of their families, as many still are today? Because declared early in the process, the embassy assumes it's a love marriage and the couple will pass through.

On the flip side, a couple that marry with the express purpose of getting a U.S. green card is considered illegitimate. Here "interest" rather than "love" is thought to define their relationship. For Togolese, however, all marriages are "interested." "A woman marries a man with money, someone who can care for her," Kodjo said one day. "A man marries a woman who will bear him children. Romance and the love you Americans imagine as the center of a marriage is not as important for us. Sure, if this couple also likes one another, all the better. But what's most important are these interests of money and children. How is a lotto visa marriage any different?"

When I pressed Kodjo on the point, he turned the question around and asked how "un-interested" European marriages are. "Don't you too marry for money or class or beauty? How many rich Americans marry poor Americans? How many white Americans marry black Americans? Not many. Few just marry as such."

"And what about," I continued, "the consular charge that the difference is that DV marriages are expedient, too interest-driven, that people are marrying just to get the visa and then divorce?" "Well, as you know," he responded, "some lottery unions end up in marriage. But also I know that many American marriages based on love end quickly as well. So I'm not sure that the length of time that a couple remains married should be determining."

"So there is no such thing as a 'faux mariage'?" I asked. "I never use that term," he said. "For me, all marriages are *arrangé et interessé*."

By Way of Conclusion

Just before they go for the embassy interview, Kodjo gives his clients a pep talk, telling them that, having been selected in the lottery, they have a right to their visa and to U.S. citizenship and that no one can take it away. If they stand strong and show courage during the interview, they will get their visas.

A fascinating moment occurred at a pre-interview session I was present at in July 2012. Kodjo ended the session by telling the couple that they, not the consul, held the "truth" about their case. The embassy knew nothing about them, he said, except what was written on their forms and what they would say during the interview. "The entire case is in your hands," he concluded. This view, that the world they constructed and performed in words constituted the truth about their world—that there was no outside to their words or to the documents, no external proof that their story wasn't true, that all was relative to that which they performed before the consul—struck me as flawless in its logic and fully in step with postcolonial times, as well as representing sage advice for the challenge ahead.

This moment also helped me make sense of a puzzling statement of Kodjo's several years earlier. In 2005, when the embassy sensed, perhaps for the first time, that there was hustling going on around the lottery, the U.S. ambassador went on Togolese television to warn against visa fraud and to say that, going forward, the consulate would assume that all who came for the DV interview were lying and that it was up to them to prove otherwise. Despite my own astonishment at this presumption—that an interviewee might be considered a fraudster until proven innocent—Kodjo was positively pleased with the ambassador's statement, saying that it confirmed what he'd assumed about the process all along and played to his strength. Namely that it was the responsibility of those being interviewed to present all the right "proof-of" papers—high school diploma, marriage certificate, papers of professional affiliation, and so on—and that if they did, they would be granted visas. Thus too, implicitly, that the consulate would have to catch the couple in a lie or an inconsistency for them to be denied. Therefore it's up to Kodjo to prepare an airtight case, for which he is famous: to produce a married couple with a perfectly believable and consistent story and with documents to match. "If that's their charge, I should win every time," he stated.

Kodjo also felt that the ambassador's televised comments were an invitation to join the fray—which is something he lives for.

Notes

1 More Togolese per capita apply for the DV each year than those from any other African country—but one index of the importance *lotto visa* has come to assume in the cultural life of this small West African country.
2 Derrida, "Différance"; Gates, "The Signifying Monkey."
3 Butler, "Gender Trouble."
4 "Pop-up" marriages—the embassy's term—are those that are added after a selectee has applied.

CHAPTER II

Dying Worlds

Kamala Visweswaran

I. Human-Elephant Conflict

Across Africa, South and South East Asia elephants have been attacking and killing human beings, leading, in the 1990s, to a new category of study among elephant researchers, human-elephant conflict (HEC). Over the past twelve years in Assam, elephants have killed 605 people; 239 since 2001 alone. In Jharkhand, along its western border with Bangladesh, 300 people have been killed between 2002 and 2004. In Sri Lanka 60 people a year for the past fifteen years have been killed by elephants (though the toll on elephants has been much higher, averaging 130 killed per year over the last decade). In Africa, from Sierra Leone to Uganda, reports of human-elephant conflict appear almost daily. In these areas, these zones of human conflict and genocide, elephants die too.

Elephants store trauma the way humans do. They respond to violence, captivity, and displacement with abnormal and violent social behavior. Male elephants in Africa have been reported to rape and kill female rhinoceroses; in some reserves male elephants are responsible for 90 percent of the deaths of other male elephants; elsewhere herds of elephants are now seen trampling and destroying entire villages. The flow of weapons through the violent conflicts of these regions has in turn transformed one of the most ordinary of criminal practices. Poaching comes to mimic the technics of violent war: hand grenades are thrown at herds of wild elephants to disable them; tusks are cut out of still living elephants, while the rest of the herd watches at a distance. The loss of elephant elders, crucial for their social networks, and the traumatic experience of seeing members of their families massacred means that the survivors, mostly females, take years to rebuild a community. At the turn of the twentieth century only 1 percent of male elephants lacked tusks; today in parts of India and Africa up to 30 percent of all male elephants born now lack tusks.

Before the brutal wars of the twentieth century came the high colonialism of the long nineteenth century. In Sri Lanka the advent of HEC is linked to the clearing of the jungles for the large tea plantations that would dominate the interior of the country. In 1948, the year of Sri Lanka's independence, the novel *Elephant Walk* by Robert Standish (pseudonym of the *Saturday Evening Post* writer Digby George Gerahty) used the intrusion of tea estates into elephant territory as the dramatic impetus for a triumphant pachydermal rampage to reclaim lost habitat. In the 1954 potboiler starring Elizabeth Taylor, however, the circus elephants on hand had to be coaxed into storming the set: so delicate was the "elephant walk" that special furniture was designed to collapse with the mere nudge of a trunk as the trained elephants carefully avoided objects placed in their path.

In recent years one of the first people to document the collapse of elephant social structure, the incidence of something like posttraumatic stress disorder among them, was the Ugandan ethologist Elizabeth Abe.[1] Her own ethnic community, the Achioli, had been violently displaced during the war with Tanzania that finally toppled Idi Amin's regime in Uganda. She and her family were refugees in Kenya in the 1970s and again in 1986 as conflict erupted between the government and the Lord's Rebel Army, an organization that routinely procured Achioli boys for its ranks by first forcing them to witness the killing of their parents. Abe reflects:

> You know we used to have villages. We still don't have villages. There are over 200 displaced people's camps in present-day northern Uganda. Everybody lives now within these camps, and there are no more elders. The elders were systematically eliminated. The first batch of elimination was during Amin's time, and that set the stage for the later destruction of northern Uganda. We are among the lucky few, because my mom and dad managed to escape. But the families there are just broken. I know many of them. Displaced people are living in our home now. My mother said let them have it. All these kids who have grown up with their parents killed—no fathers, no mothers, only children looking after them. They don't go to schools. They have no schools, no hospitals. No infrastructure. They form these roaming, violent, destructive bands. It's the same thing that happens with the elephants. Just like the male war orphans, they are wild, completely lost.[2]

Human-elephant conflict, and Abe's story of it, is not a parable of refugees being forced to live like animals or of animals becoming refugees, though we ignore the consonance at our peril. Neither is it a classic feedback loop, for this one in order to sustain itself—mass death producing more mass death—will eventually, like its subjects, be annihilated. Nor is it about the human tendency to anthropomorphize the zoological (although such criticism could be leveled at HEC studies), where perhaps a violent "animacy" co-exists.[3] Rather, I think here of a founding irony: before genocide entered the mid-twentieth-century English lexicon, Raphael Lemkin, the Latvian Jew who coined the term, struggled to differentiate targeted destruction and mass death from vandalism and barbarity but to retain the moral opprobrium associated with the latter.[4] Tellingly influenced by George Eastman's invention of the brand name Kodak as a word capture of the camera, Lemkin too sought a term that would convey in a flash the wholesale death of a kind.[5] So even as the Latin *genus*, designating family, gender, line of descent, type (from its Greek root *geno* meaning race, stock, kin) can in logic refer to a like class of objects, or in biology to a group of species exhibiting similar characteristics, out of such philological trafficking emerges a surprising taxonomic fidelity: genocide is not what happens mainly to humans; genocide is what happens to groups of species with a shared characteristic—mass death.

II. Phantom Conflict

The night of the first day back in Ahmedabad I dream:

I am in some kind of morgue. There is the feel of steel-gray walls and vacant emptiness. I have been left for dead, but the consciousness that I am still alive is on me like a dead weight, like the bodies of others I know have been tossed over me. I have been suffocating, and now I come to consciousness with a gasp. I am aware of being raped, of having been raped. I don't know whether I am in the past or present. There is an overwhelming sensation of redness that intrudes on the steel gray, just on the edge of what I can willingly see and hear. On some other plane I know there is blood everywhere. I know there is screaming: my own and that of others. I know my body has been ravaged, but I can't feel anything. The knowledge is there. But I cannot see, feel, or hear anything in this state, suspended between past and future events. I am not sure whether the violence has already happened or is about to happen again. I feel strange comfort that I am away from the violence, that it is beyond me, it cannot touch me anymore. I am aware of all this. There in that room, which is or is not a morgue. In the room where I sleep. Where I have been left for dead. Where I may no longer be alive.

Days later I read:

A newspaper report on the mysterious Vatva rapist. At first the police take the reports seriously and mount a night patrol. But when the police don't find anything, the patrol is called off. The residents are angry but know that if the police haven't seen the rapist they cannot act. The rapist, who appears on terraces where women are sleeping in the open night air or next to women's beds in their houses, is said to be tall and black with oily hair and skin. He can pass from one building to another without being seen; he has springs in his feet and is able to jump great heights and bound away from his pursuers with amazing speed. He is definitely an outsider; he is definitely Hindu, though no one dares to say it but a youth from the stricken community. Opinions are mixed as to whether he is merely a man, a man with demonic powers, a ghost (*dhaaba bhoot*, the one who haunts the terraces), or maybe even a *bhataki aatma*, the tormented soul of one who died a cruel, vicious death in the violence two years ago.

Vatva police inspector B. I. Patel says defensively, "It is not that I do not believe in the supernatural, but this particular rumor appears baseless." Does it take a Hindu policeman to miss what Muslims see? Is it a surprise that the ghost is also called *sarkari bhoot*, the government in the form of its police and officials come once again to terrify and abuse them?[6] Weeks after a beloved nineteen-year-old female college student Ishrat Raza has been killed in a police encounter over a concocted plot to kill Chief Minister Narendra Modi,[7] the police in Vatva claim there is not even the ghost of an encounter with the Vatva rapist.

The psychologists call it a form of mass hysteria. Like the Delhi Monkeyman, the Vatva rapist has the residents of Saiyedawadi and Arsh colony in a panic. The men of the *mohalla* are up in arms, guarding the neighborhood, which is too afraid to sleep. The men return home early from work so that that can take up the patrol the police have abandoned. They have chased the bhoot down dark alleys; they follow the screams of their womenfolk at night. But it is not only the women who have seen sarkari bhoot; the husbands of the women who have seen him have also spotted him; so too, the friends of those husbands. Their eyes bloodshot by morning, the men of the mohalla are missing their sleep, late for work, and losing business because of this evil, naked man; this lewd and leering *salla besahram* who threatens their women. The woman who awakened to find the bhoot next to her in her bed can hardly speak afterward; another has become possessed by its spirit. Still other women complain of red, swollen eyes and headaches that remain indefinitely after sighting the dhaaba bhoot. In the morning's light the mohallah's residents see a dead mynah hanging from a babul tree and dogs that have been slashed by knives in the night.[8] It is all real, and it is all like a bad dream.

The people of Vatva are reluctant to speak of the terror that haunts them, afraid of the ridicule and humiliation. They are used to being disbelieved. They are used to police inaction and police complicity—they are one and the same thing really. There are no First Information Reports, no complaints of the Vatva rapist on file, just as most of the rapes from the earlier violence were not reported and carried no separate FIRs. But there is a trail of raped women all the same. Only time has warped itself again. One is unsure whether the women are reacting to the rapes that already happened or are anticipating the rapes they know can happen at any time. At first I think I have only unconsciously channeled what the Vatva women describe as they lay down to their fitful, uneasy sleep, such that the contagion of their fear has also invaded my slumber. Then I realize that the women of Vatva are confronting a personification of their daily terrors; imbedded in the memory of their sisters being paraded naked through neighborhoods and villages by leering *bajrang dalis*,[9] the memory of the sexual harassment of the police during the combing operations; the fear of their men being picked up for random, but persistent POTA detentions,[10] so that the threat of the rapist becomes a way of ensuring that the men of the community return home early. To defend the community. To stalk the stalker. But also to be accounted for. Safe, in a way.

Perhaps the Vatva rapist is the phantasmatic resurfacing and recirculation of these repressed memories of violence in a place where post-traumatic stress disorder is hardly a name on a piece of paper. And yet, like the men who committed the mass violence two years ago, the Vatva rapist will never be caught. Will never stand trial. Will never be convicted in a court of law.

III. *Fieldnoting*

I want to claim the above narratives as forms of fieldnoting. In pressing the noun into a verb, however, I am not after any narrative of possession or dispossession of the object writers who are not anthropologists might also refer to as "field notes." (V. S. Naipaul once declared he took no notes to write any of his books on India, and equally smugly that the entire narrative of *Beyond Belief* was contained in nine notebooks each the size of a hundred-rupee note.)[11] Neither do I have in mind a tweeted or blogged version of "live fieldnoting" with daily entries of one to five sentences that some students are experimenting with, nor an intermediate form of writing between original field notes (to be recuperated as fetish object) and full analytic argument, but a form of writing that is ongoing and processual.[12] Fieldnoting attempts to track its sources of mediations; it does not pretend to be separate from media and other circulations of reported speech or discourse that inevitably converge upon a "field."

Fieldnoting is the process through which the field itself—its scenes and analytics—is denoted or defined, tracked through a field of proliferating associations,[13] but also a network of blockages and apprehensions. Any field, and our perception of it, shifts over time. It is both structured by the processes of accretion, sifting, and assemblage and attentive to those same processes. And yet temporality, or rather temporal suspension and drift are sparsely enough theorized. The tendency to see the mass death that genocide signifies as preceding the term's birth into language, and thus encompassing most of human history, also exceeds the parameters of the available present, so that it pushes out into "post-conflict" futures. If I started my work in Gujarat, and more locally in Ahmedabad and Baroda; even the attempt to parse who applied the term to describe the targeted killings of Muslims across Gujarat during the first several months of 2002—*genocide* is a coined term, after all; there is no equivalent in Gujarati or many Indian languages—took me farther afield, and inevitably back home.

"Traveling again. Home to nightmare."[14]

There is something about the way the experience of catastrophe—and there are none any longer the sole provenance of nature—is rendered everyday through the practices of mass media that requires attention. For has not mass media itself a distracting yet constitutive relationship to mass death? When, during the summer of 2005, I commenced Michael Ondaatje's *Coming through Slaughter* by seeing it as the story of one jazz musician's madness and devastation, after Hurricane Katrina struck and whole neighborhoods of music and life submerged, jazz audiences and communities—an entire musical heritage—engulfed, the meanings the novel might generate were also reshaped by the reportage around me. In the aftermath of sense making, as the tales of death and deprivation were still flooding in and the radio and TV were awash with "personal interest stories," I began to understand why survivors of the Gujarat massacres used the Hindi and Urdu word *tufan* (from whence the English *typhoon* is derived) to describe the violence that had befallen them.

Genocide delimits my field of work, and so news of it—a sprawling semantic field across time and space—is inescapably my object; it is intrinsic to what I call fieldnoting.[15] So it wasn't just Katrina that changed how I saw the field; it was the way the Gujarat violence played out in the print media; the way the Iraq War was always on the TV; the radio story of the artist who went to Rwanda to look at piles of bones, seeking aesthetic inspiration; the rows of photos of those killed in Cambodia, their skulls arranged apically like fruit for sale; the Darfur activists who made a video game so that teenagers could "experience" the genocide; the lawyers who brought genocide charges against the Mexican government for the massacres of UNAM students in the 1960s; the observation of Anne Frank's birthday, "the school girl whose diary introduced Americans to the story of the holocaust"; the elephants subjected to "genocide."

And later that year it was the anti-abortion rally in front of the campus gym sporting thirty-foot high posters of blown-up fetuses protesting a "holocaust of the unborn" that rearranged both my tenses and objects of description. For it seems to me that genocide simultaneously inhabits a willing subjunctive, an abject conditional (intervene, or else) and a present continuous tense; it subsumes past and future into bipolar forms of depressive realism (HEC, impunity, judicial failure) or terrorizing mania (dhaaba bhoots, fetal giants, cartoon Janjaweed). What must shift (the ground, the field; for better, for worse) to see all this as an ethnographic present?

Genocide both circumscribes my field and exceeds it, for no one yet can really explain it. Its specificities and singularities, of course, are readily described, have amassed archives and mobilized a social science, but its exponential replicability, its pluralities across time and space are not well understood (unlike other regularizing phenomena, which are amenable to the optimalities of mathematical modeling). The cladistic attempt to sort and distinguish genocide from other types of conflicts ultimately fails in trying to understand it as a distinct class of events, for its genus is one that dissolves the more those events multiply. Genocide is a multiplier, and this is not its only effect.

The sense of a field exceeding its limits is real; only partially wrought by globalization, it requires forms of writing that might layer, sequence, seriate, or reassemble it. Fieldnoting owes something to a deconstructive notion of texts, in which "they overrun the limits assigned to them . . . making them more complex; transgressing the limits of what was set up in opposition to writing (speech, life, the world, the real, history, every field of reference—to body or mind, conscious or unconscious, politics, economics, and so forth)."[16] As an open system, fieldnoting holds together apparently disparate elements, fields of reference or "plateaus" in which any number of connecting routes could exist.[17] Only method stops the assemblage once it begins, for it is in some sense inexhaustible. This is both promise and portent of the times in which we live.

IV. The Death of Form/s

Forms have to change. . . . Nothing stands still; everything has to move on. Every form which is living has to move on. To pretend to be a writer in 2005 as though you were beginning in 1955 is utterly foolish. The world has changed; the forms have changed.
—V. S. Naipaul, *New York Times* interview, 2005

A passing remark in James Clifford's introduction to *Writing Culture*, the idea of anthropologists posing as novelists manquées was made at a time when the death of the novel was already a much-rehearsed theme. John Barth's 1967 essay "The Literature of Exhaustion" is oft-cited as one of its harbingers. In fact Barth used a Borgesian conception of the Baroque as "that style which deliberately exhausts (or tries to exhaust) its possibilities and borders upon its own caricature" to suggest the "baroqueness" of literary history and its constituent forms "exhausting the possibility of novelty."[18] Amid the evanescent talk of "emergent forms," then, might we reflect upon (mourn even?) the decline of certain forms (ethnography among them) and what their survival might subtend?[19] What must die that we might better remember "how newness enters the world"?[20]

Barth himself registered less alarm than sociological prescience over the strong feelings the decline of the novel generated, noting that "one way to handle such a feeling might be to write a novel about it."

Whether historically the novel expires or persists as a major art form seems immaterial. . . . If enough writers and critics feel apocalyptical about it, their feeling becomes a considerable cultural fact, like the feeling that Western civilization, or the world, is going to end rather soon. If you took a bunch of people out into the desert and the world didn't end, you'd come home shamefaced . . . but the persistence of an art form doesn't invalidate work created in comparable apocalyptic ambience.[21]

Adorno could proclaim no poetry after Auschwitz, but Barth saw the persistence of the novel itself as both cultural fact and apocalyptic form, poised at the edge of dying worlds, if not the decline of Western civilization. Half a century later the novelist Jonathan Franzen would describe this "post-war" apocalypse as both generational and intensely personal.[22]

Jacques Derrida's classic essay "Living On" (uncoincidentally dedicated to a mischievous colleague who anonymously published "Textes: Suivi de la mort de Litterature") notes the space of suspension in which something was "over . . . and then over again" as also a space of the "brink, the edge, the verge" wherein "living on" signaled writing itself as phantasm (the victory of death over life) or pending apocalypse. How, then, might a faltering form serve as an index of the failing world of which it is but a symptom? Call this an analogism of the strategic kind.[23]

By the time Naipaul trumpeted the decline of the novel in several interviews between 1995 and 2005 ("the novel has done its work . . . there is nothing more for that form to do"), not a few critics noted that his own novelistic output had dramatically slowed. If Naipaul could claim in one of his first novels, *A Bend in the River*, that "non-fiction can distort; facts can be realigned. But fiction never lies," by 2005 he encountered a horizon where fiction itself seemed no longer a possibility; it would lead to "falsifying material." In Naipaul's words, "The fictional form would force you to do things to your material, to dramatize it in a certain way. . . . Non-fiction gave you the chance to explore . . . that other world, the one you didn't know fully." Naipaul saw the gift of great novelists as being able to "see" their societies; when the novel failed the gift, the writer's charge to "possess" one's society had to pass to a new form.[24] When narration had to salvage itself as reportage, however, Naipaul refused to see himself as a journalist, a mere writer of news,[25] but as someone who "travelled on a theme . . . to make an inquiry," taking with him "the gifts of sympathy, observation, and curiosity" developed as an imaginative writer. Naipaul's own skill set seems to recall the ethnographer's, and if it is true (regardless of whether the novel is dead) that literary non-fiction is somehow ascendant twenty-five years after *Writing Culture* raised the questions of fiction and form for anthropology,[26] what might we gain by seeing ethnography as a form of literary non-fiction, as a kind of traveling on a theme?

I am not the only one to ask this question where others have preferred the term *creative non-fiction*,[27] but in posing it anew my aim is not to referee the relationship between novelists and journalists (when not even Naipaul him-self could so do) or to engineer a disciplinary solution that merges journalism with ethnography. Indeed even to inquire into the relevance of journalism for anthropology is to recognize another death—that of the newspaper—such that the forms journalism now takes are radically altered, changed, or hybrid. The reporter and columnist Carl Hiaasen's novels about hack jour-nalists punching defunct typewriters in decrepit newsrooms vigilantly chart the demise of print journalism. Even the "new journalism" emergent in the 1960s and 1970s, and styled to the magazine-type format of the *New Yorker*, *Harper's*, or the *Atlantic Review*, now competes with blogs without word limit.

Arguably what the new journalism did most insidiously was to poach long-term investigative research from the terrain of social science. What the new journalism did most effectively was to take the immediacy of "real life" and render it both fantastic and understandable. Crime reporting moved from the daily beat of the street into "true crime" social commentary.[28] Even before Truman Capote's (1966) *In Cold Blood* pioneered the "non-fiction novel" and Norman Mailer's (1979) *Executioner's Song* finalized the third-person as its narrative strategy, Eudora Welty's 1963 short story for the *New Yorker*, "Where Is the Voice Coming From," defied coming convention by eerily inhabiting in the first person, Medgar Evers's killer, Byron de la Beck-with. Troubled and provoked by Evers's assassination, Welty, whose writing career began in journalism, thought she knew where the killer was coming from: her first-person voice was so disturbingly convincing that the *New Yorker* asked her to remove factual markers and real names from the revised text that was finally published.[29]

As interesting, for my purposes, as the non-fiction novels and stories writ-ten by journalists are writers like Naipaul—Pankaj Mishra and Amitav Ghosh among them—who work as novelists but continue with larger success in the field of literary non-fiction. Too, perhaps the best book on the Gujarat violence was written by an editor for the *Indian Express* newspaper, some-one steeped in the reportage but who made something else of it. Ghosh has described keeping field notes for a dissertation and a journal for everything else that couldn't be said in it. This sense of the expressiveness of form as at once a limit and site of dis/closure—of something that can be said in one form but not in another, as a splitting of form into its own supplement,[30] of something spoken in one language but not translatable into another—is arguably still at the heart of writing culture.

What's left about two months after an apartment complex is set on fire? After many of those who live there have been killed? And those who haven't, have flown away on wings of fear, never to return?

Not much.

It was here on the last day of the February gone by, that a mob had stood and set the buildings on fire, burnt alive 38 residents—twelve are missing to this day. The Gulbarga massacre, as it came to be called in newspapers and on TV, was one of a series across the state of Gujarat that killed over 1,000 men, women, and children, 70 percent of them Muslim, ostensibly as revenge for the death of 59 Hindu passengers in an attack on a train by a Muslim mob the previous morning. . . . .

All of the above is fact.

All of what follows is fiction.[31]

Fireprooof was not the journalist Raj Kamal Jha's first novel, but it is so far the only one on the Gujarat genocide, and amid the extended production of social science on Gujarat and its failure,[32] it is perhaps the best book that has been written on the subject. The story chronicles a father's coming to terms with the monstrous birth of his mute son, scarcely a body stem with a head and barely recognizable as human except for two large eyes. Not even properly named, it/him or "Ithim" is a kind of depersonalized testimony to humanity's truncated survival, a neonatal figure of "bare life." Jha will pull some switches between the Burn Ward and Maternity Ward, showing how the violence outside the hospital has inflicted itself on the mute witness of a child being born into the blackened, shriveled form of the recently killed, a charred strip of skin for his forehead and mid-section. As a signifying figure of dehumanization, "Ithim" refers not only to the loss of humanity of those who have watched the violence and done nothing about it, but to the possibility that the violence might have originated in this loss of humanity in the first place.

The novel is about impunity and guilt; it begins and ends with something like a First Information Report or the opening and closing statements of lawyers at trial, simulating the juridical form and language of the affidavit. But it is also an attempt at storying the dead whose stories have been lost. After the novel's opening injunction, "Don't listen to the dead, please do not listen to the dead," it inserts the testimonies of the dead, imagining what they could tell us, but as fading footnotes to the main story, in small, faint type. The novel is populated by the anonymous dead who worked in and around the hospital where Ithim is born: a ward guard, two doctors, a head nurse, a taxi driver, a teenage boy, a fruit seller, and a defiant Miss Glass, who says, "You aren't going to get me to say who I was, who I left behind. I am not going to give you a personal profile of my grief in about 350 words, in small type, single-spaced." Further along one encounters "Body 3, five years old," then "Floor Body they showed on the news and TV" and "Screaming Woman."

Fireproof is self-consciously a novel about mediation and mediatization—it destabilizes media practices by mimicking them; it plays with and upon the news, even repetitively imbedding fragments of three news photos as "evidence" in the text. One chapter, "News on TV, Man from Ukraine" surfaces the process of subject interpellation by asking the reader to recall what was being broadcast the first night of the riots: "What's its relevance now? For one, the noise from the TV, its shadows and flickers, the faces and voices of strangers [man from Ukraine, woman from South Korea] filled the room, bringing for the first time since the previous evening, a sense of the predictable and normal into my life and my home" (119).

Jha asks his readers to consider the news cycle and the fleeting images it regurgitates. His narrator surfs ninety-nine channels and does not spare the reader several passages on Guinness Book of World Record contests and human interest trivia, before he finally finds what he is looking for: "news." The reportage starts, then the sound is cut as a series of images flash by:

> This city, this afternoon, a mob looking into the camera, waving, smiling, a close-up of a body on a stretcher, its face covered but the stretcher on the floor, surrounded by several women crying. (They showed this Floor Body several times). A house on fire, a shop on fire, women and children huddled on the floor, a house on fire again, another shop on fire, a rubber tyre on fire, a car on fire, Floor Body again. The sound was back. Screaming Woman was loud, her hair across her face, several strands sprayed across her lips, blowing in the air she breathed out as she screamed.
>
> ". . . reports of deaths have come from Ahmedabad, Godhra, Vadodara, Bhavnagar, Sabarkantha, Rajkot, Panchmahals, Anand, and Kheda." Again the sound went off. (123)

Perhaps it goes without saying that these reported deaths, these images, these sounds and sound failures are all true, despite being written as fiction.

V. Anxiety/Against Method

If in some quarters *Writing Culture* was seen to reflect a "crisis in the discipline," perhaps so many years later we can see it as symptomatic of ongoing anxiety, which some have sought to solve with methods and typologies on the one hand, or instruction manuals on the other, unwittingly enacting Georges Devereaux's movement of "anxiety to method."[33] Devereaux pointed to the effects of the observer upon the observed, to the inevitable messiness of transference and counter-transference of a "field." Perhaps we are not so much in search of new methods—since all methods, as Paul Feyerabend showed (puckish anthropology notwithstanding),[34] contain their own orthodoxies—as we are in need of simple affirmation of a plurality genres, or inter-genres, some of them familiar but perhaps doing unfamiliar kinds of work; of failing as well as resurgent forms of description. If ethnography has almost been fiction or journalism, and not quite either, perhaps it must exceed or rest irresolutely between genres, as a kind of "living on" that is not yet "emergence." And where the presumption for ethnographic writing has been that intimacy holds greater value for truth telling, perhaps the journalist's more limited, even casual encounter or a novelist's deliberate break of acquaintance is adequate caution against "participant observation" becoming the one method, the one sure thing anthropology can still claim to know.

—————

Nadine Gordimer once recounted the time she wrote a novel about a revolutionary who was imprisoned and killed by the South African government.[35] She was a friend of this man and his family, knew them well without being an intimate. Sometime after the revolutionary's arrest, Gordimer, outside the prison to see one of the inmates, ran into one of the daughters in school uniform waiting in line to see her father; out of this brief encounter sprang a novel that opened with Claude Lévi-Strauss's enigmatic epitaph, "I am the place in which something has occurred."

Its first lines were "Among the group of people waiting at the Fortress was a school-girl in a brown and yellow uniform holding a green eider-down quilt, and by the loop at its neck, a hot water bottle. Certain buses used to pass that way then, and the passengers looking out will have noticed the school girl. Imagine, a school girl: she must have somebody inside."[36]

A few pages later one line on a single page marks the beginning of the narrative of *Burger's Daughter*: "When they saw me outside of the prison, what did they see?"[37] This close mirroring of the question of sight and observation, of looking and noticing a subject and of the subject in turn querying, "What did you see?" suggests the emergence of a different ethnographic relationship, ironically born through fiction.

During the several years Gordimer took to write her novel, she stayed away from the family, stopped visiting them, and ceased all contact. When she finished the novel she sent it first to the revolutionary's daughter, a seemingly strange move for a novelist, asking one of its fictional subjects to weigh in, to gauge the veracity of the novel, to test whether recognition would also constitute permission.

"This is what I saw; do you agree?"

There was silence for several weeks. . . . One afternoon she walked through my gate carrying the manuscript. So that was what it was after all, a package of paper; we sat and exchanged the usual generalities and then, in a gap, there it was between us, the novel.

I explained to her that . . . during the four years I was writing the novel, I had avoided contact with her and other surviving members of the family. I deliberately had allowed friendship to lapse. Perhaps it seems naïve, perhaps it was my quaint notion of authorial morality, perhaps it was my eccentric methodology—I had the idea that there must be no evidence, in the test of creation, that I was "studying" her in order to inform my fictions, measuring the progression of her life in the to-and-fro of past and present that delineates personality.

She said, "This was our life."

And nothing more.[38]

It seems to me that ethnography too is that record of "our life."
Of "living on," and nothing more.

Notes

I am indebted to Jim Clifford, Orin Starn, Ben Lee, Ruken Sengul, Neni Panourgia, and Charlie Piot for their comments and provocations.

1 Abe, "The Behavioral Ecology of Elephants in the Queen Elizabeth National Park, Uganda."
2 Charles Siebert, "An Elephant Crack-up?," *New York Times*, October 8, 2006.
3 See Chen, *Animacies*; Kirksey and Helmreich, "The Emergence of Multispecies Ethnography."

4 Power, *"A Problem from Hell,"* 42–43.

5 Power, *"A Problem from Hell,"* 41–42.

6 *Sarkari* loosely translates as "government," "authority," or "official."

7 See N. Ganesh and Halma Deshpande, "Could This Simple Girl Have Been an Assassin?," *Indian Express*, June 17, 2004. The trials over Ishrat Raza's killing began in 2013.

8 This account is based on the story by Bindra, "Vatva's Midnight Devil."

9 Members of Bajrang (Monkey) Dal (Army), the paramilitary wing of the Hindu Right in India.

10 The Prevention of Terrorism Act (POTA) was enacted in 2002 and withdrawn by Indian Parliament in 2004.

11 Farukh Dhondy, "In High-Tech Societies There Is No Need for an Intellectual Life," Tehelka, n.d., http://archive.tehelka.com/story_main.asp?filename =fe010704farrukh.asp.

12 There are, of course, echoes to what some have called "processual ethnography," although my emphasis is more on processes and modes of mediation. See Moore, "Explaining the Present"; Rapport, "The Narrative as Fieldwork Technique."

13 Something very similar was at work in Kim Fortun's ethnography *Advocacy after Bhopal* in which she notes that "Bhopal could not be conceived of as a case study, a bounded unit of analysis for comparative ends" (1).

14 Ondaatje, *Coming through Slaughter*, 106.

15 Or what others have called "multisited ethnography." See Marcus, "Ethnography in/of the World System."

16 Derrida, "Living On," 69.

17 My debt here to Brian Massumi's translation of Deleuze and Guattari's *Thousand Plateaus* is evident.

18 Barth, "The Literature of Exhaustion," 73.

19 George Marcus has noted that ethnography "as conventional description . . . as a contribution to theory, or as an archive of knowledge" may well be outmoded as "other genres serve these functions better. Others now do the kind of description that ethnography used to do of its old objects just as well, if not more cogently in its new terrain of interests" ("Contemporary Fieldwork Aesthetics in Art and Anthropology," 43).

20 The allusion is to Homi Bhabha's assertion of "the indeterminate temporality of the in-between that has to be engaged in creating the conditions in which 'newness enters the world'" in "How Newness Enters the World" (227).

21 Barth, "The Literature of Exhaustion," 71–72.

22 Jonathan Franzen, "What's Wrong with the Modern World?," *Guardian*, September 13, 2013, http://www.theguardian.com/books/2013/sep/13/jonathan -franzen-wrong-modern-world.

23 The gesture toward Gayatri Spivak's "strategic essentialism" may be noted here but recalls Deleuze and Guattari's critique of analogism as representation. See Deleuze and Guattari, *A Thousand Plateaus*.

24 "Novelists possess their societies. That's the most extraordinary gift that these writers gave people—the ability to see their societies." V. S. Naipaul interview, *Literary Review*, August 13, 2001.

25 "I don't like to think of it as journalism—journalism is news, an event that is important today. My kind of writing tries to find a spring, the motives of societies and cultures, especially in India. This is not journalism." Jonathan Rosen and Tarun Tejpal, "V. S. Naipaul, The Art of Fiction," *Paris Review*, Fall 1998, http://www.theparisreview.org/interviews/1069/the-art-of-fiction-no-154-v-s-naipaul. "My books have to be called 'travel writing,' but that can be misleading because in the old days travel writing was essentially done by men describing the routes they were taking. . . . What I do is quite different. I travel on a *theme*. I travel to make an inquiry. I am not a journalist. I am taking with me the gifts of sympathy, observation, and curiosity that I developed as an imaginative writer. The books I write now, these inquiries, are really constructed narratives." Ahmed Rashid, interview with V. S. Naipaul, "Death of the Novel," *Observer*, February 25, 1996.

26 See Lee Siegel, "Where Have All the Mailers Gone?," *New York Observer*, June 22, 2010, http://observer.com/2010/06/where-have-all-the-mailers-gone/; Ted Genoways, "The Death of Fiction?," *Mother Jones*, January–February 2010, http://www.motherjones.com/media/2010/01/death-of-literary-fiction-magazines-journals; Visweswaran, *Fictions of Feminist Ethnography*.

27 See Narayan, "Tools to Shape Texts" and *Alive in the Writing*.

28 As yet unresolved are my queries about why genocide as the "crime of the century" never quite enters "true crime" mode, for homicide, as Derrida suggests (*The Politics of Friendship*, x), is increasingly indistinguishable from genocide; mass murder hinges as much, if not more, on intent. Still it is the case that journalist Philip Gourevitch's award-winning book *We Wish to Inform You That Tomorrow We Will be Killed with Our Families* on the Rwanda genocide was read by many more people than Mahmood Mamdani's thorough critique of the colonial roots of the conflict, *When Victims Become Killers*.

29 See the original story, "Eudora Welty's Short Story on Medgar Evers' Death: 'From the Unknown,'" *Clarion Ledger* (Jackson, MS), June 1, 2013, http://www.clarionledger.com/article/20130602/NEWS0107/306020016/Eudora-Welty-s-short-story-Medgar-Evers-death-From-Unknown and the published version, Eudora Welty, "Where Is the Voice Coming From?," *New Yorker*, July 6, 1963, http://www.newyorker.com/archive/1963/07/06/1963_07_06_024_TNY_CARDS_000277124.

30 Neni Panourgia's engrossing ethnography, *Dangerous Citizens*, envisions its notes or *parerga* as splitting the text into a truncated body that cannot be understood without its extremities, as a Derridean supplement that both replaces and intervenes in the main text (xxv–xxvi).

31 Jha, *Fireproof*, vii–viii.

32 See Visweswaran, chapter 2, "A Thousand Genocides Now."

33 Devereaux, *From Anxiety to Method in the Social Sciences*.
34 Feyerabend, *Against Method*. See in particular chapter 17 and appendix 5.
35 Gordimer, *Writing and Being*, 11–12.
36 Gordimer, *Burger's Daughter*, 9.
37 Gordimer, *Burger's Daughter*, 13.
38 Gordimer, *Writing and Being*, 13.

Writing Culture cleared a field for an attention to emergent forms. A new object of analysis became legible and took on qualities, trajectories, aesthetics. Writing followed it, pulled into alignment with it, becoming tactile and compositional. Culture was reconceived as an assemblage of disparate and incommensurate things throwing themselves together in scenes, acts, encounters, performances, and situations. Writing became an attunement, a response, a vigilant protection of a worlding. Both writing and culture became potentially generative and capacious. Writing might skid over the surface of something throwing itself together or it might pause on a strand as it moved with other strands or fell out of synch, becoming an anomaly or a problem. Writing could be a way of thinking.

What follows here is a brief composition of precarity. I take precarity to be one register of the singularity of emergent phenomena—their plurality, movement, imperfection, immanence, incommensurateness, the way they accrete, accrue, and wear out. I write through four stories of ordinary scenes in which a form of sensing, thinking, or perceiving is emergent. The four scenes—regionality, frailty, the road, a place called Barton Springs—do not add up to a structure of precarity or some of its types. Rather the writing hones attention to the way that a thing like precarity starts to take form as a composition, a recognition, a sensibility, some collection of materialities or laws or movements. Writing culture through emergent forms means stepping outside the cold comfort zone of recognizing only self-identical objects.

Some forms of precarity are obvious and totalizing dramatizations of the thing in itself. The concept of frailty, for instance, is now a medically defined threatening condition: your weight drops below a certain point, you're not steady on your feet, you've had falls, statistically you'll be dead within three years. But other forms of precarity, and of the living in it and through it, are not metaculturally marked at all and not moralized. Precarity can take the form of a sea change, a darkening atmosphere, a hard fall, or the barely perceptible sense of a reprieve. Attachments, or ways of living, can be precious without melodrama, ordinary things that matter because they shimmer precariously. Precarity, written as an emergent form, can raise the question of how to approach ordinary tactile composition, everyday worldings that matter in many ways beyond their status as representations or objects of moralizing.

Regionality

I come from a place where the seasons are magnetized to tones of voice and a quality of light. The winter is a dark tunnel. October is saturated in color. The air is bitable. In May it swells.

At random, transient moments, a sense of being-from-here happens in a look exchanged, a town accent—a sheer recognition of a sheer recognition. These little scenes of recognition, and these sensory matters, compose place. They do not symbolize or represent it. Rather they are its always emergent forms—precise actualizations of a field of potentiality. From the perspective of acts of place and its sensory materiality, place is something that throws itself together in moments, things, in aesthetic sensibilities and affective charges.

Here the precarious, ethereal existence of a place gets hard-wired into senses in a state of sheer attunement. It is not therefore a contradiction that place, in this always emergent place, exists as an impassive corporeality. It is a mantle of redemption, a glacier of impatience, a high desert of anxiety dissected by fault lines of rage. These affects are performed in little scenes of recognition.

Habits throw themselves together into an aesthetics. Townies leave windows uncurtained and open through the night and in the deadest cold of the winter. People walk the neighborhood to peer into the scenes of people reading the paper at night or up early drinking their coffee. Lamps are favored over overhead lighting, lending texture and specificity to ordinary, no-big-deal living. Only depressives, or worse, live with curtains drawn. Drawn curtains are a physical shadow of a state of hardening, a rotting from the inside out. Curtained people are a sinkhole in the neighborhood. They suck the gestural, sensory attachments of seeing and being seen into a world in which things are dark, shadowy outlines with blank cores, like a world seen through a ripe cataract. This place needs its windows, the aesthetic of yellow light passing out to yards, the regular scenes of the precarity, and therefore intimacy, of people in place.

There are five Dunkin' Donuts in this one small town. There are ice-cream stands on every road out of town. The ice-cream cones are piled high. The milkshakes are called frappes. Coffee is the favored flavor. People line up outside at the ice-cream stand window all year long. In the winter there are always some in shorts, T-shirts, and sandals. The townie body unfazed by the cold is a little funny, endearing, a little heroic. Salt of the earth. The pinkened toes in the snow are like homing pigeons swooping the town into a good-natured wink, a shrug. Fuck it. Bring it on. This is *wicked* good.

Even iconic images of New Englandness—let's say the maple tree in October, the white colonial houses surrounding the town commons, the preponderant whiteness of the people—are the scenes of a recognition not of a naturalized order per se but of the visceral complicity of those laying claim to a composed tactility. Regionality here is the charge of the hard surface of matter pulling into precarious alignment. It seeps into what Barthes calls "the inconsequentials . . . odors, exhaustions, sounds of voices, errands, changing light."[1] The muteness of things transfixes into an aesthetic phenomenon.

When my father's heart burst on a Christmas Eve, there was an ice storm so severe that four out of ten trees in the forest snapped in half. They bent under their accruing loads through the cold night. The death snapping began in early morning. Every four or five seconds another loud crack shot through the hills. To the men up listening in amazed alarm, the sharp explosions sounded like the gunfire in Vietnam. A year later, just back to the area to live for a while, I woke to a morning refrain perfectly composed out of the regional qualities of air, light, and sound. Some men were working on trees in the street. They were calling out to each other, an intimate joking tinted by unspoken themes of competence and the human condition. It was my father's voice. The tone, the timing, the accent, the phrasing, the level of force, the purposefulness of the way that voice lived in light, with trees, in the potentiality of a laugh.

Frailty

For my mother, my father's death prompted the hard precarity of unworlding. After all those years of his failing to hold up his end of the world she was always in the middle of propping up and setting in motion, a fissure opened up and swallowed the whole thing, rage and all. She couldn't even remember what it was she had been so angry about. She said they had had a wonderful life. That winter was horrible. Help dropped by sporadically, and she would try to remember her list of things she needed help with. She became one of those doing what the living do. You make a cup of tea and an English muffin for dinner. You drive the SUV to the drugstore and back; you manage to get it into the garage without hitting the sides, but the hatch is too heavy for you to pull down; you can't even reach it, so you spend hours in the freezing garage trying to rig up something to stand on, finding a rope, trying to attach it to the latch and tie it around your waist, your fingers frozen, fumbling, you don't see well, it gets dark, you have to give up, you turn off the lights in the backseat so they won't run down the battery, you don't tell anyone. You will have to wait until someone comes to visit. Every day is now a useless expenditure of effort. Your work doesn't work anymore.

You want the spring to come; you want the beautiful winter light to stay with you a little longer today; you settle deep into the chair by the wood stove, now converted for gas; you catch a glimpse of the scene of your life and you long for it.

Numbers get hard, then impossible. You are leaving little slips of paper and little notebooks all over the house with phone numbers written on them—your kids', your sisters', your friends', your doctor's numbers. Different versions of the numbers, you're trying to record them, to find a new system that will work for you; your writing is shaky, it goes off the page and you don't even realize it. Your son finally takes your checkbook away when he finds checks half written all over the house.

You lose your license because of the eyesight; a doctor turns you in; you try to enlist help to get it back; you call your daughters with hesitant opening lines for schemes that might work, baiting them to come up with something as they used to do, increasingly desperate at their evasion, the blank where the line of a plan once happened. Now you have to rely on walking downtown for a loaf of bread or your medicine. You realize, through episodes, through experiments, through great efforts, that that's all you can carry.

One day you take a bad fall on Main Street in front of the post office as you are trying to make it to the drugstore. The cobblestones are uneven; there is a deadly large granite curb. You fall on your face. You are taken in an ambulance to the hospital. Everyone knows. Then you fall off the stool in your kitchen. Your hip breaks. You go on, clinging to your life, taking secret falls into corners until, weeks later, your situation is finally discovered. Then an operation, rehab, and home in a wheelchair. That night, in a hurricane, the waterlogged hundred-foot oak tree in the front yard falls and splits the house in half. By 5 A.M. the Channel 5 weatherman is standing on the tree shouting through the wind into a microphone and looking into your bedroom, where you have him on TV. For days the cameramen bang on the door trying to get in to get a picture of you in your wheelchair, the shut-in.

Road Registers

The U.S. road is a national macadam of living form textured into ruts, slick, black-iced patches. A thing droning, spiraling into legislation, money, road crews, place-names, city grids, the old days, the cold war, the accident, the family vacation, terrible losses, texting while driving, drinking while driving, these dead zones all along the highways, the world's largest cherry pie, a giant raisin box. Four million miles of it in the United States literally track the detritus of collective dreaming, the passing of historical presents, the spread of aggressively banal and ugly things as capitalism blanketed the country.

It is not enough to say, vaguely, that the road is an imaginary—a logic of some sort abstracted to become a thing in itself. Rather it is a thing simultaneously, coterminously real and virtual, abstract and concrete, made not of dreams per se but of laws, ordinary practices, military surges, and construction technologies. Dirt roads, city streets, the streets of gated communities, the Main Streets, the Martin Luther King Boulevards, the roads that hug the coast, all register virtualities that touch down like the path of a tornado. Sediments accrue out of contingencies. Almost accidental sensibilities spin themselves into the genres of the road trips that created the family vacation and the desperate free fall out of and into failure and abjection. The vagaries of routine and opportunity orbit the purgatory of gridlock or the fantasies of potential "home" scenes spied, in passing, on the side of the road. In the precarious circuit of the road, intensities pass from body to body—human bodies, animal bodies, machine bodies, bodies of thought, ecosystems, visceralities and noumena, histories, the seamless habitus of supermarkets and credit cards.

The road's precarity is a hinge of attunement to what might be happening in some little piece of dirt, some high-rise, some abandoned car, some perfectly ordinary road sign, a national shift in the speed limit, the revitalization of a circle of roadside cabins, a white cross, a railway crossing, a streetlight equipped with a camera, privatized fast lanes, policing, all the things people do in cars, bike lanes, a walk across country for cancer or birth defects, road rage, the only public space you can find in a desperate situation, seasonal roads formed by frozen rivers or tundra.

The road is a tone of voice, a comfort, a sleepless night, a route entombed in bodily memory, unsignified intensities, walking your kid to school hand in hand, that bad feeling when the gas prices go up so high you realize you can no longer drive, sex, Sunday drives, the old days traveling over mountain roads, the nausea in the backseat, the West Virginia drivers racing around steep blind curves they knew every inch of, the Vermont mountain road I walked one cold dark night, the footsteps following me in the woods, the sudden appearance of the aurora borealis all across the sky, hitchhiking. I remember lying awake in bed in my grandmother's house listening with dread to the whining of the trucks passing on the turnpike twenty feet from her bedroom window. I still hate the whine of tires on the road. And that turnpike.

Barton Springs

Newcomers to Austin first see Barton Springs from an elevation. You look down steep, green grassy banks shaded by century-old pecan trees to a river-pool thing a thousand feet long. Preternaturally long and as wide as the river it is. The water swells against concrete sides built by the Civilian Conservation Corps in the 1930s, its colors almost bruised with force and density. It has a brilliant green and turquoise hue. In places it goes turgid brown and even, where the plants grow thick and rise to the surface, a true black. The spring that fills the river-pool is a tear in the limestone bedrock eighteen feet below the diving board in the dead center of the thing. It pulses like a heartbeat pumping out 27 million gallons of water a day. This water churns in a cold, dense vortex like a wine cooler. It pulls body temperatures down fast on a triple-digit day. The bodies twist and flip over it, cutting the surface of the water with a belly flop or the expertise of ten thousand dives here.

At the shallow end families, young lovers, and rowdy groups of friends make their way precariously over the irregular, algae-slick rock bottom, exploring the cliffs that line one side. There are hairdos, tattoos, swimwear of all kinds, dares, refusals, splashing. People-watching is a surround-sound visual submersion experience.

At the far end are the floats. On a hot summer day it is an acre of bumper-to-bumper plastic beds in bright colors, oiled bodies, wrists and ankles hanging in the dark water. Young women strut around topless on the sidewalks. The high grassy banks are a sea of gazes and lazy talk, and drum circles, books, Frisbee throwing, dope smoking, yoga, Tai Chi.

Lifeguards perch on high stands down the length of the pool, leaning over the water like the great blue herons that lurch over its concrete sides in the early morning, piles of crawfish carcasses and fish bones at their feet. In the winter an early morning fog rises from the water. Die-hard lap swimmers troll up and down in wetsuits. At night lights sparkle across the water. There is only the sound of the quiet strokes or a giggle. There may be an element of fear.

———————

Precarity's forms are compositional and decompositional. They magnetize attachments, tempos, materialities, and states of being. Their slowed, more capacious description is a writing culture lodged in emergence, generativity, and potentiality. The writing itself attunes us to how things are hanging together or falling apart or wearing out in time that compresses or stretches out into an endurance. Such objects of analysis register the tactility and significance of something coming into form through an assemblage of affects, routes, conditions, sensibilities, and habits. Rather than rush to incorporate them into a representational order of political or moral significance, we might ask what it means to meet the world not as representation, interpretation, or raw material for exploitation but as a nearing, the ringing between composing subjects and objects "felt as ways of going on in the world," as "increases and decreases, brightenings and darkenings" in a cartography distributed across a field of intensities and durations.[2] Writing the culture of precarity's forms is one exercise in reattuning.

Notes

1 Barthes, *Incidents*, 7.
2 Heidegger, "The Thing"; McCormack, "An Event of Geographical Ethics in Spaces of Affect," 495; Deleuze, *Essays Critical and Clinical*, 145.

CHAPTER 13

Writing Culture
(or Something Like That)
Hugh Raffles

The environment itself is full of free and nonteleological energies—trade winds and storms, oceans streaming over three-fourths of the planet, drifting continental plates, cordilleras of the deep that erupt in volcanic explosions, and miles-deep glaciers piled up on Antarctica that flow into the sea and break off in bobbling icemountains. How can the passions of penguins, albatrosses, jaguars, and humans not lift their eyes beyond the nests and the lairs and the horizons? How can these passions not sink into volcanic rock and the oceanic deserts?
—Alphonso Lingis, "The Navel of the World"

The vastness of geologic time is simultaneously incomprehensible and banal. When I began writing about stone, I imagined the relation between geologic and human time as a question of scale. But now, after a year's immersion, I'm more attuned to the movements of minerals, protons, and photons, to the build-decay-uplift-assimilation and realize that what preoccupied me occupies me too. Scale is only a small question in this question.

This raises a problem relevant to this volume: What is writing culture when the object is neither human nor animal nor "multispecies" nor amenable to flattening into a network or assemblage and yet is entirely inseparable from life itself, is in fact life itself and, correspondingly, pre-, post-, necessary to, indifferent to, and transcendent of the human scale?[1]

I started with a simple question: What is stone? But soon replaced that with one which seemed more empirical: What can stone do? It didn't take long to arrive at some simple answers. Stone can endure, it can change, it can harm, it can heal. It can make you rich, it can make you poor, it can become an enemy, a friend, and a teacher. It can carry your memories and your dreams. It can build empires and bury cities. It can reveal the history of the universe. It

Figure 13.1. Photograph by the author.

can open and close the gates of philosophy. It can change the course of nature. It can change its own nature. It can empty the world of time.

Swapping nouns and adjectives for verbs and adverbs was methodologically helpful, a better place to proceed from. Verbs encircle these supremely protean things but don't encase them. Now I could place them squarely in the light and contemplate them. For example, figure 13.1 shows a stone I found on a beach in Oregon. The stone is different from every angle. Every picture I take of it manifests a different stone. Right now it feels cool in my hand, but it can also hold the heat of the sun. When it's wet, it has a dull sheen. When the right light hits it, it glows from within. It has ancient leathery skin, turtle's-neck skin, as if it's been breathing and stretching for centuries. Its dark mantle is pockmarked with the battles it's seen.

I have a story about finding this stone, and when I tell it, people say, What about the other stones? What about all the other stones on that beach that you didn't pick up, the ones that are still there in Oregon? That's a good question because the other stones, the ones the story leaves behind, the ones that remain in what we might reasonably call geologic time and only on the periphery of human time, the ones that enter human time only in their generality or in their generalized effects, affordances, and possibilities, those are the stones that raise the most challenging questions for ethnography.

So here's another stone. I encountered this one in Baishan City, Jilin Province, China, near the North Korean border. It's *songhua shi*, a type of stone that provincial officials backed by Beijing are hoping will propel the local economy (see figure 13.2).

Figure 13.2. Photograph by the author.

Reflecting on a stone not entirely unlike this, the Tang Dynasty poet-monk Wu Men wrote, "I intended to search mountains for this stone, / And, to my surprise, I found the mountains in this stone."[2]

The great Song Dynasty poet and philosopher Su Dongpo wrote, "I returned carrying the stone / And now the Eastern Sea was in my sleeve."[3]

Bai Juyi, another of the famous Tang poets, wrote, "The stones, though unable to speak, / Promised to remain my faithful friends."[4]

The authors of the early Qing *Mustard Seed Garden Manual of Painting* wrote, "In estimating people, their quality of qi is as basic as the way they are formed; and so it is with rocks. . . . How could a cultivated person paint a lifeless rock?"[5]

And Hou Kangyi, who so generously takes the time to talk when I visit his modest apartment close to the second ring road in Beijing, writes, "Stone is calm and unyielding, it is bright and it is selfless. These four qualities of a stone help me to cultivate my body and nurture my nature."[6]

Calm, unyielding, bright, selfless. These are the same four characters used by the communist poet Guo Moruo to compliment the bowl of *yuhua* (rainflower) stones—colorful pebbles from Nanjing usually displayed under water—that Zhou Enlai, the first prime minister of the People's Republic, kept near his desk.

Hou Kangyi doesn't mention Guo, but he doesn't need to because my friend Xiaoxiao Huang, translating his essay with me in a bagel store in Manhattan, instantly spots the reference, beginning a dizzying cascade of associations that begins with a famous photo of another leader, a beaming President Jiang Zemin, receiving the gift of a Kunshan stone, one of the four principal stones of ancient China praised in the *Yunlin shipu*, the first catalogue of such stones, a book published in 1125 and still a touchstone for collectors.[7] Jiang's enthusiasm raised a fever among ambitious army officers for whom—dedicated to gift-giving but cautious about cash—these rare rocks became such magical objects of possibility and desire that their excavation was soon banned for its impact on the local landscape, and arrests were being made of overeager personnel from the nearby military base. I saw one of these stones in a store in Hutai Lu market in Shanghai, a huge stone set on a waist-high platform, an immense and charismatic object that glistened startlingly with a profound otherworldliness, an unfathomable landscape of crystalline peaks, caves, and valleys—far, deep, and wide. I'm told you can travel in a stone like that if both you and it have the requisite qualities. Following the Daoist sages, you enter it, it enters you, scale collapses, and you enter, the term is *shen you*, an imaginative journey, a spirit journey, although that word *spirit* is the beginning of an endless journey in itself.[8]

Hou Kangyi was born in 1925 in what is now Dalian, the famous boom town and resort on the Yellow Sea that was then part of an embattled post-Qing Manchuria buffeted by Russia and Japan. Was he reading the Confucian classics at school and college? For forty years he taught in middle schools and universities, but I know only his life today: the modest apartment he shares with his wife, their hospitality, his carefully nurtured networks, his frequent traveling, his status as one of the country's most respected stone experts, and his new alliance with Wang Liyang, who recently published a book called *The Dao of Stone* and who told me I shouldn't judge a man's wealth from his appearance because he, Wang Liyang (actually his pen name), here in these cheap pants and ordinary jacket in his small apartment with its bad feng shui just sold a different apartment for 10 million RMB, whereas that other feng shui consultant, the one who is never separated from his mysterious Prada bag and who ferried you, Hugh, around Tianjin last week in that shiny black SUV driven by his elegantly dressed sidekick and who told you he advised KFC when they needed the most propitious arrangement for their Beijing headquarters, well, who knows what he has to his name?

In *The Dao of Stone*, Wang Liyang describes three ascending levels of stone appreciation. There is the Ordinary Dao, "directly perceived through sight." This is the external Dao that corresponds to the focus on surface form, on shape, color, texture, and pattern. Then there is the Extraordinary Dao ("the heart grasps and the senses appreciate") in which a cultivated attention to the external (*xing*, form) enables access to the internal (*shen*, spirit). And finally there are Stone Rites (*shi li*), the "superior-vehicle Dao" that draws on both the broad Confucian concept of ritual as the ground for relationships and on the Daoist language of the Daodejing through which stone lovers— seeing form but apprehending the formless—"open the stone's eyes, bathe its heart, cleanse its spirit, and dissolve into the Universe."[9]

The first two levels crop up routinely in my conversations with stone scholars. The attraction to external form (to brightly colored stones, to stones that strongly resemble propitious animals, etc.) characterizes the collecting activities of the newly rich, they say, whereas the true scholar is drawn deeper, beyond form, into the more ineffable and less calculable qualities of these objects. The superior-vehicle Dao, though, is Wang's innovation. I try to talk to him about it. So is there a Dao for every being and every object? I ask. I put this fierce-looking stone here to expel evil spirits, he tells me. Do all objects have qi? I ask. What is qi? he asks me in return.

The poetic sinologist François Jullien remarks that this type of thinking is neither epistemological nor ontological. In the formalized language of Western philosophy, he says, it is better understood as a deontological processual materialization and animation, a moral order grounded in transformation and concretion, in the great cycles of seasons, elements, substance, and matter.[10] I'm willing to make the intuitive leap and take this as an immersion in a version of geologic time, an accommodation with science that Chinese stone lovers like Hou Kangyi and Wang Liyang have been exploring explicitly since at least the Republican era, a folding that promises worldly lessons in becoming with stone, a becoming preoccupied, then occupied by stone.[11]

Figure 13.3. Francesco Ligozzi, *Dante and Virgil Descending to Hell,* 1620. Courtesy of Opificio delle Pietre Dure, Florence.

It's not so unusual. This is Francesco Ligozzi's *Dante and Virgil Descending to Hell,* painted in 1620 and now hanging in Florence in the gemlike museum of the Opificio delle Pietre Dura, a workshop set up in 1588 by Ferdinand I de' Medici, where court craftsmen produced ornamental stone inlays for the city's palaces and churches (figure 13.3).

Ligozzi painted this scene on Florentine *pietra paesina,* a local limestone that when expertly sliced and polished is so evocative of desolate landscapes and tumultuous history that it was also called "ruin marble." Ligozzi had only to add the flames, the Tuscan oak leaves, Dante, Virgil, a few sadistic demons, and the flailing, naked damned. The stone provided the rest.

Roger Caillois, the maverick postsurrealist and passionate stone collector, describes work of this type as an "alliance between the skill of the painter and the fantasies of geology."[12] It was especially popular in the court of Ferdinand's son Cosimo II, where artists also used local Arno limestone with deep and regular veining that resembles ocean waves to provide the scene for epic maritime battles and Jonah's encounter with the whale.

Caillois liked Ligozzi's painting. He detected in it "a clear case of complicity . . . between the subterranean levels of suffering and the genesis of a stone that itself comes from the depths of the earth, roasted in the heat of some non-human furnace." Caillois is taking us somewhere old, somewhere premodern that we've now forgotten so fully that it feels like somewhere new. In work like this "it is no longer a matter of the painter's whim exploiting a strange material," he says. "Instead we have an encounter between a subject and a medium which might be called a demonstration of that subject."[13]

The stone anticipates the painting, maybe even calls it forth, reels in Michelangelo's famous lines, "Nothing the best of artists can conceive / but lies, potential, in a block of stone."[14] Confronted by a fellow literati's famously pictorial marble screen, Su Dongpo, the great Song Dynasty poet-philosopher, wrote, "Now I am beginning to believe that there are artist gods."[15] Caillois says that because early modern European scholars knew that the uncanny resemblances in these stones were "sports of nature" they had every reason to think that genuine fossils were similarly natural paintings.[16] Meaningful correspondences maybe, but not manifestations of biological life in geological time.

Dipping a toe into these depths makes me feel I've been doggy-paddling in the froth of culture all these years. When I tell people about the Oregon stone, they ask me about the stones I didn't pick up, the ones that raise the most challenging questions for ethnography. What if the objects we contemplate are pre-, post-, necessary to, indifferent to, and transcendent of culture? W. J. T. Mitchell's commonsensical "paleontology of the present" that provincializes "contemporaneity from the perspective of deep time and the possible obsolescence of the human species" is suddenly itself provincialized, an insufficient starting point.[17]

Jean-Christophe Bailly enfolds human and geologic time in a processive embrace, a dissolution in porosities and exchange.[18] Tim Ingold insists that "things move and grow because they are alive, not because they have agency."[19] Elizabeth Grosz tunes in to "vibratory cosmic forces that generate the possibilities of expression and intensity."[20] For Gilles Deleuze, "a life is everywhere . . . an immanent life carrying with it the events or singularities that are merely actualized in subjects and objects."[21] How, asks Alphonso Lingis, can the passions of animals not sink into rock and desert, not sink and return?[22]

Stone, in its stillness and its resonance, pulls us vertiginously into this vastness. "It just happens to be the case," writes Bailly, "that the stone cannot be withdrawn from living . . . without living being turned into a mere category of being, a simple subtraction."[23] The stones remaining on the shore. The Eastern Sea in his sleeve. The complicit fantasies of geology. A two-billion-year timeline at the Grand Canyon.

This style of thinking makes me recall Vladimir Nabokov's warning that only one letter distinguishes the cosmic from the comic.[24] But I press on anyway, returning to the fieldwork, in this case to Beijing, to Hou Kangyi, and to Zhuangzi, my favorite Daoist sage, who tips everything into the abyss. "I'm going to try speaking some reckless words," he wrote some 2,500 years ago. "I'm going to try speaking some reckless words and I want you to listen to them recklessly. How will that be?"[25]

Acknowledgments

I have presented versions of this material at the University of Manchester, the University of Cambridge, York University, the Bard Graduate Center, and Arizona State University, as well as at the Duke *Writing Culture @ 25* conference. My thanks to everyone at these events, especially Andrea Ballestero, Anne Allison, Annmarie Mol, Charlie Piot, Christopher Carr, Chunglin Kwa, Darren Patrick, Jim Secord, Jody Berland, John Law, Ken Little, Maggie MacDonald, Miruna Achuim, Orin Starn, Peter Timmerman, Rohan Deb Roy, Simon Schaffer, and Steve Semken. Sincere thanks also to President Shou Jiahua and director Lan Guangzhao of the China View Stone Association. Thanks to Hou Kangyi, Wang Liyang, Kong Wei, Kemin Hu, and many others in the *shangshi* community, as well as to Xiaoxiao Hung, Dominic Pettman, Yen-ling Tsai, and Mei Zhan for extended dialogue, and to I-Yi Hsieh, Zhang Jingran, Yijun Wang, and Sun Zeming for their invaluable research, translation, and conceptual contributions. In addition, I am grateful to Orin Starn for his exceptional work as editor of this collection. Most of all, my thanks to Sharon Simpson for nonstop conversation and continuous inspiration on these and many other issues.

Notes

1 A question posed in direct relation to James Clifford and George E. Marcus's *Writing Culture*.
2 Men, "Cold Woods Stone Screen," 67.
3 Quoted in Hu, *The Suyuan Stone Catalog*, 103.

4 Quoted in Hu, *The Suyuan Stone Catalog*, 58.

5 Sze, *The Mustard Seed Garden Manual of Painting*, 129.

6 Kangyi, "To Be a Stone-Like Person," 2–6.

7 Available in a heavily abbreviated English edition as *Tu Wan's Stone Catalogue of Cloudy Forest*, edited and translated by Edward H. Schafer.

8 For a classic discussion of this type of scaling and its possibilities, see Stein, *The World in Miniature*, 52–77. See also Hall and Ames, *Thinking from the Han*; Zeitlin, "The Secret Life of Rocks," who emphasizes the long-standing commercialization of these stones.

9 Liyang, *Shi dao*, 123.

10 See Jullien, *Vital Nourishment*. Also Zhan, "Worlding Oneness." Jullien writes, "That is why Chinese thought has no ontology; it has no world of concrete essences. It possesses neither an individuating soul nor an opposing concept of matter. . . . It does have, though, 'materialization' by way of continuous concretion (under the yin factor), as well as 'animation,' which dispels its opacity and unfolds it (under the factor yang). Like the external world, I am shaped and kept alive by this tension between self-compensating opposites. The actualization that constitutes me (xing) is thus conceived entirely in terms of the process of concentration-emanation that brings it about" (*Vital Nourishment*, 69). Compare this with Deleuze's late concept of "a life" that is "pure immanence": "Absolute immanence is in itself: it is not in something, to something. It does not depend on an object or belong to a subject" ("Immanence," 26).

11 As an example, see Zhang Hong Zhao, *Shi ya* [Correct stones] (Beijing, 1918), reprinted in Xingzhi, *Shuo shi*. For an authoritative account of the impact of Western science in China, including geology, see Elman, *On Their Own Terms*.

12 Caillois, *The Writing of Stones*, 27.

13 Caillois, *The Writing of Stones*, 32.

14 Buonarroti, "Nothing the Best of Artists Can Conceive," 96.

15 Quoted in Hu, *Suyuan Stone Catalog*, 64.

16 Caillois, *The Writing of Stones*, 16. See also Baltrušaitis, *Aberrations*, 73–99; Mitchell's insightful discussion of fossils in *What Do Pictures Want?*, 167–87.

17 Mitchell, *What Do Pictures Want?*, 124.

18 Bailly, "The Slightest Breath (On Living)." I am grateful to Dominic Pettman for sending me this thought-provoking article.

19 Ingold, "Bringing Things to Life," 7, for which I owe many thanks to Brian Goldstone.

20 Grosz, *Chaos, Territory, Art*, 102.

21 Deleuze, "Immanence," 29.

22 Lingis, "The Navel of the World," 2.

23 Bailly, "The Slightest Breath (On Living)," 6.

24 Nabokov, *Nikolai Gogol*, 142.

25 Zhuangzi, *Basic Writings*, 42.

Abe, Eve L. "The Behavioral Ecology of Elephants in the Queen Elizabeth National Park, Uganda." PhD dissertation, Cambridge University, 1994.

Abu-Lughod, Lila. "Writing against Culture." In *Recapturing Anthropology: Working in the Present*, ed. Richard Fox, 137–62. Santa Fe, NM: School of American Research Press, 1991.

Adams, Vincanne. "Against Global Health? Arbitrating Science, Non-Science, and Nonsense through Health." In *Against Health: How Health Became the New Morality*, ed. Jonathan M. Metzl and Anna Kirkland, 40–58. New York: New York University Press, 2010.

Agha, Asif. *Language and Social Relations*. Cambridge: Cambridge University Press, 2007.

Albro, Robert. "Anthropology and the Military: AFRICOM, 'Culture,' and the Future of Human Terrain Analysis." *Anthropology Today* 26.1 (2010): 22–24.

Allison, Anne. *Nightwork: Sexuality, Pleasure, and Corporate Masculinity in a Tokyo Club*. Chicago: University of Chicago Press, 1994.

Amamiya, Karin. *Amamiya Karin no "seizon kakumei" nikki* [Amamiya Karin's diary of the "survival revolution"]. Tokyo: Shūeisha, 2009.

———. *Amamiya Karin tōsō daiarī* [Amamiya Karin's battle diary]. Tokyo: Shūeisha, 2008.

Amamiya Karin and Kayano Toshihito. *"Ikizurasa" nitsuite: Hinkon, aidentiti, nashyonarizumu* [Concerning "hardship of life": Poverty, identity, nationalism]. Tokyo: Kobunshashinsho, 2008.

Anderson, Benedict. *Imagined Communities*. Rev. ed. London: Verso, 1991.

Anderson, Warwick. *The Collectors of Lost Souls: Turning Kuru Scientists into Whitemen*. Baltimore: Johns Hopkins University Press, 2008.

Ansell, Richard, and Andrew Tinsley. "Bhopal's Never Ending Tragedy." *The Environmentalist*, October 13, 2011. Accessed March 15, 2012. http://www.environmentalistonline.com/article/2011–10–13/bhopal-s-never-ending-disaster.

Appadurai, Arjun. *Modernity at Large: Cultural Dimensions in Globalization*. Minneapolis: University of Minnesota Press, 1996.

———. *Fear of Small Numbers: An Essay on the Geography of Anger.* Durham, NC: Duke University Press, 2006.

Asad, Talal, ed. *Anthropology and the Colonial Encounter.* New York: Humanities Press, 1973.

Bailly, Jean-Christophe. "The Slightest Breath (On Living)." Trans. Matthew H. Anderson. *CR: The New Centennial Review* 10.3 (2010): 1–12.

Bakhtin, Mikhail. *The Dialogic Imagination: Four Essays.* Austin: University of Texas Press, 1981.

Bakker, Isabella, Stephen Gill, and Tim DiMuzio. "Introduction to Part IV: Human In/Security on a Universal Scale." In *Power, Production, and Social Reproduction,* ed. Isabella Bakker and Stephen Gill, 163–68. New York: Palgrave Macmillan, 2003.

Ballestero, Andrea. "Expert Attempts: Water, Collectives, Prices and the Law in Costa Rica and Brazil." PhD dissertation, University of California, Irvine, 2010.

Baltrušaitis, Jurgis. *Aberrations: An Essay on the Legend of Forms.* Trans. Richard Miller. Cambridge, MA: MIT Press, 1989.

Barth, John. "The Literature of Exhaustion." In *The Friday Book: Essays and Other Non-Fiction,* 62–76. Baltimore: Johns Hopkins University Press, 1984.

Barthes, Roland. *Camera Lucida.* New York: Farrar, Straus and Giroux, 1981.

———. *Incidents.* Berkeley: University of California Press, 1992.

Bateson, Gregory. *Naven: A Survey of the Problems Suggested by a Composite Picture of the Culture of a New Guinea Tribe Drawn from Three Points of View.* 1936. Palo Alto, CA: Stanford University Press, 1962.

Beals, Ralph. "Fifty Years in Anthropology." *Annual Review of Anthropology* 11 (1982): 1–23.

Becker, Gary, Francis Ewald, Bernard Harcourt. "American Neoliberalism: Michel Foucault's Birth of Biopolitics Lectures." May 9, 2012. Video. http://vimeo.com/43984248.

Behar, Ruth, and Deborah Gordon, eds. *Women Writing Culture.* Berkeley: University of California Press, 1996.

Behrouzan, Orkideh. "Prozak Diaries: Postrupture Subjectivities and Psychiatric Futures." PhD dissertation, MIT, 2010.

Behrouzan, Orkideh, and Michael M. J. Fischer. "Behaves like a Rooster and Cries like a [Four-eye] Canine": Nightmares, Depression, Psychiatry, and the Rise of Iranian Psychiatric Selves." In *Trauma and Mass Violence,* ed. Devon Hinton and Alex Hinton. Cambridge: Cambridge University Press, 2014.

Benjamin, Walter. *One Way Street.* 1928. London: NLB, 1979.

Bennett, Jane. *Vibrant Matter: A Political Ecology of Things.* Durham, NC: Duke University Press, 2010.

Berardi, Franco "Bifo." *The Soul at Work: From Alienation to Autonomy.* Trans. Francesca Cadel and Giuseppina Mecchia. Cambridge, MA: Semiotext(e), 2009.

Berlant, Lauren. *Cruel Optimism*. Durham, NC: Duke University Press, 2011.

Bhabha, Homi. "Articulating the Archaic: Cultural Difference and Colonial Nonsense." In *The Location of Culture*, 123–38. London: Routledge, 1994.

———. "How Newness Enters the World." In *The Location of Culture*, 212–35. London: Routledge, 1994.

Biehl, João, and Adryna Petryna. "Bodies of Rights and Therapeutic Markets." *Social Research* 78.2 (2011): 359–86.

Biehl, João, and Adryna Petryna, eds. *When People Come First*. Princeton: Princeton University Press, 2013.

Bindra, Prerna Singh. "Vatwa's Midnight Devil." *Pioneer*, July 25, 2004.

Blanchette, Jean-Francois. *Burdens of Proof: Cryptographic Culture and Evidence Law in the Age of Electronic Documents*. Cambridge, MA: MIT Press, 2012.

Boellstorf, Tom, et al., eds. *Ethnography and Virtual Worlds: A Handbook of Method*. Princeton, NJ: Princeton University Press, 2012.

Bond, David. "The Science of Catastrophe: Making Sense of the BP Oil Spill." *Anthropology Now* 3.1 (2011): 36–46.

Borofsky, Rob. *Why a Public Anthropology?* Honolulu: Center for a Public Anthropology, e-book, 2011.

Bourgois, Philippe, and Jeff Schonberg. *Righteous Dopefiend*. Berkeley: University of California Press, 2009.

Bourke-White, Margaret. "Women in Steel: They Are Handling Tough Jobs in Heavy Industry." *Life*, August 9, 1943.

Boykoff, Jules, and Maxwell Boykoff. "Journalistic Balance as Global Warming Bias: Creating Controversy Where Science Finds Consensus." *Fairness and Accuracy in Reporting*, November 1, 2004. Accessed March 15, 2012. http://www.fair.org/index.php?page=1978.

Buckley, Thomas. "'The Pitiful History of Little Events': The Epistemological and Moral Contexts of Kroeber's Californian Ethnology, 1900–1915." In *History of Anthropology*. Vol. 8: *Volkengeist as Method and Ethics: Essays on Boasian Ethnography and the German Anthropological Tradition*, ed. George Stocking, 257–97. Madison: University of Wisconsin Press, 1996.

Buonarroti, Michelangelo. "Nothing the Best of Artists Can Conceive." In *The Complete Poems of Michelangelo*, trans. John Frederick Nims. Chicago: University of Chicago Press, 2001.

Butler, Judith. *Gender Trouble: Feminism and the Subversion of Identity*. 1990. New York: Routledge. 1999.

———. *Frames of War: When Is Life Grievable?* New York: Verso, 2009.

Caillois, Roger. *The Writing of Stones*. Trans. Barbara Bray. Charlottesville: University of Virginia Press, 1985.

Callison, Candis. "More Information Is Not the Problem: Spinning Climate Change, Vernaculars, and Emergent Forms of Life." PhD dissertation, MIT, 2010.

Caputo, Philip. *Acts of Faith*. New York: Knopf, 2005.

Cefkin, Melissa, ed. *Ethnography and the Corporate Encounter: Reflections on Research in and of Corporations*. New York: Berghahn, 2010.

Centre for Science and the Environment. "Contamination of Soil and Water inside and outside the Union Carbide India Limited, Bhopal." CSE Laboratory Report. December 2009. Accessed March 15, 2012. http://www.cseindia.org /userfiles/Bhopal%20Report%20Final-3.pdf.

———. "CSE's Press Release: Dialogue on Air Pollution and Our Health." August 31, 2011. Accessed March 15, 2011. http://www.cseindia.org/content/cses-pre ss-release-dialogue-air-pollution-and-our-health.

Chan, Anita. "The Promiscuity of Freedom: Development and Governance in the Age of Neoliberal Networks." PhD dissertation, MIT, 2008.

Chen, Mel. *Animacies: Biopolitics, Racial Mattering, and Queer Affect*. Durham, NC: Duke University Press, 2012.

Clark, Grahame. "Anthropology and Human Diversity." *Annual Review of Anthropology* 8 (1979): 1–20.

Clifford, James. "Fort Ross Meditation." In *Routes: Travel and Translation in the Late 20th Century*, 225–48. Cambridge, MA: Harvard University Press, 1997.

———. "Introduction: Partial Truths." In *Writing Culture: The Poetics and Politics of Ethnography*, ed. James Clifford and George E. Marcus, 1–26. Berkeley: University of California Press, 1986.

———. "On Ethnographic Allegory." In *Writing Culture: The Poetics and Politics of Ethnography*, ed. James Clifford and George E. Marcus, 98–121. Berkeley: University of California Press, 1986.

———. "On Ethnographic Authority." *Representations* 1 (1983): 118–46.

———. "On Ethnographic Surrealism." *Comparative Studies in Society and History* 23.4 (1981): 539–64.

———. *The Predicament of Culture*. Cambridge, MA: Harvard University Press, 1988.

———. *Returns: Becoming Indigenous in the Twenty-First Century*. Cambridge, MA: Harvard University Press, 2013.

———. "Vérités partielles, vérités partials." Trans. Emir Mahieddin. *Journal des Anthropologues* 126–27:385–433.

Clifford, James, and George Marcus, eds. *Writing Culture: The Poetics and Politics of Ethnography*. Berkeley: University of California Press, 1986.

Cohen, Alex, Arthur Kleinman, and Benedetto Saraceno, eds. *World Mental Health Casebook: Social and Mental Health Programs in Low-Income Countries*. New York: Kluwer Academic/Plenum, 2002.

Cohen, Lawrence. *No Aging in India: Alzheimer's, the Bad Family, and Other Modern Things*. Berkeley: University of California Press, 2000.

———. "Operability, Bioavailability, and Exception." In *Global Assemblages*, ed. Aihwa Ong and Stephen Collier, 79–90. Oxford: Blackwell, 2005.

———. "Where It Hurts: Indian Material for an Ethics of Organ Transplantation." *Daedalus* 128.4 (1999): 135–65.

Cohn, Bernard. *An Anthropologist among the Historians and Other Essays.* Delhi: Oxford University Press, 1987.

Cole, Simon. *Suspect Identities: A History of Fingerprinting and Criminal Identification.* Cambridge, MA: Harvard University Press, 2001.

Coleman, Gabriella. *Coding Freedom: The Ethics and Aesthetics of Hacking.* Princeton, NJ: Princeton University Press, 2012.

Coleman, Penny. *Rosie the Riveter: Women Workers on the Home Front.* New York: Crown Books, 1995.

Comaroff, Jean, and John L. Comaroff. *Ethnicity, Inc.* Chicago: University of Chicago Press, 2009.

Condry, Ian. *The Soul of Anime: Collaborative Creativity and Japan's Media Success Story.* Durham, NC: Duke University Press, 2013.

Coon, Carleton. "Overview." *Annual Review of Anthropology* 6 (1977): 1–10.

Cornell, Drucilla. *The Philosophy of the Limit.* London: Routledge, 1992.

Crapanzano, Vincent. "Hermes' Dilemma: The Masking of Subversion in Ethnographic Description." In *Writing Culture: The Poetics and Politics of Ethnography,* ed. James Clifford and George E. Marcus, 51–76. Berkeley: University of California Press, 1986.

Csordas, Thomas. *Body/Meaning/Healing.* New York: Palgrave, 2002.

Das, Veena. *Critical Events.* Oxford: Oxford University Press, 1997.

———. *Life and Words: Violence and the Descent into the Ordinary.* Berkeley: University of California Press, 2006.

Dean, Kenneth, and Zheng Zenman. *Ritual Alliances of the Putian Plain.* Leiden: Brill, 2009.

De la Cadena, Marisol. "Indigenous Cosmopolitics in the Andes: Conceptual Reflections Beyond 'Politics.'" *Cultural Anthropology* 25.2 (2010): 334–70.

De la Cadena, Marisol, and Orin Starn. *Indigenous Experience Today.* New York: Berg, 2007.

de Lauretis, Teresa. Introduction to *Technologies of Gender: Essays on Theory, Film and Fiction,* 1–30. Bloomington: Indiana University Press, 1987.

Deeb, Hadi, and George E. Marcus. "Theatricality in Ethnography at the World Trade Organization: The Para-Site as Experimental Form." *Paragrana* 19.2 (2010): 137–52.

Deleuze, Giles. *Difference and Repetition.* Trans. Paul Patton. New York: Columbia University Press, 1994.

———. *Empiricism and Subjectivity: An Essay on Hume's Theory of Human Nature.* New York: Columbia University Press, 1991.

———. *Essays Critical and Clinical.* London: Verso, 1998.

———. "Immanence: A Life." In *Pure Immanence: Essays on a Life,* trans. Anne Boyman, 25–33. New York: Zone Books, 2002.

———. "Postscript on the Societies of Control." *October* 59 (1992): 3–7.

Deleuze, Gilles, and Felix Guattari. *A Thousand Plateaus.* Trans. Brian Massumi. Minnesota: University of Minnesota Press, 1987.

Derrida, Jacques. *Adieu to Emmanuel Lévinas.* Trans. Pascale-Anne Brault and Michael Naas. Palo Alto, CA: Stanford University Press, 1999.

———. "At This Very Moment in This Work Here I Am." Trans. Ruben Berezdivin. In *Re-Reading Levinas,* ed. Robert Bernasconi and Simon Critchley, 11–50. Bloomington: Indiana University Press, 1991.

———."Différance." In *Margins of Philosophy,* by Jacques Derrida. Trans. Alan Bass. Chicago: University of Chicago Press, 1982.

———. "Force of Law: The Mystical Foundation of Authority." *Cardozo Law Review* 11.5–6 (1990): 919–1045.

———. "Force of Law: The Mystical Foundations of Authority." In *Deconstruction and the Possibility of Justice,* ed. Drucilla Cornell, Michel Rosenfeld, and David Gray Carlson, 3–67. New York: Routledge, 1996.

———. *The Gift of Death.* Trans. David Wills. Chicago: University of Chicago Press, 1995.

———. "Living On." In *Deconstruction and Criticism,* by Geoffrey H. Hartman, Jacques Derrida, Harold Bloom, and Paul de Man, 254–68. 1979. London: Continuum, 2004.

———. *On Cosmopolitanism and Forgiveness.* London: Routledge, 2001.

———. *The Politics of Friendship.* Trans. George Collins. London: Verso, 2005.

———. *Writing and Difference.* Trans. Alan Bass. Chicago: University of Chicago Press, 1978.

Derrida, Jacques, with A. Dufourmantelle. *Of Hospitality.* Trans. Rachel Bowlby. Palo Alto, CA: Stanford University Press, 2000.

Devereaux, George. *From Anxiety to Method in the Social Sciences.* Paris: Mouton, 1967.

Di Leonardo, Micaela. *Exotics at Home: Anthropologies, Others, and American Modernity.* Chicago: University of Chicago Press, 2000.

Dourish, Paul, and Genevieve Bell. *Divining a Digital Future: Mess and Mythology in Ubiquitous Computing.* Cambridge, MA: MIT Press, 2011.

Du Bois, Cora. "Some Anthropological Hindsights." *Annual Review of Anthropology* 9 (1980): 1–13.

Dumit, Joseph. *Drugs for Life: How Pharmaceutical Companies Define Our Health.* Durham, NC: Duke University Press, 2012.

———. *Picturing Personhood: Brain Scans and Biomedical Identity.* Princeton, NJ: Princeton University Press, 2004.

Dumont, Louis. *From Mandeville to Marx: The Genesis and Triumph of Economic Ideology.* Chicago: University of Chicago Press, 1977.

Edelman, Lee. *No Future: Queer Theory and Death Drive.* Durham, NC: Duke University Press, 2004.

Edmonds, Alexander. *Pretty Modern: Beauty, Sex, and Plastic Surgery in Brazil.* Durham, NC: Duke University Press, 2010.

Eggan, Fred. "Among the Anthropologists." *Annual Review of Anthropology* 3 (1974): 1–19.

Ehrenreich, Barbara, and Arlie Russell Hochschild. Introduction to *Global Woman: Nannies, Maids, and Sex Workers in the New Economy,* ed. Barbara Ehrenreich and Arlie Russell Hochschild, 1–13. New York: Holt, 2002.

Elman, Benjamin A. *On Their Own Terms: Science in China, 1550–1900.* Cambridge, MA: Harvard University Press, 2005.

Engels, Friedrich. *The Origin of the Family, Private Property and the State.* Zurich, 1884.

Escobar, Arturo. "Sustainability: Designs for the Pluriverse." *Development* 54.2 (2011): 137–40.

Evans-Pritchard, E. E. *Witchcraft, Oracles and Magic among the Azande.* Oxford: Clarendon Press, 1937.

Everett, Anna. *Digital Diasporas: A Race for Cyberspace.* Buffalo: State University of New York Press, 2009.

Fabian, Johannes. *Ethnography as Commentary: Writing from the Virtual Archive.* Durham, NC: Duke University Press, 2008.

Faubion, James, and George Marcus. *Doing Fieldwork Is Not What It Used to Be: Learning Anthropology's Method in a Time of Transition.* Ithaca, NY: Cornell University Press, 2009.

Favret-Saada, Jeanne. *Deadly Words: Witchcraft in the Bocage.* 1977. Cambridge: Cambridge University Press, 1980.

Feld, Steven. *Sound and Sentiment: Birds, Weeping, Poetics, and Song in Kaluli Expression.* Philadelphia: University of Pennsylvania Press, 1990.

Feldman, Allen. *Formations of Violence: The Narrative of the Body and Political Terror in Northern Ireland.* Chicago: University of Chicago Press, 1991.

Felt, Ulrike. "Keeping Technologies Out: Sociotechnical Imaginaries and the Formation of a National Technopolitical Identity." Preprint. Department of Social Studies of Science, University of Vienna, February 2013. http://sciencestudies .univie.ac.at/publications.

Feyerabend, Paul. *Against Method.* London, Verso, 1982.

Field, Connie. *The Life and Times of Rosie the Riveter.* Film. Berkeley: Clarity Educational Productions, 1980.

Field, Les. *Abalone Tales: Collaborative Explorations in Sovereignty and Identity.* Berkeley: University of California Press, 2008.

Firth, Raymond. "An Appraisal of Modern Social Anthropology." *Annual Review of Anthropology* 4 (1975): 1–25.

Fischer, Michael M. J. "Anthropologia and Philosophia: Reading alongside Benjamin in Yazd, Derrida in Qum, Arendt in Tehran." In *The Ground Between: Anthropologists Engage Philosophy,* ed. Veena Das, Arthur Kleinman, Bhrigupati Singh, and Michael Jackson. Durham, NC: Duke University Press, 2014.

———. *Anthropological Futures.* Durham, NC: Duke University Press, 2009.

———. "Anthropology of Science and Technology." In *International Encyclopedia of the Social Sciences,* ed. Ulf Hannerz and Dominic Boyer. Forthcoming.

————. "Autobiographical Voices (1, 2, 3) and Mosaic Memory: Experimental Sondages in the (Post)Modern World." In *Autobiography and Postmodernism*, ed. Kathleen Ashley, Leigh Gilmore, and Gerald Peters, 79–114. Amherst: University of Massachusetts Press, 1994.

————. "The BAC [Bioethics Advisory Committee] Consultation on Neuroscience and Ethics: An Anthropologists' Perspective." *Innovation* 11.2 (2013): 3–5.

————. "Before Going Digital/Double Digit/Y2000: A Retrospective of Late Editions." In *Late Editions* 8: *Zeroing In on the Year 2000*, 13–34. Chicago: University of Chicago Press, 2000.

————. "Biopolis: Asian Science in the Global Circuitry." *Science, Technology, Society* 18.3 (2013): 379–404.

————. "Bombay Talkies, the Word and the World: Salman Rushdie's Satanic Verses." *Cultural Anthropology* 5.2 (1990): 107–59.

————. "Culture and Cultural Analysis as Experimental Systems." *Cultural Anthropology* 22.1 (2007): 1–65.

————. *Emergent Forms of Life and the Anthropological Voice.* Durham, NC: Duke University Press, 2003.

————. "Ethnicity and the Post-Modern Arts of Memory." In *Writing Culture: The Poetics and Politics of Ethnography*, ed. James Clifford and George E. Marcus, 194–234. Berkeley: University of California Press, 1986.

————. "Eye(I)ing the Sciences and Their Signifiers (Language, Tropes, Autobiographers): InterViewing for a Cultural Studies of Science and Technology." In *Technoscientific Imaginaries*, ed. George E. Marcus, 43–84. *Late Editions* 2. Chicago: University of Chicago Press, 1995.

————. "If Derrida Is the Gomez-Pena of Philosophy, What Are the Genres of Social Science? Just Gaming: The Y2K Computer Bug and Other Uncertainties—A Critical Simulation Game." In *Para-Sites*, ed. George E. Marcus, 15–102. *Late Editions* 7. Chicago: University of Chicago Press, 2000.

————. "Iran and the Boomeranging Cartoon Wars: Can Public Spheres at Risk Ally with Public Spheres Yet to Be Achieved?" *Cultural Politics* 5.1 (2009): 27–62.

————. "Lively Biotech and Translational Research." In *Lively Capital*, ed. Kaushik Sunder Rajan, 385–436. Durham, NC: Duke University Press, 2012.

————. "The Peopling of Technologies." In *When People Come First: Critical Studies in Global Health*, ed. João Biehl and Adriana Petryna, 347–76. Princeton, NJ: Princeton University Press, 2013.

————. "The Rhythmic Beat of the Revolution in Iran." *Cultural Anthropology* 25.3 (2010): 497–543.

————. "Technoscientific Infrastructures and Emergent Forms of Life: A Commentary." *American Anthropologist* 107.1 (2005): 55–61.

————. "Worlding Cyberspace: Towards an Ethnography in Time, Space and Theory." In *Critical Anthropology Now*, ed. George E. Marcus, 245–304. Santa Fe, NM: School for American Research, 1999.

Fortes, Meyer. "An Anthropologist's Apprenticeship." *Annual Review of Anthropology* 7 (1978): 1–30.

Fortun, Kim. *Advocacy after Bhopal: Environmentalism, Disaster, New Global Orders.* Chicago: University of Chicago Press, 2001.

———. "Ethnography in/of/as Open Systems." *Reviews in Anthropology* 32.2 (2003): 171–90.

———. "Experimenting with the Asthma Files?" Paper presented at the Digital Anthropology: Projects and Projections Panel of the 110th annual meeting of the American Anthropological Association, Montreal, November 15–20, 2011.

———. "Foreword to the 25th Anniversary Edition of *Writing Culture.*" In *Writing Culture,* by James Clifford. 1986. Berkeley: University of California Press, 2011.

———. "Toxics Trouble: Feminism and the Subversion of Science." In *Bodies in Space: Feminist Approaches to Nature and Materiality,* ed. Elvira Scheich and Karen Wagels, 234–55. Forum of Women's and Gender Studies, vol. 31. Münster: Verlag Westfälisches Dampfboot, 2011.

Fortun, Michael. *Promising Genomics: Iceland and deCODE Genetics in a World of Speculation.* Berkeley: University of California Press, 2008.

Foucault, Michel. *The Birth of Biopolitics: Lectures at the Collège de France, 1978–1979.* Trans. Graham Burchell. New York: Palgrave Macmillan, 2008.

———. *Discipline and Punish.* Trans. Alan Sheridan. New York: Pantheon, 1975.

Franklin, Sarah. *Dolly Mixture: The Remaking of Genealogy.* Durham, NC: Duke University Press, 2007.

———. *Embodied Progress: A Cultural Account of Assisted Conception.* London: Routledge, 1997.

Franklin, Sarah, and Margaret Lock, eds. *Remaking Life and Death: Towards an Anthropology of the Biosciences.* Santa Fe, NM: School of American Research, 2003.

Friedan, Betty. *The Feminine Mystique.* New York: W. W. Norton, 1963.

Furuitchi Noritoshi. *Zetsubō no kuni no kōfufukuna wakmonotachi* [Happy youth in a country of despair]. Tokyo: Kodantsa, 2011.

Garcia, Angela. *The Pastoral Clinic: Addiction and Dispossession along the Rio Grande.* Berkeley: University of California Press, 2010.

Gates, Henry Louis. *The Signifying Monkey: A Theory of African-American Literary Criticism.* New York: Oxford University Press, 1988.

Geertz, Clifford. "Blurred Genres." *American Scholar* 49 (1980): 165–79.

———. *The Interpretation of Cultures.* New York: Basic Books, 1973.

———. *Works and Lives: The Anthropologist as Author.* Palo Alto, CA: Stanford University Press, 1988.

Ghosh, Amitav. *Calcutta Chromosome: A Novel of Fevers, Delirium, and Discovery.* Delhi: Ravi Dayal, 1996.

———. *The Hungry Tide.* New York: HarperCollins, 2004.

———. *River of Smoke.* London: John Murray, 2011.

————. *The Sea of Poppies*. London: John Murray, 2008.

Gilmore, David. "Anthropology of the Mediterranean Area." *Annual Review of Anthropology* 11 (1982): 175–205.

Ginsburg, Faye. "Rethinking the Digital Age." In *The Media and Social Theory*, ed. David Hesmondhalgh and Jason Toynbee, 127–44. New York: Routledge, 2008.

Goffman, Erving. *Stigma: Notes on the Management of Spoiled Identity*. Englewood Cliffs, NJ: Prentice-Hall, 1963.

Good, Byron, et al. *A Psychosocial Needs Assessment of Communities in 14 Selected Districts in Acheh*. Banda Aceh, Indonesia: International Organization for Migration; Department of Social Medicine, Harvard Medical School; World Bank; Bakhti Husada; Universitas Syiah Kuala, 2007.

Good, Mary-Jo DelVecchio, and Byron Good. "Indonesia Sakit: Indonesian Disorders and the Subjective Experience and Interpretive Politics of Contemporary Indonesian Artists." In *Postcolonial Disorders*, ed. Mary-Jo DelVecchio Good, Sandra Hyde, Sarah Pinto, and Byron Good. Berkeley: University of California Press, 2008.

Gordimer, Nadine. *Burger's Daughter*. London: Penguin, 1979.

————. *Writing and Being*. Cambridge, MA: Harvard University Press, 1995.

Gourevitch, Philip. *We Wish to Inform You That Tomorrow We Will be Killed with Our Families*. New York: Macmillan, 1998.

Grayman, Jesse Hession. "Humanitarian Encounters in Post Conflict Acheh." PhD dissertation, Harvard University, 2013.

Green, Maia. "Framing and Escaping: Contrasting Aspects of Knowledge Work in International Development and Anthropology." In *Differentiating Development: Beyond an Anthropology of Critique*, ed. Soumhya Venkatesan and Thomas Yarrow, 42–57. New York: Berghahn Books, 2012.

Greene, Graham. *The Power and the Glory*, ed. R. W. B. Lewis and Peter J. Conn. New York: Viking, 1970.

Greenhouse, Carol. *The Paradox of Relevance: Ethnography and Citizenship in the United States*. Philadelphia: University of Pennsylvania Press, 2011.

Greenslit, Nathan. "Pharmaceutical Relations: Intersections of Illness, Fantasy and Capital in the Age of Direct to Consumer Marketing." PhD dissertation, MIT, 2007.

Greenwald, Robert, dir. *Outfoxed: Robert Murdoch's War on Journalism*. Film. New York: Brave New Films, 2004.

Grimshaw, Anna. "The Bellwether Ewe: Recent Developments in Ethnographic Filmmaking and the Aesthetics of Anthropological Inquiry." *Cultural Anthropology* 26.2 (2011): 263–86.

Grosz, Elizabeth. *Chaos, Territory, Art: Deleuze and the Framing of the Earth*. New York: Columbia University Press, 2008.

Gupta, Akhil, and James Ferguson. *Anthropological Locations: Boundaries and Grounds of a Field Science*. Berkeley: University of California Press, 1997.

Gupta, Akhil, and James Ferguson. "Beyond Culture: Space, Identity, and the Politics of Difference." In *Culture, Power, Place: Explorations in Critical Anthropology*, ed. Akhil Gupta and James Ferguson, 33–51. Durham, NC: Duke University Press, 1997.

Gupta, Akhil, and James Ferguson. *Culture, Power, Place: Explorations in Critical Anthropology*. Durham, NC: Duke University Press, 1997.

Hall, David L., and Roger T. Ames. *Thinking from the Han: Self, Truth, and Transcendence in Chinese and Western Culture*. Albany: State University of New York Press, 1998.

Hamdy, Sherine. *Our Bodies Belong to God: Organ Transplants, Islam, and the Struggle for Dignity in Egypt*. Berkeley: University of California Press, 2012.

Handler, Richard. "Critics against Culture: Jules Henry, Richard Hoggart, and the Tragicomedy of Mass Society." In *Critics against Culture: Anthropological Observers of Mass Society*, 154–85. Madison: University of Wisconsin Press, 2005.

———. "The Dainty and the Hungry Man: Literature and Anthropology in the Work of Edward Sapir." In *Observers Observed*, ed. George Stocking, 208–31. *History of Anthropology* 1. Madison: University of Wisconsin Press, 1983.

———. "Interpreting the Predicament of Culture Today." *Social Analysis* 41.3 (1997): 72–83.

———. *Nationalism and the Politics of Culture in Quebec*. Madison: University of Wisconsin Press, 1988.

Handler, Richard, and Daniel Segal. *Jane Austen and the Fiction of Culture*. Tucson: University of Arizona Press, 1990.

Hansen, Thomas Blom. *The Saffron Wave*. Princeton, NJ: Princeton University Press, 1999.

Haraway, Donna. "Situated Knowledge: The Science Question in Feminism and the Privilege of Partial Perspective." *Feminist Studies* 14.3 (1988): 575–99.

———. *When Species Meet*. Minneapolis: University of Minnesota Press, 2007.

Hardt, Michael, and Antonio Negri. *Commonwealth*. Cambridge, MA: Harvard University Press, 2009.

Harrison, Faye. *Decolonizing Anthropology: Moving Further Toward an Anthropology of Liberation*. Washington, DC: American Anthropological Association, 1997.

Havis, Richard James. "Interview with Chen Zaige." *Cineaste—America's Leading Magazine on the Art and Politics of the Cinema* 29.1 (2003): 8–11.

Heidegger, Martin. "The Thing." In *Poetry, Language, Thought*, 161–84. Trans. Albert Hofstadter. New York: Harper Colophon, 1975.

Helmreich, Stefan. *Alien Ocean: Anthropological Voyages in Microbial Seas*. Berkeley: University of California Press, 2009.

———. *Silicon Second Nature: Culturing Artificial Life in a Digital World*. Berkeley: University of California Press, 1998.

Henry, Jules. *Culture against Man*. New York: Random House, 1963.

Herzfeld, Michael. *Cultural Intimacy: Social Poetics in the Nation-State*. London: Routledge, 2004.

Heyman, Steven. "Neuroscience and Ethics." Talk at Bioethics Advisory Committee Public Consultation Session, National University of Singapore, January 10, 2013.

Ho, Dahpon David. "Sealords Live in Vain: Fujian and the Making of a Maritime Frontier in Seventeenth Century China." PhD dissertation, University of California, San Diego, 2011.

Ho, Engseng. "Empire through Diasporic Eyes: A View from the Other Boat." *Comparative Studies of Society and History* 46.2 (2004): 210–46.

———. *The Graves of Tarim: Genealogy and Mobility across the Indian Ocean.* Berkeley: University of California Press, 2002.

Hoben, Allan. "Anthropologists and Development." *Annual Review of Anthropology* 11 (1982): 349–75.

Hu, Kemin. *The Suyuan Stone Catalog: Scholars' Rocks in Ancient China*, Trumbull, CT: Weatherhill, 2002.

Hume, David. *Dialogues Concerning Natural Religion*, ed. Richard H. Popkin. Indianapolis: Hackett, 1980.

———. *An Enquiry Concerning Human Understanding.* 1748. Amherst, MA: Prometheus, 1988.

———. *A Treatise of Human Nature.* Book 1: *Of the Understanding.* 1738. Edited by D. G. C. MacNabb. Cleveland, Ohio: Meridian, 1962.

Hymes, Dell H. "Introduction to the Ann Arbor Paperbacks Edition." In *Reinventing Anthropology*, v–xlix. Ann Arbor: University of Michigan Press, 1999.

———. *Reinventing Anthropology.* Ann Arbor: University of Michigan Press, 1972.

Ingold, Tim. "Bringing Things to Life: Creative Entanglements in a World of Materials." In *Realities*, Working Paper 15. Manchester, UK: Department of Sociology, University of Manchester, 2010.

Jackson, John L., Jr. *Real Black: Adventures in Racial Sincerity.* Chicago: University of Chicago Press, 2005.

Jain, S. Lochlann. *Injury: The Politics of Product Design and Safety Law in the United States.* Princeton, NJ: Princeton University Press, 2006.

Jasanoff, Sheila. *Designs on Nature: Science and Democracy in Europe and the United States.* Princeton, NJ: Princeton University Press, 2005.

Jha, Raj Kamal. *Fireproof.* London: Picador, 2006.

Jones, Graham. *Trade of the Tricks: Inside the Magician's Craft.* Berkeley: University of California Press, 2011.

Julien, Isaac, dir. *Territories.* Video. London: Sankofa Film Collective.

Jullien, François. *Vital Nourishment: Departing from Happiness.* Trans. Arthur Goldhammer. New York: Zone Books, 2007.

Juris, Jeffrey S. *Networking Futures: The Movements against Corporate Globalization.* Durham, NC: Duke University Press, 2008.

Kahn, Jonathan. *Race in a Bottle: The Story of BiDil and Racialized Medicine in a Post-Genomic Age.* New York: Columbia University Press, 2012.

Kangyi, Hou. "To Be a Stone-Like Person." In *Wu lao hua shi* [Five masters speak of stone], ed. Lao Ying and Cai Ying, 2–6. Xi'an: Shanxi Renmin Chubanshe, 2008.

Kay, Lily. *Who Wrote the Book of Life? A History of the Genetic Code.* Palo Alto, CA: Stanford University Press, 2000.

Keane, Webb. *Signs of Recognition: Powers and Hazards of Representation in an Indonesian Society.* Berkeley: University of California Press, 1997.

———. "Sincerity, 'Modernity,' and the Protestants." *Cultural Anthropology* 17 (2002): 65–92.

Keeling, Kara. "Passing for Human: Bamboozled and Digital Humanism." *Women and Performance* 15.1 (2005): 237–50.

Keller, Evelyn Fox. "Dynamic Objectivity: Love, Power and Knowledge." In *Reflections on Gender and Science*, 115–26. New Haven, CT: Yale University Press, 1985.

Kelty, Christopher. "Collaboration, Coordination, and Composition: Fieldwork after the Internet." In *Fieldwork Is Not What It Used to Be*, ed. James D. Faubion and George E. Marcus, 184–206. Ithaca, NY: Cornell University Press, 2009.

———. "Culture In, Culture Out." *Anthropological Quarterly* 83.1 (2010): 7–16.

———. *Two Bits: The Cultural Significance of Free Software.* Durham, NC: Duke University Press, 2008.

Kernaghan, Richard. *Coca's Gone: Of Might and Right in the Huallaga Post-Boom.* Palo Alto, CA: Stanford University Press, 2009.

Kessler, Ronald C., et al. "The Global Burden of Mental Disorders: An Update from the WHO World Mental Health (WMH) Surveys." *Epidemiologia e psichiatria sociale* 18.1 (2009): 23–33.

Kidder, Tracy. *Mountains beyond Mountains: The Quest of Dr. Paul Farmer, a Man Who Would Cure the World.* New York: Random House, 2003.

Kirksey, S. Eben, and Stefan Helmreich. "The Emergence of Multispecies Ethnography." *Cultural Anthropology* 25.4 (2010): 545–76.

Kleinman, Arthur, Veena Das, and Margaret Lock, eds. *Social Suffering.* Berkeley: University of California Press, 1997.

Kothari, Uma. "Authority and Expertise: The Professionalisation of International Development and the Ordering of Dissent." *Antipode* 37 (2005): 425–46.

Krogman, Wilton. "Fifty Years of Physical Anthropology." *Annual Review of Anthropology* 5 (1976): 1–14.

Kulke, Herman, K. Kesavapany, and Vijay Sakhula, eds. *Nagapattinam to Suvarnadwipa: Reflections on the Chola Naval Expeditions to Southeast Asia.* Singapore: Institute of Southeast Asian Studies, 2009.

Kumar, Richa. "The Yellow Revolution in Malway: Alternative Arenas of Struggle and the Cultural Politics of Development." PhD dissertation, MIT, 2009.

Kuntsman, Ada, and Rebecca Stein. *Another War Zone: Social Media and Military Occupation in Israel.* Palo Alto, CA: Stanford University Press, 2014.

Kuo, Pao Kun. "Descendants of the Eunuch Admiral." In *The Complete Works of Kuo Pao Kun*. Vol. 4: *Plays in English*, ed. C. J. W. L. Wee. Singapore: Theater Practice and Global Publishing, 2012.

Kuo, Wen-Hua. "The Voice on the Bridge: Taiwan's Regulatory Engagement with Global Pharmaceuticals." *East Asian Science, Technology and Society: An International Journal* 3.1 (2009): 51–72.

Lacoue-Labarthe, Philippe. "The Echo of the Subject" in *Typography: Mimesis, Philosophy, Politics*, 139–207. Palo Alto, CA: Stanford, 1998.

Lahsen, Myanna. "Knowledge, Democracy and Uneven Playing Fields: Insights from Climate Politics in—and between—the U.S. and Brazil." In *Knowledge and Democracy: A 21st-Century Perspective*, ed. Nico Stehr, 163–81. London: Transaction, 2008.

———. "Seductive Simulations: Uncertainty Distribution around Climate Models." *Social Studies of Science* 35 (2005): 895–922.

Lahsen, Myanna, with Gunilla Oberg. *The Role of Unstated Mistrust and Disparities in Scientific Capacity*. Linköping: Swedish Institute for Climate Science and Policy Research, Linköping University, 2006. https://polopoly.liu.se/content/1 /c4/10/58/Lahsen%20oberg%20pdf%20final%20version%202006.pdf.

Landecker, Hannah. *Culturing Life: How Cells Became Technologies*. Cambridge, MA: Harvard University Press, 2007.

Lanoo, Michael. *Malformed Frogs: The Collapse of Aquatic Ecosystems*. Berkeley: University of California Press, 2008.

Lassiter, Luke Eric. *The Chicago Guide to Collaborative Ethnography*. Chicago: University of Chicago Press, 2005.

Latour, Bruno. *A Cautious Prometheus? A Few Steps toward a Philosophy of Design (with Special Attention to Peter Sloterdijk)*. Paris: Mendeley Universal, 2008.

———. "Why Critique Has Run out of Steam." *Critical Inquiry* 30.2 (2004): 225–48.

Lepinay, Vincent. *Codes of Finance: Engineering Derivatives in a Global Bank*. Princeton, NJ: Princeton University Press, 2011.

Lévi-Strauss, Claude. *The Naked Man*. Vol. 4: *Mythologiques*. 1971. Trans. Doreen and John Weightman. New York: Harper and Row, 1981.

Lewis, Herbert. *In Defense of Anthropology: An Investigation of the Critique of Anthropology*. Piscataway, NJ: Transaction, 2013.

Lingis, Alphonso. "The Navel of the World." In *Dangerous Emotions*, 1–21. Berkeley: University of California Press, 2000.

Livingston, Julie. *Improvised Medicine: An African Oncology Ward in an Emerging Cancer Epidemic*. Durham, NC: Duke University Press, 2013.

Liyang Wang. *Shi dao* [The dao of stone]. Beijing: Xueyuan Chubanshe, 2010.

Lotfalian, Mazyar. "Aestheticized Politics, Visual Culture, and Emergent Forms of Digital Practice." *International Journal of Communication* 6 (2012): 1–20.

Lucy, John A. *Reflexive Language: Reported Speech and Metapragmatics*. Cambridge: University of Cambridge Press, 1993.

Lutz, Catherine, and Anne Lutz Fernandez. *Carjacked: The Culture of the Automobile and Its Effect on Our Lives.* New York: Palgrave Macmillan, 2010.

MacKenzie, Donald. *An Engine, Not a Camera: How Financial Models Shape Markets.* Cambridge, MA: MIT Press, 2008.

MacNabb, D. G. C., ed. Introduction to *A Treatise of Human Nature.* Book 1: *Of the Understanding,* by David Hume. 1738. Cleveland, Ohio: Meridian, 1962.

Makihara, Miki, and Bambi B. Schieffelin. *Consequences of Contact: Language Ideologies and Sociocultural Transformations in Pacific Societies.* Oxford: Oxford University Press, 2007.

Mamdani. Mahmood. *When Victims Become Killers.* Princeton, NJ: Princeton University Press, 2001.

Marchetti, Gina. "From Mao's 'Continuous Revolution' to Ning Ying's Perpetual Motion (2005): Sexual Politics, Neoliberalism, and Postmodern China." In *Chinese Women's Cinema: Transnational Contexts,* ed. Lingzhen Wang, 191–212. New York: Columbia University Press, 2011.

Marcus, George E. "Afterword: Ethnographic Writing and Anthropological Careers." In *Writing Culture: The Poetics and Politics of Ethnography,* ed. James Clifford and George E. Marcus, 262–94. Berkeley: University of California Press, 1986.

———. "Collaborative Options and Pedagogical Experiment in Anthropological Research on Experts and Policy Processes." *Anthropology in Action* 15.2 (2008): 47–57.

———. "Contemporary Fieldwork Aesthetics in Art and Anthropology: Experiments in Collaboration and Intervention." In *Ethnographica Moralia: Experiments in Interpretive Anthropology,* ed. N. Panourgia and G. Marcus, 29–44. New York: Fordham University Press, 2008.

———. "Contemporary Problems of Ethnography in the Modern World System." In *Writing Culture: The Poetics and Politics of Ethnography,* ed. James Clifford and George E. Marcus, 165–93. Berkeley: University of California Press, 1986.

———. "Ethnography in/of the World System: The Emergence of Multi-Sited Ethnography." *Annual Review of Anthropology* 25 (1995): 95–117.

———. "Ethnography Two Decades after Writing Culture: From the Experimental to the Baroque." *Anthropological Quarterly* 80.4 (2007): 1127–46.

———. Introduction to *Para-Sites: A Casebook against Cynical Reason,* ed. George Marcus, 1–13. Chicago: University of Chicago Press, 2000.

———, ed. *Late Editions: Cultural Studies for the End of the Century.* 8 vols. Chicago: University of Chicago Press, 1992–2000.

———. "Rhetoric and the Ethnographic Genre in Anthropological Research." *Current Anthropology* 21 (1980): 507–10.

———. "The Uses of Complicity in the Changing Mise-en-Scène of Anthropological Fieldwork." *Representations* 59 (1997): 85–108.

Marcus, George, and James Clifford. "The Making of Ethnographic Texts: A Preliminary Report." *Current Anthropology* 26 (1985): 267–71.

Marcus, George, and Dick Cushman. "Ethnographies as Texts." *Annual Review of Anthropology* 11 (1982): 25–69.

Marcus, George, and Michael Fischer. *Anthropology as Cultural Critique*. Chicago: University of Chicago Press, 1986.

Marcus, George, and Michael Fischer. *Anthropology as Cultural Critique: An Experimental Moment in the Human Sciences*. Chicago: University of Chicago Press, 1999.

Mascia-Lees, Frances, Patricia Cohen, and Colleen Ballerino Cohen. "The Postmodern Turn: Cautions from a Feminist Perspective." *Signs* 15.1 (1989): 7–33.

Masco, Joseph. *Nuclear Borderlands: The Manhattan Project in Post–Cold War New Mexico*. Princeton, NJ: Princeton University Press, 2006.

Massumi, Brian. *Parables of the Virtual: Movement, Affect, Sensation*. Durham, NC: Duke University Press, 2002.

Matsutake Worlds Research Group. "A New Form of Collaboration in Cultural Anthropology." *American Ethnologist* 36.2 (2009): 380–403.

McCance, Dawn. *Posts: Re Addressing the Ethical*. Albany: State University of New York Press, 1996.

McCormack, Derek P. "An Event of Geographical Ethics in Spaces of Affect." *Transactions of the Institute of British Geographers* 28 (2003): 488–507.

McIntosh, Laurie. "Before and After: Terror, Extremism, and the 'Not So New' Norway." *African and Black Diaspora* 7.1 (2014): 70–80.

McKinnon, Susan, and Sydel Silverman, eds. *Complexities: Beyond Nature and Nurture*. Chicago: University of Chicago Press, 2005.

Mead, Margaret. "Changing Styles of Anthropological Work." *Annual Review of Anthropology* 2 (1973): 1–26.

Men, Wu. "Cold Woods Stone Screen." In *The Suyuan Stone Catalog: Scholars' Rocks in Ancient China*, by Kemin Hu, 67. Trumbull, CT: Weatherhill, 2002.

Mitchell, David Stephen. "The Art of Fiction No. 204." Interview by Adam Begley. *Paris Review* 193 (summer 2010). http://www.theparisreview.org/interviews/6034/the-art-of-fiction-no-204-david-mitchell.

———. *Cloud Atlas*. New York: Random House, 2004.

———. *The Thousand Autumns of Jacob de Zoet*. New York: Random House, 2010.

Mitchell, W. J. T. *What Do Pictures Want? The Lives and Loves of Images*. Chicago: University of Chicago Press, 2006.

Mnookin, Jennifer. "Images of Truth: Evidence, Expertise and Technologies of Knowledge in the American Courtroom." PhD dissertation, MIT, 1999.

Montoya, Michael. *Making the Mexican Diabetic: Race, Science, and the Genetics of Inequality*. Berkeley: University of California Press, 2011.

Moore, David Chioni. "Anthropology Is Dead, Long Live Anthro(a)pology: Poststructuralism, Literary Studies, and Anthropology's 'Nervous Present.'" *Journal of Anthropological Research* 50.4 (1994): 345–65.

Moore, Sally Falk. "Explaining the Present: Theoretical Dilemmas in Processual Ethnography." *American Ethnologist* 14.4 (1987): 727–36.

Muehlebach, Andrea. *The Moral Neoliberal Italy: Welfare and Citizenship in Italy.* Chicago: University of Chicago Press, 2012.

Mullings, Leith. "President's 2012 Report to the Membership." *Anthropology News* (January/February 2013): 24–25.

Muñoz, José Esteban. *Cruising Utopia: The Then and There of Queer Futurity.* Durham, NC: Duke University Press, 2009.

Murphy, Robert. *The Dialectics of Social Life.* New York: Basic Books, 1971.

Murray, C. L., and Alan D. Lopez. *The Global Burden of Disease: A Comprehensive Assessment of Mortality and Disability from Diseases, Injuries and Risk Factors in 1990 and Projected to 2020.* Cambridge, MA: Harvard University Press, 1996.

Murray, Stephen. "Ralph Beals." In *Presidential Portraits,* ed. Regna Darnell and Frederic Gleach, 133–36. Washington, DC: American Anthropological Association, 2002.

Myerhoff, Barbara. *In Her Own Time: The Final Fieldwork of Barbara Myerhoff.* Santa Monica, CA: Direct Cinema, 1985.

Myers, Natasha. "Modeling Proteins, Making Scientists: An Ethnography of Pedagogy and Visual Cultures in Contemporary Structural Biology." PhD dissertation, MIT, 2007.

Nabokov, Vladimir. *Nikolai Gogol.* New York: New Directions, 1961.

Nakane, Chie. *Tate shakai no ningen kankei* [Human relations in a vertical society]. Tokyo: Kodansha, 1967.

Narayan, Kirin. *Alive in the Writing, Crafting Ethnography in the Company of Chekov.* Chicago: University of Chicago Press, 2012.

———. "Tools to Shape Texts: What Creative Nonfiction Can Offer Ethnography." *Anthropology and Humanism* 32.2 (2007): 130–44.

Navarro, Tami, Bianca Williams, and Attiya Ahmad. "Sitting at the Kitchen Table: Fieldnotes from Women of Color in Anthropology." *Cultural Anthropology* 28.3 (2013): 443–63.

Negri, Antonio. *The Political Descartes: Reason, Ideology and the Bourgeois Project.* 1970. Trans. Matteo Mandarini and Alberto Toscano. London: Verso, 2007.

NHK Muen shakai purojekuto. *Muen shakai: Muenshi sanman-nisennin no shōgeki* [Relationless society: The shock of 32,000 relationless deaths]. Tokyo: Bungei shunjū, 2010.

Novak, David. *Japanoise: Music at the Edge of Circulation.* Durham, NC: Duke University Press, 2013.

Obarrio, Juan. "Postshamanism." *Cultural Studies Review* 13.2 (2007): 166–89.

Ondaatje, Michael. *Coming through Slaughter.* New York: Vintage, 1976.

Ong, Aihwa, and Stephen Collier. *Global Assemblages: Technology, Politics, and Ethics as Anthropological Problems.* Oxford: Blackwell, 2005.

Ortner, Sherry. "Theory in Anthropology Since the Sixties." *Comparative Studies in Society and History* 26.1 (1984): 126–66.

Osanloo, Arzoo. *The Politics of Women's Rights in Iran.* Princeton, NJ: Princeton University Press, 2009.

Otto, Ton, and Nils Bubandt. *Experiments in Holism: Theory and Practice in Contemporary Anthropology*. Oxford: Wiley-Blackwell, 2010.

Ozden, Canay. "Vernacular Economics and Smart Electricity Grids: How Traders, Engineers, and Economists Make Markets Differently." PhD dissertation proposal, MIT, 2012.

Ozkan, Esra. "Executive Coaching: Crafting a Versatile Self in Corporate America." PhD dissertation, MIT, 2007.

Panagia, Davide. "Inconsistencies of Character: David Hume on Sympathy, Intensity, and Artifice." In *Deleuze and Philosophy*, ed. Constantin V. Boundas, 85–97. Edinburgh: Edinburgh University Press, 2006.

Panourgia, Neni. *Dangerous Citizens*. New York: Fordham University Press, 2009.

Paxson, Heather. *The Life of Cheese: Crafting Food and Value in America*. Berkeley: University of California Press, 2012.

———. "Post-Pasteurian Cultures: The Microbiopolitics of Raw-Milk Cheese in the United States." *Cultural Anthropology* 23.1 (2008): 15–47.

Perin, Constance. *Shouldering Risks: The Culture of Control in the Nuclear Power Industry*. Princeton, NJ: Princeton University Press, 2005.

Perrow, Charles. *Normal Accidents: Living with High-Risk Technologies*. New York: Basic Books, 1984.

Peters, John Durham. *Speaking into the Air: A History of the Idea of Communication*. Chicago: University of Chicago Press, 1999.

Petryna, Adriana. *Life Exposed: Biological Citizens after Chernobyl*. Princeton, NJ: Princeton University Press, 2002.

———. *When Experiments Travel: Clinical Trials and the Global Search for Human Subjects*. Princeton, NJ: Princeton University Press, 2009.

"A Plea to Abandon Asthma as a Disease Concept." *Lancet* 368.9545 (2006): 1415–16.

Polier, Nicole, and William Roseberry. "Tristes Tropes: Postmodern Anthropologists Search for the Other and Find Themselves." *Economy and Society* 18.2 (1989): 245–64.

Pollock, Anne. *Medicating Race: Heart Disease and Durable Preoccupations with Difference*. Durham, NC: Duke University Press, 2012.

Power, Samantha. *"A Problem from Hell": America and the Age of Genocide*. New York: Basic Books, 2002.

Pradhan, Rajesh. *When the Saints Go Marching In: The Curious Ambivalence of Religious Sadhus in Recent Politics in India*. Delhi: Orient Blackswan, 2013.

Prentice, Rachel. *Bodies in Formation: An Ethnography of Anatomy and Surgery Education*. Durham, NC: Duke University Press, 2012.

Rabinow, Paul. *Making PCR: A Story of Biotechnology*. Chicago: University of Chicago Press, 1995.

———. *The Accompaniment: Assembling the Contemporary*. Chicago: University of Chicago Press, 2011.

———. "Representations Are Social Facts: Modernity and Post-Modernity in Anthropology." In *Writing Culture: The Poetics and Politics of Ethnography*, ed. James Clifford and George E. Marcus, 234–61. Berkeley: University of California Press, 1986.

Rabinow, Paul, and Gaymon Bennett. *Designing for Human Practices: An Experiment with Synthetic Biology*. Chicago: University of Chicago Press, 2012.

Rajagopal, Arvind. *Politics after Television: Hindu Nationalism and the Reshaping of the Indian Public*. Cambridge: Cambridge University Press, 2001.

Rapport, Nigel. "The Narrative as Fieldwork Technique: Processual Ethnography for a World in Motion." In *Constructing the Field*, ed. Vered Amit, 71–95. London: Routledge, 2000.

Redfield, Peter. *Life in Crisis: The Ethical Journey of Doctors without Borders*. Berkeley: University of California Press, 2013.

Rheinberger, Hans-Jorg. "Experimental Systems, Graphematic Spaces." In *Inscribing Science: Scientific Texts and the Materiality of Communication*, ed. Timothy Lenoir, 285–303. Palo Alto, CA: Stanford University Press, 1998.

Rhodes, Lorna. *Total Confinement: Madness and Reason in the Maximum Security Prison*. Berkeley: University of California Press, 2004.

Rhys, Lloyd. *Jungle Pimpernel: The Story of a District Officer in Central Netherlands New Guinea*. London: Hodder and Stoughton, 1947.

Riggs, Marlon. *Black Is, Black Ain't*. San Francisco: California Newsreel, 1994.

———. *Tongues Untied: Black Men Loving Black Men*. San Francisco: Frameline, 1989.

Rist, Gilbert. *The History of Development*. London: Zed Books, 1997.

Robbins, Joel. "Beyond the Suffering Subject: Towards an Anthropology of Good." *Journal of the Royal Anthropological Institute* 19.3 (2013): 447–62.

Rogers, Susan Carol. "Notes from the President." *SAE Bulletin* 1.1 (1987): 1, 3.

Ronell, Avital. *The Test Drive*. Champaign: University of Illinois Press, 2005.

Roosth, Sophia. "Crafting Life: A Sensory Ethnography of Fabricated Bodies." PhD dissertation, MIT, 2010.

Rosaldo, Renato. "From the Door of His Tent: The Fieldworker and the Inquisitor." In *Writing Culture: The Poetics and Politics of Ethnography*, ed. James Clifford and George E. Marcus, 77–97. Berkeley: University of California Press, 1986.

Rose, Nikolas, and Joelle Abi-Rachelle. *Neuro: The New Brain Sciences and the Management of the Mind*. Princeton, NJ: Princeton University Press, 2013.

Rushdie, Salman. *Midnight's Children*. 1981. London: Vintage, 1995.

———. *The Satanic Verses*. 1988. London: Vintage, 1998.

Rutherford, Danilyn. "Sympathy, State Building, and the Experience of Empire." *Cultural Anthropology* 24.1 (2009): 1–32.

Sahlins, Marshall. *Culture and Practical Reason*. Chicago: University of Chicago Press, 1976.

Sanal, Aslihan. *New Organs within Us: Transplants and the Moral Economy*. Durham, NC: Duke University Press, 2011.

Sangren, P. Steven. "Rhetoric and the Authority of Ethnography: 'Postmodernism' and the Social Reproduction of Texts." *Current Anthropology* 29.3 (1988): 405–35.

Schafer, Edward H., ed. and trans. *Tu Wan's Stone Catalogue of Cloudy Forest*. Berkeley: University of California Press, 1961.

Schatzberg, Eric. "Technik Comes to America: Changing Meanings of Technology before 1930." *Technology and Culture* 47 (2006): 486–512.

Schilling, Thomas. "The Social Implications of Digital Mapmaking among Insect Ecologists, Geologists, and Aboriginal First Nations Heritage Consultants." PhD dissertation proposal, MIT, 2013.

Schneider, David. *American Kinship: A Cultural Account*. Englewood Cliffs, NJ: Prentice-Hall, 1968.

Schroedinger, Erwin. *What Is Life? The Physical Aspect of the Living Cell*. Dublin: Dublin Institute for Advanced Studies, Trinity College, 1944. http://whatislife .stanford.edu/LoCo_files/What-is-Life.pdf.

Schwarz, Heinrich. "Techno-Territories: The Spatial, Technological and Social Reorganization of Office Work." PhD dissertation, MIT, 2002.

Segal, Daniel, and Sylvia Yanagisako, eds. *Unwrapping the Sacred Bundle: Reflections on the Disciplining of Anthropology*. Durham, NC: Duke University Press, 2005.

Shamsie, Kamila. *Burnt Shadows*. London: Bloomsbury, 2009.

Shiva, Vandana. *Water Wars: Privatization, Pollution and Profit*. Boston: South End Press, 2002.

Siegal, Bernard. "Foreword." *Biennial Review of Anthropology* 1 (1959): v–vi.

Siegal, Bernard, and Alan Beals. "Foreword." *Biennial Review of Anthropology* 5 (1967): v–vi.

Siegel, James T. *Fetish, Recognition, Revolution*. Princeton, NJ: Princeton University Press, 1997.

Silverstein, Michael. "'Cultural' Concepts and the Language-Culture Nexus." *Current Anthropology* 45.5 (2004): 621–52.

———. "Shifters, Linguistic Categories, and Cultural Description." In *Meaning in Anthropology*, ed. Keith H. Basso and H. A. Selby, 11–55. New York: Harper and Row, 1976.

Slade, Giles. *Made to Break: Technology and Obsolescence in America*. Cambridge, MA: Harvard University Press, 2006.

Soto Laveaga, Gabriela. *Jungle Laboratories: Mexican Peasants, National Projects, and the Making of the Pill*. Durham, NC: Duke University Press, 2009.

Sourcewatch. "Monsanto's High Level Connections to the Bush Administration." n.d. Accessed March 15, 2012. http://www.sourcewatch.org/index.php?title =Monsanto's_High_Level_Connections_to_the_Bush_Administration.

Spivak, Gayatri Chakravorty. *Other Worlds: Essays in Cultural Politics*. New York: Methuen, 1987.

———. *Outside in the Teaching Machine.* New York: Routledge, 1993.

SRI Consulting. "The American Environmental Values Survey, 2006: American Views on the Environment in an Era of Polarization and Conflicting Priorities." October 2006. Accessed March 15, 2012. http://ecoamerica.typepad.com /blog/files/ecoAmerica_AEVS_Report.pdf.

Starn, Orin. "Here Come the Anthros (Again): The Strange Marriage of Anthropology and Native America." *Cultural Anthropology* 26.2 (2011): 179–204.

———. *Ishi's Brain: In Search of America's Last "Wild" Indian.* New York: W. W. Norton, 2004.

Stein, Rolf A. *The World in Miniature: Container Gardens and Dwellings in Far Eastern Religious Thought.* Trans. Phyllis Brooks. Palo Alto, CA: Stanford University Press, 1990.

Stocking, George. *Delimiting Anthropology: Occasional Inquiries and Reflections.* Madison: University of Wisconsin Press, 2001.

———. *Race, Culture, and Evolution.* New York: Basic Books, 1968.

Strathern, Marilyn, ed. *Audit Cultures.* London: Routledge, 2000.

———. *Commons and Borderlands: Working Papers on Interdisciplinarity, Accountability, and the Flow of Knowledge.* Oxford: Sean Kingston, 2004.

Suchman, Lucy. "Anthropological Relocations and the Limits of Design." *Annual Review of Anthropology* 40 (2011): 1–18.

Sunder Rajan, Kaushik. *Biocapital: The Constitution of Postgenomic Life.* Durham, NC: Duke University Press, 2006.

———, ed. *Lively Capital: Biotechnologies, Ethics, and Governance in Global Markets.* Durham, NC: Duke University Press, 2012.

Sze, Mai-mai, ed. and trans. *The Mustard Seed Garden Manual of Painting (1679–1701).* Princeton, NJ: Princeton University Press, 1956.

Taussig, Michael. *Mimesis and Alterity: A Particular History of the Senses.* New York: Routledge, 1993.

———. *Shamanism, Colonialism, and the Wild Man: A Study in Terror and Healing.* Chicago: University of Chicago Press, 1991.

Tett, Gillian. *Fool's Gold: The Inside Story of J. P. Morgan and How Wall St. Greed Corrupted Its Bold Dream and Created a Financial Catastrophe.* New York: Free Press, 2009.

Theidon, Kimberly. *Intimate Enemies: Violence and Reconciliation in Peru.* Philadelphia: University of Pennsylvania Press, 2012.

Tocqueville, Alexis de. *Democracy in America.* Vol. 2. 1840. Trans. Henry Reeve. New York: Knopf, 1945.

Trouillot, Michel-Rolph. "Anthropology and the Savage Slot." In *Recapturing Anthropology: Working in the Present,* ed. Richard G. Fox, 17–44. Santa Fe, NM: School for American Research Press, 1991.

Tsing, Anna. "The Global Situation." *Cultural Anthropology* 15.3 (2000): 327–60.

Tyler, Stephen A. "Post-modern Ethnography: From Document of the Occult to Occult Document." In *Writing Culture: The Politics and Poetics of Ethnography,* ed. James Clifford and George Marcus, 122–40. Berkeley: University of California Press, 1986.

Urban, Greg. *Metaculture: How Culture Moves through the World*. Minneapolis: University of Minnesota Press, 2001.

Venkatesan, Soumhya, and Thomas Yarrow, eds. *Differentiating Development: Beyond an Anthropology of Critique*. New York: Berghahn Books, 2012.

Vine, David. *Island of Shame: The Secret History of the U.S. Military Base on Diego Garcia*. Princeton, NJ: Princeton University Press, 2009.

Virno, Paolo. "Natural-Historical Diagrams: The 'New Global' Movement and the Biological Invariant." In *The Italian Difference: Between Nihilism and Biopolitics*, ed. Lorenzo Chiesa and Alberto Toscano, 131–47. Melbourne: re.press, 1999.

Visweswaran, Kamala. *Fictions of Feminist Ethnography*. Minneapolis: University of Minnesota Press, 1994.

Wagner, Roy. *The Invention of Culture*. Englewood Cliffs, NJ: Prentice-Hall, 1975.

Wallace, Anthony. "Revitalization Movements." *American Anthropologist* 58.2 (1956): 264–81.

Weber, Samuel. *Return to Freud: Jacques Lacan's Dis-location of Psychoanalysis*. Cambridge: Cambridge University Press, 1991.

Weeks, Kathi. *The Problem with Work: Feminism, Marxism, Antiwork Politics, and Postwork Imaginaries*. Durham, NC: Duke University Press, 2011.

Weiss, Margot. *Techniques of Pleasure: BDSM and the Circuits of Sexuality*. Durham, NC: Duke University Press, 2011.

Whorf, Benjamin Lee. *Language, Thought, and Reality*. Cambridge, MA: MIT Press, 1956.

Wiegman, Robyn. *Object Lessons*. Durham, NC: Duke University Press, 2012.

Williams, Raymond. *Culture and Society: 1780–1950*. New York: Columbia University Press, 1958.

World Bank. "Indonesia's PNPM Generasi Program: Final Impact Evaluation Report." Jakarta: World Bank Jakarta Office, 2012.

Wylie, Sara. "Corporate Bodies and Chemical Bonds: An STS Analysis of the American Natural Gas Industry." PhD dissertation, MIT, 2010.

Xingzhi Sang, ed. *Shuo shi* [On stones]. Shanghai: Shanghai Keji Jiaoyu Chubanshe, 1993.

Xuan Jiang. "The Global Diffusion and Variations of Creative Industries for Urban Development: The Chinese Experience in Shanghai, Beijing and Guangzhou." PhD dissertation, University of Delaware, 2011.

Yanagisako, Sylvia, and Daniel Segal, eds. *Unwrapping the Sacred Bundle: Reflections on the Disciplining of Anthropology*. Durham, NC: Duke University Press, 2005.

Yuasa Makoto. *Hanhinkon: "Suberidaishakai" kara no dasshutsu* [Reverse poverty: Escape from a "sliding down society"]. Tokyo: Iwanami shinsho, 2008.

Zeitlin, Judith T. "The Secret Life of Rocks: Objects and Collectors in the Ming and Qing Imagination." *Orientations* 30.5 (1999): 40–47.

Zhan, Mei. "Worlding Oneness: Daoism, Heidegger, and Possibilities for Treating the Human." *Social Text* 29.4 (2012): 107–28.

Zhuangzi. *Basic Writings*. Trans. Burton Watson. New York: Columbia University Press, 2003.

Zota, Ami. "Oral Contraceptives Are Not a Major Estrogen Source in Drinking Water." *Environmental Health News*, December 7, 2010. Accessed March 15, 2011. http://www.environmentalhealthnews.org/ehs/newscience/birth-contr ol-not-major-estrogen-source-in-water.

ANNE ALLISON is a professor of cultural anthropology and women's studies at Duke University. A specialist in contemporary Japan, she studies the interface between material conditions and desire, fantasy, and imagination across various domains, including corporate capitalism, global popular culture, and precarity. Allison is the author of *Nightwork: Sexuality, Pleasure, and Corporate Masculinity in a Tokyo Hostess Club* (1994), *Permitted and Prohibited Desires: Mothers, Comics, and Censorship in Japan* (1996), *Millennial Monsters: Japanese Toys and the Global Imagination* (2006), and *Precarious Japan* (2013).

JAMES CLIFFORD is Professor Emeritus in the History of Consciousness Department at the University of California, Santa Cruz, where he taught for three decades. He is best known for his historical and literary critiques of anthropological representation, travel writing, and museum practices. Clifford has just published *Returns: Becoming Indigenous in the Twenty-First Century* (2013), a book that is the third in a trilogy. The first volume, *The Predicament of Culture* (1988) juxtaposed essays on twentieth-century ethnography, literature, and art. The second, *Routes: Travel and Translation in the Late 20th Century* (1997) explored the dialectics of dwelling and traveling in postmodernity. The three books are inventive combinations of analytic scholarship, meditative essays, and poetic experimentation.

MICHAEL M. J. FISCHER is Andrew W. Mellon Professor in the Humanities and a professor of science and technology studies at MIT. He is the author of *Iran: From Religious Dispute to Revolution; Anthropology as Cultural Critique* (with George Marcus); *Debating Muslims: Cultural Dialogues in Postmodernity and Tradition* (with Mehdi Abedi); *Emergent Forms of Life and the Anthropological Voice; Mute Dreams, Blind Owls, and Dispersed Knowledges: Persian Poesis in the Transnational Circuitry;* and *Anthropological Futures.* Most recently he has been doing fieldwork on Biopolis and the life sciences, educational reform, and aging initiatives in Singapore.

KIM FORTUN is a professor and the chair of the Department of Science and Technology Studies at Rensselaer Polytechnic Institute. She is the author of the award-winning *After Bhopal: Environmentalism, Disaster, New World Orders* (2001), and coedited the journal *Cultural Anthropology* with Mike Fortun. Among her many publications, she wrote the new foreword to the twenty-fifth-anniversary second edition of *Writing Culture*. She is now working on a book called *Making Environmental Sense* about how information technology, theory, and culture have shaped the environmental field over the past two decades.

RICHARD HANDLER is a cultural anthropologist who has written on nationalism and the politics of culture, museums and the representation of history, anthropology and literature, and the history of Boasian anthropology. He is currently a professor of anthropology and the director of the Program in Global Studies at the University of Virginia.

JOHN L. JACKSON JR. is the Richard Perry University Professor of Communication, Africana Studies, and Anthropology at the University of Pennsylvania. Before coming to Penn, Jackson taught in the Department of Cultural Anthropology at Duke University and spent three years as a Junior Fellow at the Harvard University Society of Fellows. Jackson received his BA in communications (radio, TV, film) from Howard University and his PhD in anthropology from Columbia University. As a filmmaker he has produced fictional films and documentaries that have screened all around the world, including Amsterdam, Jamaica, Trinidad and Tobago, Curaçao, London, Puerto Rico, Toronto, and South Africa. He has published several books: *Harlemworld: Doing Race and Class in Contemporary Black America* (2001); *Real Black: Adventures in Racial Sincerity* (2005); *Racial Paranoia: The Unintended Consequences of Political Correctness* (2008); *Thin Description: Ethnography and the African Hebrew Israelites of Jerusalem* (2013); and *Impolite Conversations: On Race, Politics, Sex, Money, and Religion* (2014, with Cora Daniels). His most recent film, codirected with the anthropologist Deborah Thomas, is *Bad Friday: Rastafari after Coral Gardens* (2012).

GEORGE E. MARCUS is Chancellor's Professor of Anthropology at the University of California, Irvine. Previously he was for twenty-five years the chair of the Anthropology Department at Rice University during its period of creative influence amid an era of critical thinking about culture and methods. He now directs a center for ethnography devoted to refitting those methods for a very different era of intellectual challenge.

CHARLIE PIOT is a professor of cultural anthropology at Duke University, where he has a joint appointment in African and African American studies. His area of specialization is the political economy and cultural history of rural West Africa. His first book, *Remotely Global: Village Modernity in West Africa* (1999), attempted to retheorize a classic out-of-the-way place as within the modern and global. His recent book, *Nostalgia for the Future: West Africa after the Cold War* (2010), explores shifts in Togolese political culture during the 1990s, a time when the NGOs and charismatic churches took over biopolitics, reorganizing social and political life in the absence of the state. His current project is on Togolese who apply for and attempt to game the U.S. Diversity Visa Lottery.

HUGH RAFFLES is a professor of anthropology and the director of the Graduate Institute for Design, Ethnography and Social Thought at the New School. He is the author of *In Amazonia: A Natural History* (2002), *Insectopedia* (2010), and a forthcoming ethnography of rocks and stones.

DANILYN RUTHERFORD received her doctorate in anthropology with a minor in Southeast Asian studies from Cornell University in 1997. She is the author of two books: *Raiding the Land of the Foreigners: The Limits of the Nation on an Indonesian Frontier* (2003) and *Laughing at Leviathan: Sovereignty and Audience in West Papua* (2012). She has taught at Goldsmiths College, the University of Chicago, and, most recently, the University of California, Santa Cruz, where she is a professor and chair. She is a past president of the Society for Cultural Anthropology. Her research has long focused on the disputed Indonesian half of New Guinea and has involved fieldwork and archival research in West Papua, the Netherlands, and the United States. She is currently finishing a project on affect and technology in colonial state-building. She is taking small steps toward her next project, which will focus on belief, secularism, and speech therapy in the United States.

ORIN STARN is a professor of cultural anthropology and history at Duke University. Starn is the author of *Nightwatch: The Politics of Protest in the Andes* (1999), *Ishi's Brain: In Search of America's Last "Wild" Indian* (2004); and *The Passion of Tiger Woods: An Anthropologist Reports on Golf, Race, and Celebrity Scandal* (2013). His edited volumes include *The Peru Reader: History, Culture, Politics* (with Carlos Iván Degregori and Robin Kirk, 2005); *Between Resistance and Revolution: Cultural Politics and Social Protest* (with Richard G. Fox, 1997); and *Indigenous Experience Today* (with Marisol de la Cadena, 2007). He has also written for the *Los Angeles Times*, the *Huffington Post*, and the *Chronicle of Higher Education* and appeared on NPR, ESPN, and many other radio and TV programs. Starn is now doing new research in Peru and on the experience of Latina housecleaners in the United States.

KATHLEEN STEWART is a professor of anthropology at the University of Texas, Austin. She writes on place, the senses, affect, nonrepresentational theory, the ordinary, worlding, and ethnographic writing as a form of theory. Her experiments in ethnographic creative nonfiction attempt to capture or help compose modes of living as they come into being. Her first book, *A Space on the Side of the Road: Cultural Poetics in an "Other" America* (1996) received the Chicago Folklore Prize and the Victor Turner Award for Best Ethnography. *Ordinary Affects* (2007) approaches ordinary intensities in circulation as a plane of expressivity that is more than representational. Her current book project, *Worldings*, is written as a prism of shards or angles on the phenomena of worldings throwing together as refrains, rhythms, tactile compositions, sensory labors, atmospheric attunements, and the arc of a life. She has recently published articles in *Cultural Anthropology*, *Environment and Planning D*, *Communication and Critical/Cultural Studies*, *Cultural Geographies*, *Geographical Review*, *Anthropology Now*, *Journal of Folklore Research*, and *The International Encyclopedia of Social and Behavioral Sciences*.

MICHAEL TAUSSIG is a self-indulgent fictocritical writer of two performed theater pieces (*The Berlin Sun Theater* and *The Sea Theater*) as well as several books with philosophical, anthropological, and quite often Colombian themes, including *Beauty and the Beast* (2012); *The Nervous System* (1991); *My Cocaine Museum* (2004); and *Shamanism, Colonialism and The Wild Man* (1991).

KAMALA VISWESWARAN teaches anthropology at the University of Texas, Austin. She has done research in Tamil Nadu and Gujarat, India. She is the author of *Fictions of Feminist Ethnography* (1994) and *Un/common Cultures* (2010) and the editor of *Perspectives on Modern South Asia* (2011) and *Everyday Occupations: Experiencing Militarism in South Asia and the Middle East* (2013). She is currently working on two book manuscripts: "Histories of Rights, Histories of Law" and "A Thousand Genocides Now: Gujarat in the Modern Imaginary of Violence."